Resources, Rights and Cooperation:

A Sourcebook on Property Rights and Collective Action for Sustainable Development

CAPRi

CGIAR Program on Collective Action and Property Rights (CAPRi)
International Food Policy Research Institute (IFPRI.org)
2033 K Street NW, Washington, D.C. 20006 USA
www.capri.cgiar.org

Table of Contents

Table of Contents

Table of Contents

Table of Contents

Acknowledgments

The secretariat of the CGIAR Systemwide Program on Collective Action and Property Rights (CAPRi), the producers of this sourcebook, gratefully acknowledges the contribution of many people who made this book possible. First and foremost, we thank our Executive Committee members for their endorsement, excitement, and support of the whole process, and Patti Kristjanson (ILRI), Pablo Eyzaguirre (Bioversity International), and Juan Camilo Cárdenas (Universidad de los Andes, Bogotá), who dedicated their time to carefully review and revise each article. Leticia Merino (Universidad Nacional Autónoma de México), Namita Mishra and Venkat Raj (Foundation for Ecological Security, Anand) also made valuable contributions as advisors for the sourcebook. We are especially grateful to Nancy Johnson (ILRI) for working closely with Helen Markelova to lead the process and helping us fulfill this long-standing wish.

Julian Gonsalves deserves special credit for advising us on our training approach, conceiving the sourcebook, and guiding us through the process of making the book and the posters happen. Julian and his team (in the Philippines, editors Claudia Svetlana Z. Cabrera, Bernadette Joven, Butch Pagcaliwagan, Lorna Calumpang, Josephine Bo, Lily Ann Lando, and Kim Escobin, desktop publishing specialist Noreen Carada and Charmaine Leynes and illustrator Roger Villar; and in Goa, India, editors Miguel Braganza, Kashinath G. Hiremath, and Rena Menezes Fernandes, illustrators Alexyz Fernandes, Prasanth A.V., Kedar Dhondu, and Justin Lobo, and desktop publishing specialists Supresh A. Kharbe and Clifford Fernandes) have done an immense job of turning dense research papers into user-friendly, readable materials suitable for a wide audience.

We sincerely thank Joy Caminade who took time during a busy season at work to ensure that the writeshop went smoothly and efficiently. The Goa team, led by Roque Fernandes, not only made the final writeshop possible, but also welcomed us to their beautiful state with open arms and created a great working atmosphere that allowed us to finalize the volume.

We would also like to express our gratitude to the governments of Norway and Italy and the World Bank for their continued support of CAPRi's work, including this volume and much of the underlying research. We are thankful to Betsy Pereira (IFPRI) for providing logistical support for the sourcebook process.

Finally, we are most grateful to the numerous authors whose works are included in this volume. We believe that their research will inspire and instruct the users of the sourcebook and will contribute to improvements in the livelihoods of many indirect beneficiaries of this book. We appreciate your intellectual contributions to the CAPRi program over the years, and hope that this sourcebook will enable your research findings to reach a broader audience.

Ruth Meinzen-Dick
CAPRi Secretariat

Acknowledgments

Executive Committee

Patti Kristjanson (ILRI)
Pablo Eyzaguirre (Bioversity International)
Juan Camilo Cárdenas (Universidad de los Andes, Bogotá)
Nontokozo Nemarundwe (PhytoTrade Africa, Harare)
K.V. Raju (Institute for Social and Economic Change, Bangalore)

Advisor

Leticia Merino (Universidad Nacional Autónoma de México)
Namita Mishra
Venkat Raj (Foundation for Ecological Security, Anand)

Production Team – Core Group

Nancy Johnson (ILRI)
Helen Markelova (IFPRI)
Ruth Meinzen-Dick (IFPRI)
Julian Gonsalves - Consultant

Editors

Philippines
Claudia Svetlana Z. Cabrera
Bernadette Joven
Butch Pagcaliwagan
Lorna Calumpang
Josephine Bo
Lily Ann Lando
Kim Escobin
Renell Pacrin
Dulce Dominguez

Goa, India
Roque Fernandes
Joy Caminade
Miguel Braganza
Kashinath G. Hiremath
Rena Menezes Fernandes

Illustrators

Alexyz Fernandes
Ariel Lucerna
Roger Villar
Prasanth A.V.
Kedar Dhondu
Justin Lobo

Layout

Celso Amutan
Charmaine Leynes
Noreen Carada
Supresh A. Kharbe
Clifford Fernandes

Preface

The Systemwide Program on Collective Action and Property Rights (CAPRi) is an intercenter initiative of the Consultative Group on International Agricultural Research (CGIAR) that was created in 1995. The CAPRi program promotes, facilitates, and conducts collaborative research on institutions and rights that relate to agriculture and natural resource management. The collaboration includes researchers and practitioners from CGIAR centers, national agricultural research institutions, universities, NGOs, and development organizations. All 15 CGIAR centers and over 400 institutions from developed and developing countries are currently members of CAPRi.

The overarching goal of CAPRi is to contribute to policies and practices that reduce rural poverty by analyzing and disseminating knowledge on the ways that collective action and property rights institutions influence the efficiency, equity, and sustainability of natural resource use and technological innovation in agriculture. Because natural resource management (NRM) issues are at the forefront of the development agenda, a thorough understanding of the factors that contribute to sustainable management is critical to the formulation of viable strategies to enhance resource productivity, both now and in the future.

CAPRi has compiled a substantial body of empirical research on the formation and effectiveness of voluntary, community-level organizations, collective action, and property rights institutions, including common property, in a range of developing regions and contexts. In addition to agriculture and NRM, CAPRi works on rural markets, risk and vulnerability, and climate change, as well as cross-cutting topics of poverty reduction and gender. Addressing these complex interactions between institutions, natural resources, and livelihoods requires an interdisciplinary approach that combines insights and methods from social and natural scientists as well as the rich body of knowledge held by rural people.

CAPRi has three main objectives: to contribute to research, to influence policy, and to build the capacity of national and international researchers to study collective action and property rights. The working papers series (www.capri.cgiar.org) contains over 100 papers based on original research and synthesis that have made a major contribution to improving understanding of the role of collective action and property rights in agriculture, NRM, and poverty reduction in developing countries. On the basis of this research, numerous research and policy briefs have been produced that translate research findings into concrete recommendations for policymakers and practitioners.

Preface

CAPRi conducted its first training course in 2004 in Nairobi, Kenya. Additional courses were conducted in 2005 (Hyderabad, India), 2007 (Bangalore, India), and 2010 (San Salvador, El Salvador). Given their success and the growing demand, the scaling up of the training program was beyond CAPRi's capacity and mandate. In response, an assessment of capacity building strategies recommended producing a sourcebook that would capture and disseminate the results of the large body of CAPRi research.

This first CAPRi sourcebook is a fitting commemoration of the 15th anniversary of CAPRi. Unique among other training materials, it is based directly on the experiences and lessons of research on CAPRi core themes from around the world. The presentation is simple and straightforward, but it is based on sound underlying research. The objective of the book is to build capacity of research and development organizations to recognize the importance and relevance of CAPRi concepts and to apply the lessons and methods from CAPRi research in their work with communities, policymakers, and other stakeholders. It is our hope that it will serve not only as a relevant and practical guide for development practitioners, trainers, and policymakers, but will also be used in universities and other institutions of higher learning.

Foreword

The capacity to tackle major challenges facing society depends on our ability to work together voluntarily, globally as well as locally, and to devise and maintain a diverse range of institutions for governing ourselves and our resources. Why people cooperate and how cooperation can be catalyzed and supported are two of the most important questions facing science and society. The answers will not come from a single discipline within social science or even from social scientists alone. To date, major advances in understanding complex policy questions have come from comparative work across methods and disciplines. This often happens serendipitously; systematic collective action among researchers may be a precursor to understanding and enabling collective action more generally.

The understanding generated by collaborative research is too important to be left to researchers alone. It has important practical applications for sustainable management of resources and for poverty reduction. The complexity of institutional arrangements can be daunting for non-specialists, but simplistic "solutions" that are often promoted as panaceas cannot solve complex problems. What we need are clear ways to relate the insights from research to the experiences of development practitioners.

The CGIAR Systemwide Program on Collective Action and Property Rights (CAPRi) plays a critical role in bringing together a diverse set of actors including theoretical and applied researchers from social and natural sciences, policymakers, and practitioners from developed and developing countries. CAPRi facilitates not only knowledge generation, but also dialogue, comparative analysis, and mutual learning. Considerable diversity and healthy debates exist within CAPRi. Trust and respect are common denominators, a factor that strongly supports collective action and helps to explain the Program's successful 15-year history.

This sourcebook draws on the experiences, lessons, and principles derived from a body of research spanning disciplines, countries, and sectors. It addresses the challenges of sustaining collective action and securing property rights in agriculture, natural resource management, and rural development more generally. Targeted towards development practitioners, the text communicates concepts, empirical findings, and their implications for action in clear language. It offers frameworks, guidelines, methods, and tools for addressing institutional issues in development work. What it does not offer are panaceas. The topics addressed in the sourcebook are inherently complex, and the goal is not to simplify them but rather to learn to manage this complexity. Furthermore, the Sourcebook will help equip development practitioners, policymakers, and others interested in sustainable development to learn how to cope more effectively with complexity.

Elinor Ostrom

Senior Research Director, Workshop in Political Theory and Policy Analysis,
Indiana University

Research Professor and Founding Director, Center for the Study of Institutional Diversity,
Arizona State University

Introduction

What is a Sourcebook?

A sourcebook is a collection of short readings that present the key results and, most importantly, implications for action from over 15 years of research on property rights and collective action for poverty alleviation and sustainable development by CAPRi members, partners, and associated organizations. The sourcebook is designed to provide both a general orientation to the issues as well as practical insights on how to address specific, real-world problems.

The sourcebook is divided into eight sections, each addressing an important aspect of property rights and collective action on which CAPRi has generated a significant body of research. Also included a glossary of relevant terms. The pieces in each section were specially selected to cover different aspects of each topic and to complement each other in terms of the range of experiences available from different regions and contexts. In its entirety, the sourcebook is a comprehensive synthesis of key concepts, insights, and lessons from Asia, Africa, and Latin America. It is important to note, however, that the articles are also explicitly designed to stand alone so that they can be used individually or re-combined with pieces from the same or other sections, depending on the needs of the user.

How to use the Sourcebook

Most users of the sourcebook may not read it from cover to cover because it is designed primarily as a reference guide. Instead, they may search for information on a specific topic, resource, method, or region. The table of contents was designed to make it easy for users to identify relevant materials from different parts of the sourcebook. However, readers may find it useful to begin with Chapter 1, which presents an overall framework for understanding the relevance of collective action and property rights for sustainable development.

Since the sourcebook's primary target audience is field-based practitioners, the readings present theory and analysis in simple terms and extract practical lessons for action. The sourcebook was not designed as a research reference and therefore does not go into detail on research methods and approaches. Nonetheless, researchers may find the sourcebook useful to identify relevant studies, as well as to see the kinds of results and conclusions that can be drawn from applied research on collective action and property rights. Each piece is based on a research paper, noted in the "Source" box on the first page. Suggested readings at the end are provided for those who would like more information.

Introduction

How this Sourcebook was developed

This sourcebook was developed from original research outputs identified by the CAPRi team, mainly from the research work it supported via its global network, supplemented by key pieces from other experts.

Most of the readings are from social science researchers working in the fields of agriculture, natural resource management, and poverty reduction, often as part of multidisciplinary teams. In addition, many of the pieces are based on "research for development" that involved not only scientists, but also development practitioners and communities.

A team of editors and artists in the Philippines helped repackage longer articles into short, succinct, user-friendly materials. This compilation was critically reviewed by a CAPRi Executive Committee at a review-writeshop held in Goa, India, October 27-30, 2009. Articles were further revised and improved upon during this workshop, where specialized assistance was provided by a local team of editors, artists, and a graphic design team. The original authors then approved the repackaged versions of their original articles before they were sent for copyediting and final layout in the Philippines. A series of posters was also produced as part of this same effort, but are packaged as a complementary publication (Resources, Rights and Cooperation: Education Poster Resources). These were initially developed in the Philippines, but further revised and amended with new artwork in Goa, India. A CD is also available which contains electronic versions of the original papers, the repackaged articles, and the posters. The sourcebook is also available online at www.capri.cgiar.org.

Chapter 1

Fundamentals of Collective Action and Property Rights

Collective Action and Property Rights for Sustainable Development

Institutions for collective action and systems of property rights shape how people use natural resources. These patterns of use in turn affect the outcomes of people's agricultural production systems. Together, mechanisms of collective action and property rights define the incentives people face for undertaking sustainable and productive management strategies, and they affect the level and distribution of benefits from natural resources. The linkages between property rights, collective action, and natural resource management have important implications for technology adoption, economic growth, food security, poverty reduction, and environmental sustainability. Yet, despite their importance in people's lives, property rights and collective action are often undervalued, and when they are recognized, often misunderstood.

SOURCE:

Meinzen-Dick, R. and M. di Gregorio. 2004. *Collective Action and Property Rights for Sustainable Development: Overview.* 2020 Focus Brief 11. International Food Policy Research Institute, Washington, D.C.

Property Rights and Collective Action

Collective action is often considered narrowly in terms of formal organizations, and property rights only in terms of formal titles issued by the government. In fact, they are much more than that.

Collective action can be defined as voluntary action taken by a group to achieve common interests. Members can act directly on their own or through an organization. In the context of natural resource management, even deciding on and observing rules for use or non-use of a resource can be considered collective action, and it can be instituted through common property regimes or through coordinated activities across individual landholdings.

Sources of Property Rights

There are multiple sources of property rights, including:

- International treaties and law;
- State (or statutory) law;
- Religious law and accepted religious practices;
- Customary law, which may be formal written custom or living interpretations of custom;
- Project (or donor) law, including project or programme regulations;
- Organisational law, such as rules made by user or non-user groups; and
- The marketplace.

Property rights can be defined as "the capacity to call upon the collective to stand behind one's claim to a benefit stream," according to Bromley (1991). Rights do not necessarily imply full ownership or the sole authority to use or dispose of a resource; different individuals, families, groups, or even the state often hold overlapping use and decision-making rights. To be secure, rights should be of sufficient duration to allow one to reap the rewards of investment and should be backed by an effective, socially sanctioned enforcement institution. This institution is not always the government; communities or other institutions may provide the backing.

Links to Sustainability of Natural Resource Management and Agricultural Systems

Figure 1 shows how property rights and collective action affect the application of agricultural technologies and natural resource management practices. Conventional on-farm technologies like improved, high-yielding crop varieties (HYVs) have a short, usually seasonal, time horizon. They can be adopted by a single farmer—even by a tenant. Other technologies may require longer time horizons between adoption and payoff. In those situations, farmers need secure tenure (property rights) to have the incentive and authority to adopt. For example, tenants are often not allowed to plant trees, or lack incentives to build terracing.

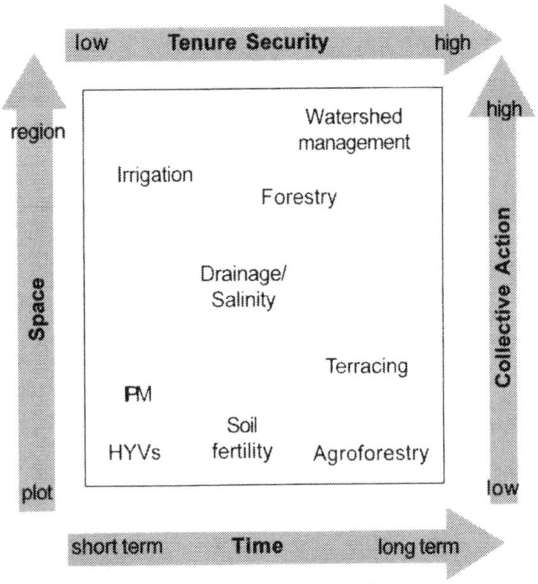

Figure 1: The Role of Collective Action and Property Rights in Natural Resource Management.

Moving from on-farm technologies to those that operate at larger spatial scales implies a greater need for collective action to make the technology work. Integrated pest management (IPM), for example, must be coordinated across farms. Most natural resource management practices have both long time, and large spatial scales. Both property rights and collective action are therefore crucial for the management of forests, rangelands, fisheries, watersheds, or irrigation systems that serve more than a single farm. In some cases, the scale of the resource to be managed may go beyond what can be done by voluntary collective action by a community. Federations of user groups may sometimes be able to manage larger resources, but often the state or even international bodies become critically important partners. In these cases, co-management between the community and government, rather than government management alone, often leads to better outcomes.

Without property rights, there is no incentive to protect the resource, so it becomes degraded over time.

> **Rights Defined**
>
> The way rights are defined determines whether people are included in or excluded from the control of a vital resource for their lives. Holding property rights is thus empowering to individuals or groups, particularly control rights that recognize authority over how the resource is managed.

Property rights and collective action also affect natural resource management and agricultural production systems in interaction with other factors such as information, wealth, risk, labor, and marketing. Collective action and networks among community members can facilitate access to information and even allow farmers to participate in technology development. Ownership of assets can serve as collateral for obtaining credit. Microfinance programs have shown that action through groups can also provide access to credit, with social bonds providing collateral.

Rights over property, function as a buffer against risk, especially environmental events and loss of other livelihoods. Similarly, collective action enables risk sharing and inspires mechanisms for collective self-help. Collective action and reciprocity arrangements offer ways to overcome labor shortages, especially for practices that require intense labor effort in concentrated periods. Property rights and collective action are also interdependent. This is particularly clear in the case of common property regimes, where holding rights in common reinforces collective action among members, and collective action is needed to manage the resource. Maintaining property rights can require collective action, especially in the case of landscape-level resources and where outsiders challenge local claims.

Links to Poverty Reduction

Property rights and collective action affect people's livelihoods. The most vulnerable and marginalized rural groups often lack access to resources (that is, they have no or insecure property rights) and find participation in collective action too costly because of lack of time or other resources. Enhancing rights to relatively small homestead plots can increase food security by allowing women to grow food in gardens, and rights to common property often provide insurance for the poor. Tenure security provides key assets for poverty reduction, allowing the poor to help themselves by growing food, investing in more productive activities, or using property as collateral for credit. Collective action can increase food security through mutual insurance.

Both property rights and collective action are empowerment tools, as poor people often have difficulty making their voices heard. Interventions to strengthen their property rights or to help them participate in collective activities improve their bargaining positions. Security of rights and the capacity to manage local common resources allow people to make decisions while taking the future into consideration. This longer-term approach generally translates into more environmentally sustainable management practices and a healthier resource base for future generations.

Property Rights Regime: The Case of Western Ghana Forests

The customary system of acquiring land in Western Ghana by clearing forests to make agricultural fields gives one a claim over the land. This system came under pressure from increasing population. Agroforestry, particularly cocoa production, became more profitable than shifting cultivation, which created local pressure to individualize land tenure. Though individualization of tenure frequently led to women losing their customary access to land, in this case the introduction of cocoa increased the demand for women's labor. Men needed to provide incentives for their wives to work in the cocoa fields.

Although land was customarily held only by men, women acquired use rights through their relationships with men, and traditional "gifting" ceremonies, witnessed by the community, were adapted so husbands could transfer individual land rights to their wives in exchange for labor on the cocoa fields. Thus, with the introduction of cocoa, customary practices were used to adapt the land tenure and give women relatively secure rights to land and trees.

Implications for Policy and Practice

Many countries are now adopting policies to devolve the management of forests, fisheries, irrigation, watersheds, or rangelands to local communities or to develop some form of co-management between the state and communities. In addition, community-driven development initiatives are helping local organizations set priorities for local public service spending and to provide services such as schools and health centers. For these programs to succeed, effective collective action within communities is essential.

Successful collective action does not always emerge, especially where traditional management institutions like pastoral communities on rangelands have been weakened by migration or excessive state intervention. Government agencies need to work with communities to strengthen local management institutions and allow more local decision-making without imposing external rules.

Devolution programs that transfer management responsibility for natural resources from government agencies to farmers often fail to transfer corresponding rights. Yet rights over the resource are needed to provide groups with the incentives to conserve and even invest in the resources. Without recognized decision-making rights, the groups lack the authority to manage the resource or to stop members or outsiders from breaking the rules. Recognized property rights not only reinforce collective action needed for collective management, but also provide security for individuals and households.

There are many ways of strengthening property rights for the poor. Many government and non-government organizations involved in community development are addressing collective action issues, through revolving credit or livestock schemes, agricultural extension groups, or domestic water supply. There is a wealth of practical experience on ways to organize or strengthen collective action. Researchers have documented factors that affect collective action, but their findings are often based on a few successful case studies. Much more needs to be learned about what approaches foster collective action that continues beyond project intervention, as well as about how externally induced organizations interact with indigenous institutions for collective action.

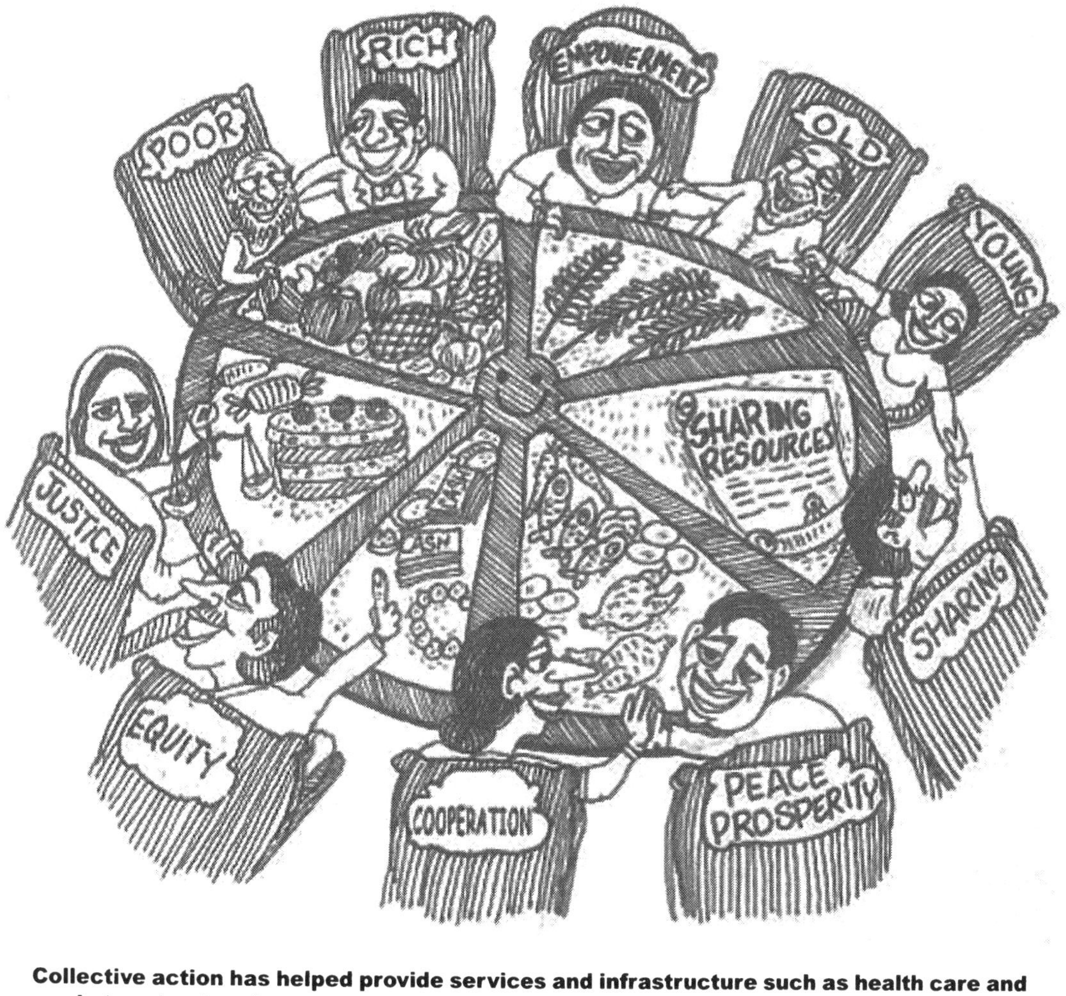

Collective action has helped provide services and infrastructure such as health care and roads to schools, where governments alone failed to do so.

Suggested Readings

Bromley, D. 1991. *Environment and Economy: Property Rights and Public Policy.* Cambridge, MA: Basil Blackwell.

Knox, A., R. Meinzen-Dick and P. Hazell. 1998. *Property Rights, Collective Action, and Technologies for Natural Resource Management*. CAPRi Working Paper 1. International Food Policy Research Institute: Washington, D.C. (http://www.capri.cgiar.org/pdf/capriwp01.pdf). Also visit the CAPRi website at http://www.capri.cgiar.org.

Meinzen-Dick, R., A. Knox and M. Di Gregorio (eds). 2001. *Collective Action, Property Rights, and Devolution of Natural Resource Management: Exchange of Knowledge and Implications for Policy.* Feldafing, Germany: German Foundation for International Development [DSE]/Food and Agriculture Development Centre (http://www.capri.cgiar.org/workshop_devolution.asp)

Meinzen-Dick, R., A. Knox, F. Place and B. Swallow (eds). 2002. *Innovation in Natural Resource Management: The Role of Property Rights and Collective Action in Developing Countries.* Baltimore: John Hopkins University Press.

Understanding Property Rights

People often think of property rights in a narrow sense as ownership – the right to completely and exclusively control a resource. However, property rights are better understood as overlapping "bundles" of rights. There are many combinations of such rights, but they can often be grouped as:

SOURCE:

Meinzen-Dick, R., R. Pradhan and M. di Gregorio. 2004. *Collective Action and Property Rights for Sustainable Development: Understanding Property Rights*, 2020 Focus Brief 11. International Food Policy Research Institute, Washington, D.C.

- **Use rights** – such as the right to access the resource (for example, to walk across a field), withdraw from a resource (pick wild plants), or exploit a resource for economic benefit (commercial fishing); and

- **Control or decision-making rights** – such as the rights to management (plant a crop), exclusion (prevent others from accessing the field), or alienation (rent out, sell or give away the rights).

These rights may also be conditioned by the amount, timing, and other aspects of resource use and management. Several individuals or groups may have different kinds of rights over the same resource. For example, all members of a community may be allowed to bathe in a river or collect drinking water, but only certain farmers may be permitted to draw water to irrigate a field or to decide how to distribute that water in the dry season.

At the same time, the state may claim ultimate "ownership" of the water, including the right to reassign it to others. Even on land declared as state forest land, individuals from a community may have the right to collect medicinal plants or fallen branches for firewood (use), local groups may have the right to plant trees (management) and guard them (exclusion), but the state may retain the right to approve any felling of trees and to collect revenue from users.

Legal Pluralism: Many Sources of Rights

To recognize property rights in practice, we need to look beyond state-issued titles to the resource. As illustrated in Figure 1, there are multiple sources of property rights, including:

- International treaties and law;
- State (or statutory) law;
- Religious law and accepted religious practices;
- Customary law, which may be formal written custom or living interpretations of custom;
- Project (or donor) law, including project or program regulations; and
- Organizational law, such as rules made by user groups.

The co-existence of these laws does not mean that all laws are equal, or equally powerful. Each is only as strong as the institution that stands behind it. Often, state law is more powerful and used by government officials, for example, to declare and enforce forests as state property. Statutory law is also used by powerful outsiders, such as logging companies with concessions in customary lands, to claim resources in ways that are not locally recognized as legitimate. On the other hand, actions of local communities, such as petitioning, demonstrations, and roadblocks, are ways of claiming locally recognized rights as well as seeking recognition of their rights by the state.

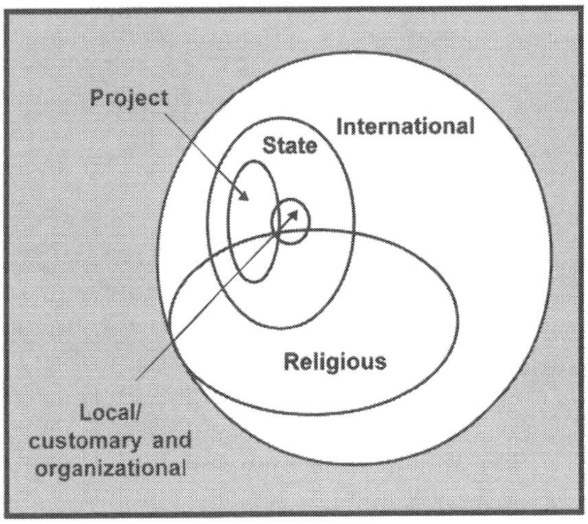

Figure 1. Co-Existing Multiple Resources of Property Rights.

In some cases, state law is not as relevant as the village, ethnic community, or user group in determining property rights on the ground. For example, state laws on inheritance are often ignored in favor of religious laws or local custom. Research has shown that state titling programs do not always provide stronger security than customary rights and may even be a source of insecurity for women and households with less information or fewer connections to obtain government land registration.

While legal pluralism can create uncertainty because rival claimants can use a large legal repertoire to claim a resource, multiple legal frameworks also provide flexibility for people to maneuver in their use of natural resources.

Property Rights as Dynamic Systems

Often, the more variable the resource, the more flexible are the property rights that develop over it. Water rights are particularly fluid, changing by season and year, depending on the availability of the resource and demands for water. Similarly, many customary rangeland management systems negotiate access rights depending on factors like weather and the social relations between the

groups. This flexibility provides a measure of security in times of drought or other disasters, by creating reciprocal expectations of resource sharing between groups.

Another source of change in property rights comes from interaction between types of law. These different legal frameworks do not exist in isolation, but influence each other. Changes in state law can influence local custom, and changes in customary practices can also lead to changes in state law.

For state law to be effective on the ground, effective implementation is required. Legal literacy programs may be needed to inform the public – and even government officials – about changes in the laws.

How exactly these different legal orders influence each other depends on power relationships between the "bearers" of different laws. Power relationships also determine the distribution of rights and whether people can effectively claim their rights. Actual rights on natural resources are therefore a product of locality, history, changes in resource condition and use, ecology, and social relationships and are subject to negotiation. Thus, in practice, property rights are not cast in stone or in title deeds, but negotiated.

Property Rights, Responsibilities, and Devolution Programs

Effective resource management entails balancing benefit entitlements and the responsibilities that come with property rights. After failing to effectively manage natural resource systems centrally, many governments are now undertaking decentralization and devolution programs to transfer responsibility for resource management to local governments and user groups. Unfortunately, many such programs emphasize the transfer of responsibilities without transferring the corresponding rights. As a result, user groups may lack the incentive, and even the authority, to manage the resource.

When devolution programs do transfer rights over resources to user groups or local government, that particular institution becomes the gatekeeper that determines individuals' rights over the resource. An effective voice in those organizations becomes essential in exercising any decision-making rights over the resource. This situation can be especially problematic for women when formal rules limit membership to the "head of household", or where social norms make it unacceptable for women to speak up in public. Because strengthening the control rights of some means restricting the use rights of others, those who are not members of the groups in question may have less access to the resource.

Thus, while effective transfers of rights and responsibilities from centralized government agencies to local organizations can lead to more sustainable resource management, authorities must give due attention to the equity outcomes, especially noting who loses access to resources.

Implications

Although property rights have a powerful influence on human welfare and natural resource management, this institution is complex. Property rights do change over time, but legislative reform alone is unlikely to alter the manifestation of property rights on the ground. Rather, change occurs through social and power relations and negotiations between different groups, who may appeal to a variety of legal bases for claiming property rights. Instead of looking for simple "solutions" to property rights issues, it is more useful to try to understand the complexity.

This approach involves looking at the claims and the bases of the claims made by individuals, groups, or government entities to different bundles of rights over the resource, and at the different types of laws that pertain to the use or management of the resource. Security of tenure is important, but so is flexibility to respond to changing conditions that affect resource use and property rights.

Suggested Readings

Bruns, B. R., and R. Meinzen-Dick (eds). 2000. *Negotiating Water Rights.* New Delhi and London: Vistaar Publications and Intermediate Technology Development Group Publishing.

Meinzen-Dick, R. and R. Pradhan. 2002. *Legal Pluralism and Dynamic Property Rights*. CAPRi Working Paper 22. Washington, D.C.: IFPRI. (http://www.capri.cgiar.org/pdf/capriwp22.pdf)

Spiertz, J. and M. G. Wiber (eds). 1996. *The Role of Law in Natural Resource Management.* The Hague, The Netherlands: VUGA.

Understanding Collective Action

Collective action can be understood as an action or series of actions taken by a group of individuals to achieve common interests. It can be voluntary for some or obligatory for others, such as compulsory membership in water users' associations. The efforts of hired or forced workers do not constitute collective action.

SOURCES:

McCarthy, N. 2004. *Local-level Public Goods and Collective Action,* Focus Brief 11, International Food Policy Research Institute, Washington, D.C.

Meinzen-Dick, R., M. Di Greogorio and N. McCarthy. 2004. *Methods for Studying Collective Action in Rural Development*. CAPRi Working Paper No. 33. International Food Policy Research Institute, Washington, D.C.

Ostrom, E. 2004. *Understanding Collective Action*. 2020. Focus Brief 11. Food Policy Research Institute, Washington, D.C.

While collective action is often considered the activities of formal organizations, many formal organizations exist on paper only and do not foster any real collective action. On the other hand, much collective action occurs informally through social networks or even through people coming together temporarily for specific purposes. Therefore, it can be an event (e.g. an organized march), a process (e.g. a series of participatory exercises), or an organization (e.g. microfinance group). Since members can act directly on their own or through an organization, collective action should not be equated with an organization.

Collective action can also occur at non-local levels or across levels of stakeholders as a voluntary action between local and non-local actors. For example, organizations can form a coalition based on their mutual interests. In addition, local communities can work together with local government officials and private sector representatives to ensure access to forests and forest resources.

Collective action can help groups of smallholder producers link with other members of the commodity value chain for joint marketing ventures. However, contractual obligations between the members of a value chain or other stakeholders are not considered collective action, since this type of arrangement is not voluntary.

Collective action affects people's livelihoods. It can increase opportunities for income generation through microfinance groups, serve as protection in times of shocks through mutual insurance schemes, and improve provision and access to public services through community-driven development programs. It is particularly important for natural resource management as the poor organize around access to and governance of vital resources.

Collective Action Institutions

Institutions are the rules or constraints that shape political, economic and social interaction. They set and limit the choices of individuals, and they provide the incentives that affect human behavior, which in turn determine outcomes. Institutions can arise either spontaneously, when decision makers organize themselves, or be planned by an outside authority.

Institutions provide a means of living and working together. Through institutions, individuals act with others to produce benefits that they could not produce by acting alone. Consequently, institutions may encourage collective action and cooperation.

Institutions important for collective action include:

- Informal constraints (sanctions, taboos, customs, traditions, codes of conduct);
- Formal rules (constitutions, laws); and
- Rules, norms, and strategies used in repeated interactions.

Rules are the shared prescriptions (e.g. must, must not, or may) that are enforced by agents who are responsible for monitoring conduct and imposing sanctions. These working rules determine eligibility to decide, actions allowed or constrained, group rules, procedures to follow, information to be provided, and payoffs to specific actions. Norms, on the other hand, are the shared prescriptions that are self-enforced and do not rely on material sanctions or inducements.

Incentives for Collective Action

Collective action is costly in terms of time and the missed benefits of acting alone, but people participate in collective action when the benefits outweigh the costs. Five common incentive structures for local-level collective action contribute to the creation of local-level public goods.

Table 1: Different Incentive Structures Affect Ease of Collective Action.

Situation	Example	Role of Group	"Game" Structure
Everyone is better off contributing, even if no others contribute.	Increasing returns to public good, e.g. pest management.	Share information, coordinate activities.	Coordination game.
An individual is better off contributing if no one else does, but if others contribute, the individual would rather "free ride".	Livestock herd mobility.	Coordinate activities, especially taking turns for repeated contributions.	Chicken game.
Individual prefers to contribute if all others do, but not contribute if no one else does.	Building community infrastructure (building or bridge).	Assure each member that others will also contribute.	Assurance game.
Individual prefers not to contribute if no one else does and also free ride, if all others contribute — even if all would be better off if all contribute.	Soil erosion or agroforestry in variable environments.	Convince members to contribute, punish free riders (most difficult).	Prisoner's dilemma.

Principles for Successful Local Collective Action

Sometimes, the benefits from collective activities cannot be withheld from people who do not participate in the collective effort. For example, planting of vegetation along riverbanks to reduce runoff and erosion will benefit all, even those who have not participated.

In this case, some people will be tempted not to help with the planting, since they can enjoy the benefits anyway. This is called "free riding" and can break down cooperative effort. Collective rules on use, monitoring, and sanctioning can help reduce the likelihood of free riding, by reducing the incentives to free ride as well as assuring other members that their peers will also contribute.

Although CA is important for the poor for many reasons, various factors determine whether collective action emerges and how well it performs. Some principles can explain why it seems to work better in some contexts than others. Policies, programs or other interventions that focus exclusively on formal organizations often hamper the emergence and undermine the effectiveness of collective action.

Design Principles for Effective Management of the Commons

1. Group boundaries are clearly defined.
   Example: defined members of a forest users' association and the boundaries of the area they manage.

2. Rules governing the use of collective goods are well matched to local needs and conditions.
   Example: rules on who can graze or harvest different products at different times of the year, prohibition on logging close to water sources, or members' contributions to firefighting or replanting.

3. Most individuals affected by these rules can participate in modifying the rules.
   Example: a group can set harvesting rules and modify them in a drought year.

4. The rights of community members to devise their own rules is respected by external authorities.
   Example: the government respects by-laws that the local users develop.

5. A system for monitoring behavior exists; the community members themselves undertake this monitoring.
   Example: group members watch each other and patrol to make sure outsiders are not breaking the rules.

6. A graduated system of sanctions is used.
   Example: the first time someone is caught breaking the rules they are told not to do it again; after that there are increasing fines for overgrazing.

7. Community members have access to low-cost conflict resolution mechanisms.
   Example: local groups are able to discuss and resolve local disputes, and call on government to help resolve disputes with outsiders.

8. For resources that are parts of larger systems, there are nested enterprises (supportive links) between local groups and higher-level organizations.
   Example: local user groups managing part of a large forest are members of a federation of user groups that manages the whole forest, and has links to government agencies as well. In Nepal, forest user groups are even federated to the national level and work with the government to represent their members' interests in forest management policy.

Suggested Reading

Ostrom, E. 1990. *Governing the Commons: The Evolution of Institutions for Collective Action.* New York, NY, U.S.A.: Cambridge University Press.

Collective Action in Poverty Reduction Programs

SOURCE:

Meinzen-Dick, R. and M. di Gregorio. *2005. The Role of Collective Action in Fighting Hunger.* In: Sanchez, P. (ed). *Halving Hunger: It Can Be Done.* United Nations Development Programme.

Over half of the hungry people in the world are small-scale farmers, herders, and fishers, who produce food but cannot reliably feed themselves and their families. Nevertheless, poor people are themselves working to improve their lives. Even when their individual resources may be weak, working together can help overcome limitations of wealth, farm size, and bargaining power. Collective action can provide an instrument for addressing poverty through natural resource management, income generation, reducing vulnerability, providing critical services, and allocation of rights. Collective action offers the potential to build assets and overcome poverty traps.

Programs Built on Collective Action

Over the years, there have been well-documented experiences of collective action initiatives that have been effective in the areas of agriculture and natural resource management, marketing, and service delivery. The following scenarios illustrate situations when collective action was effective in achieving some levels of success, in improving the well-being of the poor.

- ***Pooling of resources or joint investment can enhance the productivity of smallholders.*** Conventional on-farm technologies like improved crop varieties can be adopted by a single

farmer, even a tenant; however, farmers may jointly invest in equipment or irrigation. Moving on from on-farm technologies to those that operate at larger spatial scales, there is greater need for collective action to make the technology work.

- ***Collective action is vital in common property management.*** Village commons provide firewood, grazing, or water that households need on a regular basis to supplement private land. In times of crisis, people may rely even more heavily on the commons, and thus common property resources provide a safety net to reduce vulnerability. Across the various resource sectors — irrigation, watershed management, fisheries, forestry, and rangelands — two major challenges surface: provision of the initial investment and regulation of ongoing harvesting and protection of the resource.

- ***Devolution and co-management elicit collective action.*** The last decades have witnessed governments managing natural resources in a more decentralized manner in collaboration with local communities. Devolution or decentralized management work by the principle of subsidiarity, wherein natural resource management is seen to be more effective when local people are involved. The strategy has shown that local people are more capable of monitoring and enforcing rules at their level, monitoring costs are much lower, and accessibility to valuable local knowledge helps fine-tune management practices and maintain ecosystem balances. Additionally, it empowers local communities, which depend largely on the resource base and have a stake in its conservation and sustainability for their food and livelihoods. The supporting role of government institutions in the devolution scheme, where authority is transferred to local users, should also be realized in terms of providing security of rights to users. Some forms of co-management arrangements between the community and government often lead to better outcomes than when the government or user groups try to manage by themselves.

Increasing Milk Production in India through Cooperatives

Milk cooperatives in India have stimulated great increases in production and availability of dairy products throughout the country by collecting milk from over 10 million producers, 60 percent of whom are small or marginal farmers or landless. A three-tiered cooperative structure with professional staff links local collection with processing plants and marketing to distribute the milk to consumers, returning the profits to the producer members, rather than to middlemen.

- ***Collective action opens up market opportunities for smallholders.*** Smallholder farmers often have very limited access to agricultural inputs, due to the unavailability of either resources or money. From a trader's viewpoint, the transaction cost in supplying to smallholders is higher than dealing with just a few large farmers. Marketing cooperatives have played a major role in addressing these problems by providing inputs and credit to farmers and purchasing and aggregating the outputs of many farms.

- ***Community-driven development requires collective action.*** Community-driven development (CDD) has been gaining recognition for its potential in establishing cooperation for many development programs for poor or marginal sectors of society. In CDD, poor people in communities are supposed to set the agenda for development activities, working in collaboration with demand-responsive agencies, whether government or non-government organizations (NGOs), to provide technical support and backup.

  The relevance of collective action for CDD programs is twofold: *collective action is an important pre-condition and predictor for the success of* CDD *programs*, and CDD programs aim at *strengthening capacity for collective action.* The first point speaks of collective action as a vehicle for creating local organizations as well as resource management groups, which are crucial for undertaking CDD programs.

Factors Contributing to Collective Action

Development projects achieve more success if collective action is present, though it cannot be expected to be present always. It is therefore important to determine where collective action is likely to arise, identify where additional efforts are needed to strengthen collective action, particularly when expanding beyond initial pilot sites, and know the conditions where the poor and food — insecure can involve themselves in the process.

- ***Collective action transpires when the benefits in managing the resource collectively outweigh the costs of cooperation.*** A resource is of value to the users and they will work together if the returns justify the effort. This implies that collective action is not likely to arise in areas of extreme environmental degradation. Yet, it is often the most degraded lands that are transferred under "joint forest management", or irrigation systems that have ceased to function, and are very expensive to run. In such cases, the state may need to intervene to rehabilitate the resource first.

Why Some Decentralization Efforts Failed

- Decentralization policies are often undertaken partially. Management duties and costs may have been transferred to local authorities, but relevant rights and access to benefit shares are less likely to be transferred.
- Devolution, if only undertaken partially, can actually strengthen the control of local branches of government over the resource and in effect, further reduce access of local communities.
- Even if there are structures and institutions in place to devolve authority to local users, elite capture is still a risk, where resource is managed only in the interest of a few of right holders.

- ***Past successful experience in collective action or a history of cooperation facilitate further cooperation.*** Development projects that entail cooperation among participants should, before instituting new groups, investigate existing group formation, associations, and informal networks and try to link the new activity to successful existing groups. Programs should be careful not to overload such groups with new activities.

- ***Diversity in a group can work positively.*** In terms of wealth and skills differences, diversity in a group can be an asset to a certain extent, as it allows the group to take advantage of the individual characteristics of its members. However, sharp inequalities in wealth and income may also render the collective action unsuccessful, as it engenders diversified interests within the group. Moreover, if benefits accrued through collective management are not shared equally, but instead according to wealth or status, indicating capture by a sub-group, collective action is likely to break down. The presence of a strong group identity is likely to indicate high potential for collective action.

- ***Collective action is more favorable if channeled by effective agents.*** Appropriate skilled leadership, well-connected to outside institutions, complements the enrichment of social capital in fostering successful collective action.

- ***Cooperation is easier to achieve in areas of stable population.*** Repeated interactions among the same set of people generally increase the incentives to cooperate, and reduce the transaction costs as people get to know each other and establish common rules and norms. A high turnover of population makes collective action more difficult. Out-migration creates more "exit options" that reduce the need for cooperation, and rapid increases in population may also place pressure on resources.

Collective action empowers women to engage in livelihood activities that could potentially improve their household income.

- ***Access to markets can increase potential benefits from collective action for different activities (marketing) and thus foster cooperation in new areas.*** Market development affects the likelihood of cooperation in different and often conflicting ways. Increased access to markets not only reduces people's dependence on natural resources, but also often introduces a new way of resolving risks that collective management of natural resource used to address, especially if access to the credit market is increased.

- ***An enabling institutional environment provides a platform for collective action.*** This holds true, particularly when the authority of local organizations is recognized and backup sanctions to enforce collective management rules or forums for dispute resolution are provided. Paramount to this is the recognition of external authorities that lo-

Cases when Collective Action is NOT Likely to Emerge

- *Wrong presumptions.* It should not be presumed that devolution programs and community-driven development projects then by local government structures or user organizations always possess the capacity to manage resources on their own, or that new organizations can be easily set up and will certainly be able to undertake collective action. This is not always the case.
- *Loss of trust* in external or collective institutions.
- *Negative and recurrent disappointing experiences* as a consequence of the involvement of powerful external interest groups.
- Corruption and rent-seeking, and non-compliance with rules by members.
- *Exclusion of very poor and marginalized people.* Initial cost of participation, time constraints, and distance in spatial or social (e.g., gender, education) terms are some of the factors that impede poor and marginalized people from participating actively in development endeavors.

cal organizations are capable of crafting their own rules of conduct and sanctioning and monitoring mechanisms.

Policies that Promote Collective Action

There are no blueprint approaches for getting people to work together everywhere. Governments should not rush to set targets for how many organizations should be formed or registered, as many of these never function. However, the following provide some guidelines for external programs that try to promote real collective action.

1. In terms of policies, governments should first look for factors that prevent people from working together. Some regulations may be needed to provide an assurance that particular target groups are being included and served, but imposing too many rules or processes will restrict local involvement.

2. Responsibilities need to be balanced with real rights. Without this, the group does not have the authority to make decisions, which will limit the extent of local participation, even if people are willing to be involved. Moreover, rights provide important incentives for people to take on responsibilities. Nonetheless, where resources are transferred to local organizations, it is essential to check whether local organizations are excluding certain people, e.g. women or those from certain castes or ethnic groups.

3. International organizations and donors can encourage the active involvement of local organizations in the design and implementation of projects, sharing experiences of what has worked—and what has not. At the same time, they should be careful not to over emphasize collective action, as it is too important to become a fad. Rather, it should be recognized as vital to ensuring food security, with important spillovers to other sectors, and that the underlying institutions therefore merit concerted investment.

4. Development NGOs have a wealth of experience in working with community groups, fostering the collective action and empowerment of those who have often been excluded. The constraint is often one of scale: even relatively large NGOs have only worked in a small fraction of the communities where poverty is prevalent. Sharing experiences among NGOs, and using their staff to train others, provide mechanisms to expand their contributions.

Collective action offers many opportunities for addressing poverty and enhancing welfare. Many challenges are being faced by concerned local groups — particularly those based in poor communities — which hinder them from contributing to collective endeavors. However, where joint investment or cooperative efforts can be potentially built, then substantial investments on the part of governments, international organizations, donors, development agencies, civil society, research institutions — and most of all, by poor people themselves are very much required.

Suggested Readings

Agrawal, A. 2001. *Common Resources and Institutional Sustainability.* In: Ostrom, E., T. Dietz, N. Dolsak, P. C. Stern, S. Stonich, and E. U. Weber (eds). *The Drama of the Commons.* Washington, D.C.: National Academy Press.

Bruns, B. and P. C. Bruns. 2004. *Strengthening Collective Action.* 2020 Focus Brief 11, International Food Policy Research Institute, Washington, D.C. http://www.ifpri.org/2020/focus/focus11.htm.

Krishna, A. 2003. *Understanding, Measuring and Utilizing Social Capital: Clarifying Concepts and Presenting a Field Application from India.* Working Paper No. 28. Collective Action and Property Rights for Poverty Reduction (CAPRi). International Food Policy Research Institute: Washington, D.C. [online] http://www.capri.cgiar.org/pdf/capriwp28.pdf

Meinzen-Dick, R.S., A. Knox , F. Place and B. M. Swallow (eds). 2002. *Innovation in Natural Resource Management: The Role of Property Rights and Collective Action in Developing Countries*. Baltimore and London: The Johns Hopkins University Press.

Swallow, B. and F. Place. 2002. *Assessing the Relationships Between Property Rights and Technology Adoption in Smallholder Agriculture: A Review of Issues and Empirical Methods.* In: Meinzen-Dick, R., A. Knox, F. Place and B. M. Swallow (eds). *Innovation in Natural Resource Management: The Role of Property Rights and Collective Action in Developing Countries.* Baltimore and London: The Johns Hopkins University Press.

Wollenberg, E. and D. Edmunds. 2003. *Local Forest Management: The Impacts of Devolution Policies*. Earthscan Publications.

Sourcebook on **Resources, Rights, and Cooperation**, produced by the CGIAR Program on Collective Action and Property Rights (CAPRi)

Property Rights:
Issues and Challenges

Rights over land and other natural resources play a fundamental role in human society. The distribution of wealth and poverty is a reflection of underlying property rights. However, reforming property rights to give poor women and men greater access and stronger control over resources is not an easy task.

SOURCE:

Meinzen-Dick, R., P. Kameri-Mbote and H. Markelova. 2007. *Property Rights for Poverty Reduction.* 2020 Focus Briefs on the World's Poor and Hungry People. Washington, DC: IFPRI. International Food Policy Research Institute, Washington, D.C.

Property Rights Provide Assets for Livelihoods

Land is a critical asset for the rural poor. It fulfills important economic functions by providing a means of livelihood through the production and sale of crops and other products. It can also serve as collateral for credit or be sold to start up another income-generating activity. Landless people are excluded from these opportunities, which is why they are often among the poorest. Landless people depend on employment from other farmers or non-farm income sources, but the growth and stability of such employment also depend on the growth of incomes and spending in local farming.

For those with access to land, the strength of their rights over the land shapes their incentives for continued production, ensuring both their food security and a steady supply to the local market.

Thus, land rights affect food security from the individual to the national level. Research suggests that land tenure increases investment in the human capital of children. Therefore, property rights are particularly important in shaping who has entitlements to food and may serve as an instrument to prevent the inter-generational transmission of poverty.

Land provides a buffer in times of shocks. When unemployment or food prices are high, those who have access to land can turn to their farm for self-employment and food production. In cases of crop failure or other distress, landowners can sell or mortgage their land to meet basic consumption needs, which gives them more stability than the landless who lack this buffer.

Landlessness and Poverty

Data from South Asia, home to 40 percent of the world's poor, show that poverty is strongly associated with landlessness and insecure access to land.

- In India, over 30 percent of the landless and near-landless (less than 0.2 ha) live in poverty.
- In Bangladesh, those with less than 0.2 ha make up two-thirds of the poor.

Those with secure rights to land also benefit when its value increases, either selling at higher prices or putting the land to more profitable uses. For example, with urban expansion, even small farmers can make large profits by converting their land to housing, whereas those who have been using the land without secure ownership rights will be squeezed out. Nevertheless, land sales do not always benefit the poor in the long-run if they are distress sales or based on incomplete information about the value of their land. Alternative assets or livelihoods are needed so that land sales do not lead to greater impoverishment.

Property Rights Include Common Property

It is not only agricultural land that matters. Without water, crops will not grow, so irrigation supplies are vital in dry areas, and everyone needs access to water for drinking, cooking, bathing, and washing. Trees — whether in forests or other types of land — are critical for fruits, fuel, home construction, medicines, and craft supplies. Rangelands provide food for livestock. Wetlands offer a range of food, medicines, housing, or craft supplies. Water bodies are a source of fish and other aquatic plants and animals. All of these resources play a critical role as a major or supplemental source of livelihoods.

Many of these resources are commonly rather than individually owned. Access to the commons is also a key source of food, income, and productive resources (such as water, fuel, building materials). In fact, common property areas such as wetlands, forests, and pastures, cover over 30 percent of the total land area in Africa.

The Poor and their Landlessness

In India, community forests contribute up to 29 percent of the income of poorer households, adding US $5 billion a year.

In Zimbabwe, the poorest 20 percent of the population generate up to 40 percent or more of their total income from the commons.

Social, Political, and Household Implications of Property Rights

In many rural societies, land ownership is an indication of a person's social identity. For example, the term *balabbat*, for landholder in highland Ethiopia, literally means "a man who has a father."

Landholding also shapes access to many government services, influence in local politics, participation in social networks, and intra-household relations. Extension agents focus their attention on landowners, often to the exclusion of their wives, children, or tenants. Membership in many water

Table 1. The Multiple Functions of Land Rights	
Functions	**Examples**
Economic functions	• Productive activities (farming, livestock rearing) • Land sales and rentals • Benefits from land appreciation • Investment incentive effects
Food security	• Source of food and income • Buffer against sudden price increases
Reduced vulnerability/shock mitigation	• Source for food and employment • Collateral for credit • Income from land sales and rentals
Social functions	• Social standing/bargaining position, within household, community, and nation • Membership of groups • Cultural identity • Religious functions
Conservation	• Authority to make decisions, investments • Incentives for sustainable management

users' associations is restricted to landowners, depriving others of a voice in the management of this critical resource.

Whole communities are too often deprived of government services because they are not recognized as landowners. Globally, control over land and territories has become a major issue for ethnic minorities and indigenous communities.

Secure land rights enable the poor to participate in the political process without fear of losing their source of livelihood. Therefore, securing property rights for the disadvantaged elements of a rural community can increase their participation in community life and forge a presence in the local political arena, which can have direct positive effects on their well-being.

Women's Property Rights

The distribution of property rights within the household matters. When women depend on fathers, husbands, sons or other men for land, their access depends on the quality of relations with that man. Wives too often lose their land when they are widowed or divorced.

Women with secure rights to land are more likely to engage in independent economic activities and have stronger bargaining power in the household and community. This, in turn, contributes to the welfare of the household and investment in the education and welfare of their children.

Property Rights and Promoting Sustainable Practices

Long-term security of land tenure provides an incentive to invest in production and conservation technologies that can improve crop yields and facilitate the more sustainable use of land and other natural resources. People will not make such long-term investments unless they have the rights to plant, harvest, and benefit from those investments, which are linked with rights to the land. Even within the household, if women or young people do not have land rights, they cannot make such investments. Thus, property rights are a tool in promoting environmentally sound management.

Challenges in Strengthening Property Rights

Efforts to create policies and programs that promote tenure security face many challenges. No universal prescription applies, because tenure regimes need to adapt to the nature of the resource and the society in which they operate. Systems that are appropriate in irrigated areas may not work for rangelands or forests; those that are suitable in a highly individualized society may not be appropriate where traditions of collective resource management are strong, and vice versa.

Property Rights have Complex Meanings and Sources

To create effective poverty reduction strategies based on enhancing tenure security, it is important to remember that, for rural people, land is a critical asset that has multiple functions and meanings. In addition to its economic function as a source of food production and income, land has social and political value, as well as important religious and cultural meanings (ancestral lands, for example). For many indigenous people, land has implications for the identities of individuals and communities. Therefore, policies that address only the economic value of the resource land may be resisted, occasionally violently.

To understand the complexity of property rights in practice, it is important to move beyond state-issued land titles to recognize the existence of multiple sources of property rights. In any given community, access to land and related resources may depend on the following types of laws and interactions among them:

- International treaties and law;
- State (or statutory) law;
- Religious law and practices;
- Customary (formal and informal) law;
- Project and donor rules (including project or program regulations); and
- Organizational rules (such as rules made by users' groups).

Policies that consider only state law may undermine the access to and use of land on which local people depend. When government legal systems are more accessible to those with education, money, or central location, the poor and marginalized may depend more on customary or religious bases for claiming rights to resources. However, it is important not to idealize, as customary practices can also disadvantage women or poorer people. In such cases, government intervention can help strengthen the claims of weaker members. This process is not automatic, however, a woman may not want to incur social sanctions by claiming stronger land rights from her husband, or a tenant may not want to risk losing other help from a landlord-patron. Legal reforms can provide a foundation for change, but if they are to have any effect, they must be carefully implemented to ensure that people know about the laws and have access to the relevant authorities.

What matters is not necessarily full "ownership" of land but tenure security. Many people have restricted, overlapping, or conditional rights to use and manage resources, such as to graze animals or harvest certain products from land officially "owned" by the state or by other people. Simplifying land rights to give complete authority to the owner of the land in the name of apparent efficiency can cut off these other claims, which are important for the livelihoods, social standing, or security of others. When these claims are eliminated, the poor and marginalized often suffer most.

Land is Scarce

Another challenge is the fact that there is only so much land. With a growing population and related needs for food, water, and other resources, the rural poor will continue to be disadvantaged in their quest for secure livelihoods. In many developing countries where other economic activities are lacking, land continues to be the main productive resource, and both the economy and people's livelihoods depend heavily on agricultural and other natural resources. However, the holding of land may be skewed in favor of some groups, excluding the poor.

In some cases, the poor are forcefully removed from land to make way for what are deemed to be more productive uses of land such as foreign investment, urban development, or new infrastructure like dams. Dispossession from land entails loss of the resources that people depend on for their livelihoods. When poor people have been exercising rights to land without formal legal recognition and the rights granted to new users have their basis in law, poor people risk losing their rights without compensation. In such a context, compensation must address the unjust expropriation and extinction of the rights of the poor.

When common property is expropriated, whole groups may need to be compensated. Justice also demands that the terms of compensation be mutually agreed to by all concerned parties, which may include restitution of the land when possible. Because land has many continuing values besides its "sale" price, a lumpsum payment may be inadequate, especially when the money can be siphoned away to cover immediate expenses. Instead, alternative assets that provide a flow of benefits need to be identified.

The Poor are Diverse

The third challenge is ensuring the inclusion of all the poor. Among people identified as poor and excluded from landownership and access, there are other forms of exclusion based on caste, gender, and age. Targeting the poor as monolithic communities may result in greater marginalization for some segments of the rural population.

What can be Done?

Policies are needed to ensure that the poor have secure access to land and other vital resources. Law remains a useful policy instrument in allocating property rights, as it can be used creatively to change property rights holdings and to ensure that the poor have access to the land they need for survival. Nonetheless, because property rights must be tailored to the physical, social, and economic context, there are no universal prescriptions. Policies must consider not only economic productivity, but also issues of equity and less tangible considerations like the social or religious significance attached to land.

- *Ensure Access by the Poor.* Once a country establishes normative procedures on inclusion, it must ensure that the poor have access to these provisions. The impact of policies must enable a poor rural woman to have secure tenure that enables her to invest in and benefit from the land, her community must have rights over resources, her household within the community must have rights to the land, and she must have secure rights within her household. If these conditions are not in place, different policies may be needed to address problems at each level.

These policies could include stronger recognition of community rights to common property, the provision of credit or rental markets to help make land available to landless households, and changes to family and inheritance law to give women stronger rights over land.

- *Build on Customary Arrangements.* Effective land policies must take into account that in many rural areas, government land administration systems are very different from the customary arrangements. Imposing land titling policies that ignore traditional tenure regimes might take a long time to implement (given the absence of supporting infrastructure) and lead to greater impoverishment and inequality in landownership. In addition, interventions that promote individualized land rights and disregard existing or potentially beneficial common property provisions can worsen the distribution of land within the community. Therefore, statutory land titling policies must be carefully selected and harmonized with existing arrangements.

- *Acknowledge the Many Values of Land.* Property rights should be framed in a way that recognizes the multiple values of land — as an economic resource that should be managed productively, a significant resource to which members of society should have equitable access, a finite resource that should be utilized sustainably, and a cultural heritage that should be conserved for future generations. This approach ensures the inclusion of diverse interests, values, and persons in property relations and enhances the visibility of less obvious vulnerabilities.

When new users come in with statutory legal rights, poor people's rights are often obliterated without compensation.

Suggested Readings

Kameri-Mbote, P. and J. Onyango Oduor. 2007. *Following God's Constitution: The Gender Dimension in the Ogiek Claim to Mau Forest Complex.* In: Hellum, A. and J. Stewart. 2007. *Paths Are Made by Walking: Human Rights Interfacing Gendered Realities and Plural Legalities.* Harare: Weaver Press.

Meinzen-Dick, R.S. and R. Pradhan. 2002. *Legal Pluralism and Dynamic Property Rights.* CAPRi Working Paper 22. International Food Policy Research Institute, Washington, D.C.

Mwangi, E. (ed). 2007. *Land Rights for African Development: From Knowledge to Action.* CAPRi Policy Brief 5. International Food Policy Research Institute: Washington, D.C.

Collective Action:
Issues and Challenges

SOURCE:

Thorp, R., F. Stewart and A. Heyer. 2005. *When and How Far is Group Formation a Route Out of Chronic Poverty?* World Development 33(6): 907–920.

Groups are of fundamental importance to economic, social, and political outcomes. Group formation among the poor may affect poverty directly, via improved income generation, or indirectly via empowerment and political action. Groups can be important vehicles for representing and promoting the interests of their members. In a number of significant ways, however, the chronically poor are disadvantaged in group formation, and this may form a significant part of the vicious circle and dynamics of chronic poverty.

Different Groups with Different Functions

Market Failure or Efficiency Functions. To overcome market failures such as externalities associated with non-excludability, groups or collective action are needed to produce public goods. There are three types of market failure groups: producers' associations, credit and savings groups, and natural resource management organizations.

Empowerment

Empowerment often means having secured and greater control over the decision-making process.

Claims Functions. These arise where a primary purpose of a group is to advance the claims of its members to power and/or resources. Examples of these are lobby groups, trade unions, women's groups, associations of the poor such as the landless. For these groups to be successful, the mobilization of mutually beneficial social networks and institutions is important.

Pro Bono Functions. Pro bono functions aim to alter the distribution of benefits within society, but they are (in theory) mainly directed toward individuals outside the group, in contrast to claims groups. Pro bono functions are performed by groups in the public sector, or nongovernment organizations (NGOs), and are typically associated with the provision of services such as health, education, or microcredit. Groups fulfilling pro bono functions also often contribute to overcoming market failures, such as externalities or indivisibilities, and to claims goals.

Credits and Savings Groups

For credits and savings groups, the control of capital and management rest entirely with the group, and thus, levels of autonomy and responsibility are high. Operating through a group instills the discipline to save through group encouragement and solidarity, which would be hard to achieve individually. Groups in this sense play a protective role against the demands of kin and clan, which can be crucial for women members.

Factors Inhibiting Successful Group Formation among the Poor

Groups potentially do offer an escape from poverty. However, the poor may be less likely to form groups in the first place, or to make a success of groups. The poorest may typically be excluded from successful groups. Following are the main factors inhibiting successful group formation among the poor and, in particular, the poorest:

Lack of Assets

Poverty, and in particular chronic poverty, is associated with lack of education, capital, labor, social status, and other assets. Yet, these make important contributions to group formation and organizations. Hence, the poor are structurally weak in terms of group formation, relative to others in society. In relation to market failure groups, the poor often cannot make productive contributions that make their inclusion worthwhile, which results in what some have analyzed as a middling effect, whereby the poorest and the richest tend to be excluded from groups. While the rich may not need groups in order to produce efficiently, the poorest may be excluded because they have no assets to contribute to group enterprises.

Lack of Access to Markets

Unequal access to networks results in asymmetric information about opportunities. In particular, the poor often lack access to social networks, which can be a major handicap to the success of groups. For the chronically poor, a lack of social networks may also inhibit group formation in the first place, as destitution leaves little space for networking.

In addition, deprivation tends to worsen some forms of conflict and thereby damages the trust essential for networking and economic exchange more generally. In turn, the resulting limited and biased economic networks among the poor, generally strongest within their own income group, limit knowledge about and access to market opportunities. Flawed access to market information is worsened by the isolation of rural poverty.

The Case of Thailand and South Asia

In Thailand, despite the adoption by the state of legislation to promote community forestry, certain groups has not been able to benefit from this due to lack of political entitlements, including immigrants of the last 100 years who were not able to obtain citizenship.

In South Asia, social stratification explains why cooperation is almost totally absent in some regions and a common feature of others. This seems especially true where caste and ethnic factors interact with class. For example, in the wet rice areas of West Bengal, the only "cooperation" found is a form of forced labor for building roads. In many countries, immigrants, squatters, and scavengers suffer from similar disadvantages in terms of their status and political entitlements, which makes it hard for them to organize and act as a group.

Lack of Rights

Access to political institutions seems to have a crucial bearing on the ability of groups to succeed among the poor. This is strongly influenced by the enforcement of rights or political entitlements, while a lack of citizenship, territorial claims, influence, and so forth can be crippling.

Leadership

Group formation often needs a catalyst, the nature of which is crucial. Leadership, whether from inside or outside the group, has generally been vital for group success. Internal leadership is the healthiest form, subject to achieving the fine balance between leadership and domination/exploitation.

Dependence on External Intervention

Many successful group ventures among the poor depend on external actors such as the state, an NGO, or social activists. The poorer the group, the more important the outsider's role is; though internal leadership can be successful. Yet, such external leadership roles typically go wrong, in which case the poor, by their very dependence on such actors, are placed at a disadvantage.

In many cases, it is the appropriation of groups for ideological, political, or economic ends external to the group's objectives that results in disaster. Forestry groups and microfinance groups are often subordinated to external objectives (environmental conservation, financial sustainability, etc.) resulting in a lack of genuine participation and the disempowerment of the so-called beneficiaries.

The very poor are often excluded or exploited in group ventures.

Groups and the Very Poorest

The problem for efficiency groups is that they are more often than not, exclusive. The landless people are usually automatically excluded from agricultural production ventures. Many microfinance groups exclude the poorest, and where they are included, they are usually exploited. Although claims groups, which are about voice, are less likely to exclude, problems of inclusion might arise from factors such as caste, gender, and ethnicity. Some might exclude for cohesion as in the case of South African housing groups which excluded the poorest, the majority of whom were illegal immigrants.

Policy Implications and Recommendations

There is a need for concerted efforts to qualify the widespread propagation of market norms and to emphasize those of trust and cooperation. International organizations, NGOs, and governments can make contributions in a variety of ways, including in their own modes of operation and in the recommendations they make and the demands they impose on developing country institutions. Successful groups among the poor do exist, and it should be the policy of national and local governments to document and publicize such successes and to promote their replication.

- Most structures of government (and aid policy) need to be reviewed to make them supportive of groups for the poor.
- Legal systems should be reviewed to ensure they do not discriminate against the asset — poor.
- Credit systems can be geared to be more favorable to groups incorporating poor people. In India, for example, banking regulations require a certain proportion of lending to low-income activities.
- Public expenditure in relation to infrastructure, education, and training in particular needs to be reviewed to assess and improve its impact on pro-poor group functioning.
- Effective policies of decentralization, based on devolution of power and resources, with adequate support to enhance accountability and promote understanding of group formation, can be an important mechanism of support for many of the group activities and in turn be helped by the prevalence of proactive groups, generating a virtuous cycle. However, local governments too can be subject to elite pressure groups.

Specific efforts are needed either to extend groups among the poor to include the poorest, or by implementing special initiatives geared toward the poorest. The policies of governments and NGOs toward group formation among the poor should seek to promote inclusiveness in coverage, through training programs, institutional arrangements, leadership development, and ways in which groups are held accountable.

There will always remain challenges in group formation, but the overall effects of groups — creation of self-esteem, empowerment, shared identity, and mutual support — appear to outweigh all such challenges.

Suggested Readings

Agarwal, A., and C.C. Gibson. 1999. *Enchantment and Disenchantment: The Role of Community in Natural Resource Conservation*. World Development, 27(4), 629-649

Heyer, J. and F. Stewart. et al (eds) 2002. *Group Behaviour and Development: Is the Market Destroying Cooperation?* Oxford: Oxford University Press.

Molinas, J. R. 1998. *The Impact of Inequality, Gender, External Assistance and Social Capital on Local-Level Cooperation*. World Development 26(3): 413-431.

Olson, M. 1965. *The Logic of Collective Action. Public Goods and the Theory of Groups*. Cambridge, MA: Harvard University Press.

Sourcebook on **Resources, Rights, and Cooperation**, produced by the CGIAR Program on Collective Action and Property Rights (CAPRi)

Collective Action, Empowerment, and Conflict Mediation

The notion of 'empowerment' has been more often deductively claimed than carefully defined or inductively assessed. In Indonesia, the Kecamatan Development Program (KDP) provides a good example on how program empowers participants (especially members of marginalized groups) by building their capacity to manage local conflict.

SOURCE:

Gibson, C. and M. Woolcock. 2005. *Empowerment and Local Level Conflict Mediation in Indonesia: A Comparative Analysis of Concepts, Measures, and Project Efficacy.* Policy Research Working Paper 3713. The World Bank.

Organized collectives — unions, political parties, village councils, women's groups, etc. — are fundamental to people's capability to choose the lives they have reason to value. They provide an arena for formulating shared values and preferences and instruments for pursuing them, even in the face of "powerful opposition" (Evans, 2002).

A growing body of research on deliberative decision-making processes has hypothesized a range of mechanisms by which institutional innovations might empower members of marginalized groups. They generally agree that closely tying the exercise of public power to active and broad citizen participation can, under certain conditions, expand the influence of disenfranchised groups.

When the currency of public exchange and decision-making becomes fairness-based reasoning itself, weaker voices can more easily be heard. In such cases, socially marginalized groups may develop the tools to influence productive conflicts about the purposeful structuring of future undertakings by newly formed groups. By generating more open and accessible forums for productive, inter-group conflict, deliberative democratic arrangements give marginalized groups a seat at the table with more powerful interests. More importantly, they also codify deliberation itself, its overarching value of fairness- and reason-based group decision-making, as the preferred currency of social exchange, which facilitators and a set of incentives for participation by women and the poor are structured to support.

It can be expected that there are substantial qualitative differences between the routines by which people and groups interact, shaped by different concentrations, and types of group influence. Most obviously, a conflict management routine that emerges from high concentrations of power will generally perpetuate group inequalities, while forms of shared or countervailing power may generate more discretion for marginalized groups.

Defining Empowerment

Empowerment is the process of enhancing individual or group capacity to make choices and transform those choices into desired actions and outcomes. It is an increasingly popular term that suggests an emerging, shared understanding that marginalized individuals and groups often possess limited influence in shaping decision-making processes that affect their well-being. Still, relatively little reliable empirical work exists to show whether and how Community-Driven Development (CDD) or other projects increase this influence, thereby improving development processes and outcomes.

Shared or Countervailing Power

The notion of countervailing power grew largely out of the analysis of interest group politics in adversarial arenas. It referred to the ability of trade unions, consumer organizations, and other organized interest groups to mold government rules and regulations that kept highly concentrated American industries in check following World War II.

The form of countervailing power underlying successful experiments with participatory collaboration differs substantially from that which evolves in adversarial arenas. In part, collaborative countervailing power refers to the ability of otherwise disadvantaged groups to put in place a wholly different kind of rule for group decision-making: the principle of fairness itself. The convergence of fairness-based deliberation as a decision rule, with collaboration as an institutionalized style of collective decision-making, discourages the perpetuation of prefabricated interests by pre-formed groups and encourages the exploration of joint interests by new, (often) functionally-oriented identity groups.

In practice, the rise of such routines partially neutralizes elites' prior advantages in organization, knowledge, intensity of interest, rhetorical capabilities, and agenda-setting ability, thereby diminishing several key tools of exclusion and subjugation. One potential result of this shift is a broader distribution of influence between marginalized and dominant groups.

Organized collectives provide an arena for formulating shared values and preferences and instruments for pursuing them, even in the face of powerful opposition.

Two analytically crucial parameters of comparison arise for those interested in understanding the routines governing both local-level conflict management and inter-group power relationships: fairness-based versus purely interest-based decision rules and adversarial versus collaborative types of forums. Distinct sources, forms, functions, and effects correspond to distinct combinations of each, and determining the qualities of various combinations is the task of empirical analysis. Although the growing literature on participatory collaboration suggests that the most durable forms of empowerment require both countervailing power and collaborative forums, evidence suggests that such happy combinations are rare. More often, conflict management routines feature one, the other, or neither.

Collaborative Forums

Collaborative forums encourage routines of speaking, acting, and group decision-making within which more and less powerful groups define, defend, and represent their interests with less of an orientation toward niche preservation and more of an orientation toward exploring shared preferences. Where forums encourage identity groups to recognize other identity groups in shared social space as potential allies rather than enemies, the potential for marginalized individuals to form coalitions and to begin acting collectively and with more influence ultimately rises.

The Power of Collective Action in Resolving Conflict: The Case of Sumorobangun Dam

In one case from the village of Biting in Ponorogo, East Java, an extended conflict over the repair of a leaky dam served as a flashpoint for the organization of farmers and other villagers dependent on its empty reservoir for irrigation. At the beginning of the conflict, the group mostly used bureaucratic channels to request repairs to the Sumorobangun Dam. After writing a series of letters to the District Legislative Assembly (DPRD) Head and the District Head, starting in 1996, the farmers' group felt their demands for action had fallen upon deaf ears and began expressing their sense of rejection and anger destructively. As farmers suffered more and more from the water scarcity, frequent arguments and limited small-scale violence broke out, including a hoe fight between two family members that resulted in head injuries but no deaths.

As unrest peaked in 2001, the farmers' group changed its tactics. In organizing a public demonstration, the group mobilized a broad web of social networks that included teachers, police, civil servants, rice paddy owners/farmers, and paddy workers from four sub-districts. This mobilization caught the attention of a candidate from a locally weak political party who was running for a DPRD seat and took the opportunity to apply pressure on the incumbent. Together, hundreds of villagers blockaded a key road connecting two districts, and in the middle of the road set up two chairs facing the dilapidated dam. By demanding that the two officials view the condition of the dam and witness the hundreds of villagers demanding its repair, the farmers' group finally solicited a response.

The DPRD Deputy Head arrived on the scene and committed to fixing the dam, a promise the district government ultimately fulfilled one year later. Additionally, a subsequent flurry of peaceful and fruitful activism ensued surrounding government compensation for lands previously inundated by the dam. These groups used the conflict to develop new, more effective routines for promoting their interests from below.

In this case, the farmers' group actually channeled protracted and escalating conflict into a unifying routine of speaking and acting that generated iterative results. On the one hand, appealing to a broad group of protestors generated significant negotiating power for the farmers because while the DPRD incumbent and his challenger could afford to ignore one demographic slice of the sub-district, both had a clear incentive to respond to the broader spectrum and more sizable numbers of potential voters who protested. On the other hand, the farmers' use of the richly symbolic protest action of blocking a road with a crowd of villagers and two empty chairs was a public performance that transformed their new association into a powerful force.

Collective action can empower people and bring about change. In Indonesia, a successful demonstration for the repair a dam solicited a positive response from the government.

Nevertheless, both theory and empirical observation reveal that marginalized groups often wield little clout, suffer from unstable preferences, and may be unaccustomed to confidently representing their preferences in formal associational settings. Without tools of speaking and acting in such settings, they inevitably struggle to be taken seriously by actors who have mastered (and indeed may have invented) dominant norms and rules of interaction. To counter this inherent disadvantage, to avoid being exploited, and to establish collaboration as the preferred norm of interaction within a forum, marginalized groups have to fill the power vacuum with demonstrable proof of their particular abilities.

Channeling Escalating Conflict into Dialogue

The Sumorobangun Dam case illustrates how a coalition of marginalized villagers revised the dominant practical and discursive routines for managing an ongoing conflict. By using a highly symbolic language of public protest, they exposed shared interests between natural allies, whose commonalities had previously gone unrecognized and unused.

The dam case was a telling example of a locally — organized coalition of marginalized groups mobilizing around an issue at a strategic time and with highly innovative discursive and practical tactics that more powerful authorities could not ignore. Numerous attempts to persuade officials to fix the dam using conventional tactics, letter writing, personal lobbying, and formal complaints to public authorities, ultimately failed. In the 2001 protest, which followed three years of the Kecamatan Development Program, a massive community development project focused on community participation in decision-making, in Biting, succeeded for a number of reasons. For one, they generated new, highly symbolic norms that established weaker and traditionally less organized groups as capable of challenging the dominance of sub-district authorities around a certain issue.

Suggested Readings

Evans, P. 2002. *Collective Capabilities, Culture and Amartya Sen's Development as Freedom.* Studies in Comparative International Development 37(2): 54-60.

Fung, A. and E. Wright. 2003. *Deepening Democracy: Institutional Innovations in Empowered Participatory Governance.* London: Verso.

Galbraith, J.K. 1956. *American Capitalism: The Concept of Countervailing Power.* New York: Houghton Mifflin.

Chapter 2

Rights to Resources and Collective Action for Agriculture

Influence of Property Rights and Collective Action on the Choice of Technology

The technologies people use play a fundamental role in shaping the efficiency, equity, and environmental sustainability of natural resource management (NRM). However, improved agricultural and natural resource technologies are of little value unless they are judged to be appropriate by farmers and subsequently adopted. There are many factors constraining farmers' technology choices, but the lack of secure property rights has been commonly identified as an important barrier to adoption, particularly for longer-term investments in tree crops and improvements to natural resources.

SOURCE:

Knox, A., R. Meinzen-Dick and P. Hazell. 1998. *Property Rights, Collective Action and Technologies for Natural Resources Management.* CAPRi Working Paper No. 1. International Food Policy Research Institute, Washington, D.C.

For technologies and NRM practices that require farmers to make joint decisions and cooperate in their implementation, inadequate and ineffective institutions for managing collective activity can be a constraint to adoption. Property rights and collective action are also important in determining who benefits from productivity increases (equity), both directly by determining who can reap the benefits of improvements in factor productivity, and indirectly through their effects on land markets, access to credit, etc.

Factors Influencing Technology Choices

Infrastructure

Unless the appropriate physical, economic, and institutional information infrastructure is in place, farmers may be unable to acquire technological inputs or market their outputs. Roads, electricity, water supplies, availability of improved seeds and other key inputs, as well as access to market outlets, are considerations for technology adoption by farmers.

Information

Information is a critical dimension of technology choices. Farmers must know that new technologies exist and how these could help them in terms of improving yields and increasing profits. Effective extension services can accelerate information dissemination on the profitability and risks associated with new technologies.

Effective extension services can accelerate dissemination on the profitability and risks associated with new technologies.

Risks

Farmers are more likely to take on risks associated with the adoption of a new technology if they have the capability and enough assets (i.e. risk-reducing options) to manage risks. These options may include livestock and crop diversification, inter-cropping, and plot scattering. Some of the risk-coping strategies may include use of savings or credit, storage, family support networks, and asset markets.

Wealth and Credit

Wealth provides a household with the option to acquire and use technologies. However, the lack of wealth need not be a constraint to technology adoption if households have access to credit and savings services.

Labor

Labor bottlenecks can be a significant constraint to the use of some technologies. Unless local labor markets are elastic, increases in demand for labor can raise seasonal wage rates and quickly dampen the profitability of new technologies, particularly for farms that require more than family labor alone. New cropping systems and technology may alter social relations, reduce labor requirements and exclude families from access to land resources between harvest and in field margins.

Access to credit and savings services allows farmers to purchase needed technological inputs.

Price Policy

The profitability of new technologies is affected by input and output prices, both of which are influenced by market fluctuations and government policies such as subsidies and support prices.

Environmental Conditions

Technologies may be unsuitable beyond the bounds of certain physical, socio-economic, cultural, and political environments. For example, agroecological conditions have prevented the use of high-yielding varieties (HYVs) in areas with low rainfall (and insufficient irrigation facilities), unfavorable micro-climates, and poor soils. Social biases toward technology arising from institutions and power structures can also preclude adoption. Cultural restrictions are a factor, too. In some regions of Africa and Asia, women are not allowed to plant trees and unable to participate in many agroforestry technologies.

Property Rights

Property rights provide the incentive and authority to make long-term investments. If there is a long time between investing in a new technology and getting the returns (e.g. planting a tree or terracing a field), farmers will not have the incentive to make the investment unless they have secure, long-term property rights. In many cases, tenants or those who are using the resource without full rights to it may even be prohibited from making such long-term investments. However, secure tenure does not necessarily mean full ownership or government-issued titles. Customary rights or long-term leases provide enough security for investment in many contexts.

Collective Action

In addition to joint investment in the purchase, construction, or maintenance of technologies, actions such as decision-making and implementation of rules to exploit (or refrain from exploiting) a resource; representing the group to outsiders; and mechanisms for sharing information and other resources are especially relevant for agriculture and natural resource management techniques.

Having group representatives to voice out concerns to outsiders is important in reaching common goals related to agriculture and natural resources management.

Linkages Between Property Rights and Collective Action

Collective action is often needed to uphold common, as well as private, property rights, and the adoption of large-scale technologies and NRM practices. Integrated pest management (IPM) practice, for example, requires substantial space to operate effectively, and hence is facilitated by collective action to coordinate its adoption.

Technology and Property Rights and Collective Action: A Two-Way Mapping

Well-defined and secure property rights to common pool resources are highly important for the poor, particularly poor women. Effective poverty alleviation strategies need to support common property regimes which enhance the production of common pool resources over the long-term and ensure fair distribution to more marginalized interest groups.

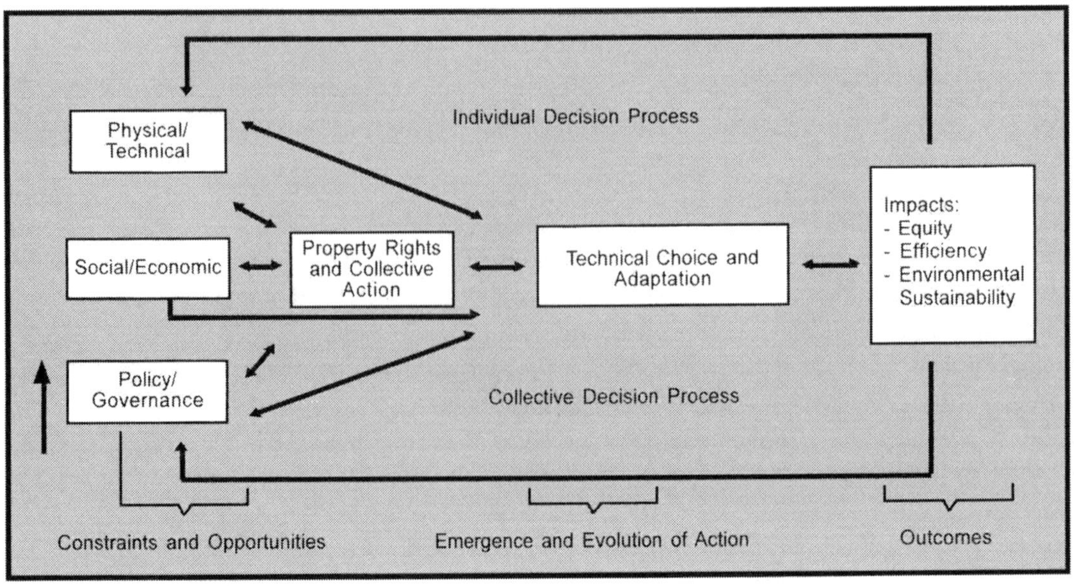

Figure 1. Conceptual Framework: Indirect Effects on Technology Adoption via Property Rights and Collective Action.

Figure 1 illustrates how other constraints interact with property rights and collective action to influence the decision to adopt a technology.

P*hysical/technical factors* affecting adoption include agro-climatic conditions (including risk) or infrastructure.

Social and economic factors include human capital (information), economic risk, social networks, wealth, credit availability, labor patterns, and social norms.

Policy and governance factors affecting adoption include pricing policies or legislation regarding resource use.

There is a two-way mapping between traditional constraints, on the one hand, and property rights and collective action, on the other, which subsequently influences choice of technology. Similarly, technologies and their adoption can stimulate institutional change. For example, the introduction of integrated pest management technologies has fostered increased levels of community and inter-community organization, and planting trees can strengthen tenure security. As Figure 1 indicates, property rights and collective action can also influence outcomes of efficiency, equity, and environmental sustainability. These factors then feed back on the environmental and institutional conditions, for example, through population growth or changes in the physical condition of the resource.

Implications for Efficiency, Equity, and Environmental Sustainability

Adoption of new technologies is not an end in itself, either for agricultural researchers, policymakers, or people who employ them in farming or for managing natural resources. Rather, the outcome of technological change should be evaluated in terms of the contribution to broader goals of sustainable development. Growth, poverty alleviation, and environmental sustainability form a "critical triangle" for development. Although there may be trade-offs between these three objectives, they are all necessary and interlinked.

The degree of tenure security within a community or among communities is not necessarily uniform. Wealth, power, and status are factors in determining one's tenure security and thus shape equity and environmental outcomes. Collective action becomes a critical component of tenure security in common property regimes, and a means of coordinating resource management across private holdings.

Greater control over resources tends to enhance men's influence over community power structures and wield political leverage with government officials and others responsible for technology distribution as well as infrastructure and market development.

The same is true for the wealthier strata of society. Technologies and their supporting infrastructure will therefore mainly reflect the interests of men who control the most substantial resources, unless a sufficient degree of collective action emerges. These actions should be capable of reshaping political outcomes so that government and other suppliers of technology and infrastructure intervene with policies to override these biases.

Greater integrated community participation in decision-making on the design, implementation and adaptation of technologies may not only ensure that the new technology does not disproportionately and inefficiently increase the workload of marginalized groups, but actually functions to reduce overall labor inputs.

Suggested Readings

Eyzaguirre, P. B. 1988. *Competing Systems of Land Tenure in an African Plantation Economy. In:* Downs, R.E. and S. P. Reynas (eds). *Land and Society in Contemporary Africa.* Hanover, N.H.: University Press of New England.

Place, F., M. Roth and P. Hazell. 1994. *Land Tenure Security and Agricultural Performance in Africa: Overview of Research Methodology.* In: Bruce, J. W. and S. Migot-Adholla (eds). *Searching for Land Tenure Security in Africa.* Washington, D.C.: The World Bank.

Place, F. and B. Swallow. 2000. *Assessing the Relationships Between Property Rights and Technology Adoption in Smallholder Agriculture: A Review of Issues and Empirical Methods.* CAPRi Working Paper 2. Washington D.C.: IFPRI.

Swallow, B., R. Meinzen-Dick, T. Williams and T. A. White. 1997a. *Multiple Functions of Common Property Regimes.* EPTD Workshop Summary Paper No. 4. International Food Policy Research Institute: Washington, D.C.

Sustained Collective Action for Integrated Pest Management

SOURCE:

Ravnborg, H. M. 2004. *Collective Action and Property Rights for Sustainable Development: Collective Action in Pest Management.* 2020 Focus Brief 11, International Food Policy Research Institute, Washington, D.C.

Every year, crop and animal pests deprive farmers of significant parts of their production. It is estimated that 10–40 percent of the world's gross agricultural production is destroyed by agricultural pests. These pests include a huge variety of different organisms, not only insects, mites, worms, rodents, and birds, but also, in a broader sense, all organisms such as weeds, fungi, bacteria, and viruses. The variety of pests and their interactions with other ecosystem conditions make pest problems very diverse and often complex, so solutions to single pest problems must vary substantially. Some pests can be controlled by individual farmers; others are amenable to public programs like aerial spraying. Many pest management approaches, however, call for neighbors to work together. Collective action is particularly important for reducing pesticides in agriculture.

Integrated Pest Management

Integrated Pest Management (IPM) is an ecosystem approach to crop production and protection that combines different management strategies and practices to grow healthy crops and minimize the use of pesticides (Source: FAO).

Often, the best results occur when the majority of farmers in an area adopt integrated pest management (IPM) practices, such as combining occasional use of pesticides with crop rotation or intercropping of different crops or varieties. Convincing neighboring farmers to adopt such practices in a coordinated fashion is, thus, a key to success. This need is especially great when the integrated approach involves allowing some crop losses to achieve greater overall profits, as well as to reduce environmental pollution and health hazards from heavy pesticide use. In such cases, successful pest management has both a spatial and a temporal dimension.

- First, IPM depends upon being implemented in a coordinated fashion over a wide geographic area. Thus, pest management is more effective if required institutions are in place to stimulate and facilitate coordinated or collective management efforts.

- Second, although in some cases a pest is controlled once and for all over a short period of time, in other cases pest management is a continuous effort that requires sustained collective action. This commitment in turn requires a certain degree of stability in the group undertaking. Under certain conditions, secure property rights might contribute to ensure such stability, but they are no guarantee.

Many other factors contribute to farmers' decisions about whether to continue farming in an area, such as the existence of alternative livelihood options in and outside the area, a sense of belonging to an area, and local cultural and social settings.

The Case of Collective Action in Pest Management

Leaf-cutting ants are a serious problem for farmers in many parts of Latin America. These ants are capable of destroying an entire cassava plot or one or more fruit trees overnight. There are simple technical options for controlling the ants, such as the regular pumping of insecticide into the anthill.

Ants, however, do not respect farm boundaries. Farmers who control anthills on their own fields might still face damage to their crops caused by ants coming from neighboring fields where no control measures are taken. Actions by individual farmers acting alone in cases like these can also raise new problems. The extensive use of pesticides on some farms may drive pests to fields of others or cause the pests to develop localized resistance to pesticides. Likewise, if farmers use pesticides that kill not only the pests but also their enemies, neighboring farmers who introduce or encourage the presence of predators may find that their predator populations never reach a viable size.

Gaining Farmers' Support for Collaboration

One obstacle to coordinated pest management is the view of farmers as sovereign decision makers. In many places, farmers are reluctant to interfere with the farming practices of others because this action might be perceived as a reproach and thus endanger future relationships and reciprocity. A key challenge therefore is to create institutions that encourage neighboring farmers to participate in coordinated pest management so that the individual farmer does not need to approach his or her neighbors.

Recognizing the transboundary nature of pest management problems helps to legitimize the otherwise socially unacceptable interference with the farming practices of others. In the case of ant control in Colombia, a joint community map of the location of anthills and their potential radius of crop damage, superimposed on a map of farm boundaries, provided an important illustration of the transboundary nature of the ant control problem. With the help of the map and the backing of external facilitators, farmers could calculate the average number of anthills affecting each plot and the number of anthills actually located on plots belonging to other farmers.

Since pests cross farm boundaries, joint action to control them is needed.

In many cases, external support is needed to help systematize the ecological and entomological observations and treatments upon which the need for coordinated pest management is based. Institutions such as farmer field schools or an agricultural extension service might be feasible options for providing this external support.

Farmers are more willing to participate in coordinated pest management when low-cost, economically feasible technical options are available. Which options are considered low cost and economically feasible obviously depends upon the context, i.e. the potential damage caused by the pest as well as the resources available to the individual farmer. Not surprisingly, the more widespread and severe the damage caused by pests and the less demanding and costly the technical control option, the easier it will be to persuade farmers to participate in coordinated pest management.

Hence, in areas with no previous experience of coordinated pest management, it is wise to begin by embarking on pest management problems that:

- are widespread (that is, they should affect the majority of farmers so that a large proportion of farmers will choose to participate in the coordinated pest management effort);
- are amenable to low-cost management options so that the poorest farmers are not prevented from participating in the coordinated pest management effort; and
- can be dealt with effectively at a relatively limited spatial scale so that farmers do not become frustrated at having to coordinate their pest management efforts with distant and perhaps unknown farmers.

Coordinated action in pest management takes into account both the spatial and temporal dimensions of pest ecology.

Because of the transboundary nature of many pest problems, technical solutions, whether based on the use of pesticides or on biological principles, are rarely sufficient. To be effective, such technical solutions need to be implemented in a coordinated fashion among farmers within a given area. Coordination, however, often represents a major challenge.

In areas with no previous experience of coordinated pest management, it is best to start on pest management problems that are widespread, have low-cost solutions, and are of limited spatial scale. Under these conditions, it is easier for farmers to mutually monitor compliance with agreed management practices. Widespread and consistent compliance will, in turn, facilitate the gradual development of trust among neighboring farmers, which is so important when, as in integrated pest management, short-term individual gains must be balanced against longer term collective interests.

Suggested Readings

Pretty, J. 2002. *Regenerating Agriculture: Policies and Practice for Sustainability and Self-Reliance.* London: Earthscan.

Ravnborg, H. M., A. M. de la Cruz, M. P. Guerrero and O. Westermann. 2002. *Collective Action in Ant Control*, p. 257-271. In: Meinzen-Dick, R., A. Knox, F. Place and B. Swallow (eds). *Innovation in Natural Resource Management: The Role of Property Rights and Collective Action in Developing Countries.* Baltimore: Johns Hopkins University Press.

Management of Irrigation Systems: From Government to Water User Associations

SOURCE:

Vermillion, D.I. 2004. *Irrigation, Collective Action, and Property Rights.* 2020 Focus Brief 11, International Food Policy Research Institute, Washington, D.C.

Approximately 40 percent of the world's food and 60 percent of its grain are produced under irrigation. Between 1900 and 1950, the total area under irrigation worldwide nearly doubled, from 48 million hectares to 94 million hectares. By 2000, it had reached 240 million hectares. The expansion entailed expensive infrastructure and strained governments' capacity to afford and manage these systems.

During the past two decades, there has been a shift of direct management of irrigation systems to regulation of the water sector. This management mechanism includes provision of support services and capacity building among water user associations and irrigation service providers. More than 40 developing countries in Africa, Latin America, and the Middle East have adopted programs to transfer the management of irrigation systems from government agencies to water user associations.

Governments have realized that enlisting water user participation helps in meeting the costs of operating, maintaining, rehabilitating, and upgrading irrigation systems.

State-Owned Versus Traditional Irrigation Systems

Traditional irrigation systems are developed and managed by local farmer groups. In many cases, such systems have been operated, maintained, and improved by local people for decades and even centuries. Research shows that these systems last because they are founded on locally-derived principles of water and land rights, rules, and obligations.

State-sponsored irrigation systems, on the other hand, are normally established without consulting the water users or making them participate in the decision-making process. Water users, in turn, do not have a sense of ownership over or responsibility for these systems. For this reason, farmers are unwilling to pay irrigation service fees. When governments are unable to mobilize adequate resources to finance irrigation, the condition of the infrastructure and quality of water services decline further. In addition, traditions sometimes break down because of state-sponsored development.

Water Users' Property Rights

Sometimes, irrigation management transfer programs overlook transferring property rights, authority, and strategic planning to change the roles and modalities of government.

The most important rights of water users are the following:

Sustaining irrigation systems. Water users help in maintaining, upgrading, repairing, and sustaining irrigation systems.

- the right to use, both on individual farms and for the irrigation system as a whole, a certain amount or share of water of an acceptable quality;
- the right to cultivate land and what crops to plant, with collective protection against conversion of irrigated land to other uses;
- the right to use, repair, and improve irrigation infrastructure;
- the right to determine what irrigation services will be provided and by whom;
- the right to adopt rules, irrigation service plans, and budgets;
- the right to establish, collect, and use an irrigation service fee (without having to transmit funds to the government);
- the right to assign penalties, settle disputes, and obtain legal support;
- the right to give consent to or refuse external assistance; and
- the right to maintain representation in a higher level public council at the river basin or district level.

Government and Water Users Partnership

For irrigation systems to be productive and sustainable, water users must play a larger role in their governance, financing, and management.

Governments should create a new partnership with water users to empower water user associations with property rights and governing authority, ensure that governments provide support services and regulate the sector at the macro level, and establish cost sharing for irrigation investment.

From international experience, irrigation sector reform programs should establish both a policy working group and a national secretariat to guide and coordinate the planning and implementation of the reform process. The process should include:

- strategic, participatory planning;
- research and stakeholder consultations;
- mobilization of political support;
- design and adoption of an appropriate policy, legal, institutional, and regulatory framework;
- strategy to coordinate lending and technical assistance;
- articulating needs for and sources of support services;
- public awareness campaigns; and
- monitoring, evaluations, and course corrections.

The partnership between government and water users should be redefined to involve the farmers in managing irrigation systems. Investing in organizing farmers to manage irrigation systems is as important as investing in irrigation infrastructure.

Water users as decision makers. State-sponsored irrigation systems should consult water users to engender a sense of ownership and responsibility for these systems.

The Case of South Sumatra

In South Sumatra, Indonesia, the government, with no local participation from the local community, installed a water division box on a site where farmers had previously used a traditional water-proportioning weir. After construction of the new division box, the farmers promptly reinstalled their proportioning weir just below it, in order to maintain traditional water rights. This case illustrates the importance of designing property rights, local institutions, and infrastructure in an integrated way.

Suggested Readings

Ostrom, E. 1992. *Crafting Institutions for Self-Governing Irrigation Systems.* San Francisco: Institute for Contemporary Studies Press.

Subramanian, A., N.V. Jagannathan and R. Meinzen-Dick (eds). 1997. *User Organizations for Sustainable Water Services.* World Bank Technical Paper No. 354. Washington, D.C.: World Bank.

Vermillion, D. L., and J.A. Sagardoy. 1999. *Transfer of Irrigation Management Services: Guidelines.* FAO Irrigation and Drainage Paper No. 48. Rome: Food and Agriculture Organization of the United Nations.

Collective Action for Sustainable Water Harvesting Irrigation

Collective action for water harvesting irrigation (WHI) refers to the joint or collective effort of farmers in getting and using water for crop, animal, household, or other purposes.

SOURCE:

Scott, C.A. and P. Silva-Ochoa. 2001. *Collective Action for Water Harvesting Irrigation in the Lerma-Chapala Basin, Mexico.* CAPRi Working Paper No. 20. International Food Policy Research Institute, Washington, D.C.

Organized water user groups also handle external representation with government programs and external demands (either competing or complementary) for water and other resources. In water-scarce areas, the goal is for farmers to produce high crop yields with less water, which can be achieved when farmers collectively manage the water resources available to them.

Why Collective Action?

- It makes participatory management of water resources possible — community members then have a stake in making decisions.

- It promotes equity and efficiency in water distribution — no member can monopolize the use of water resources, and distribution scheduling is normally based on optimizing conveyance efficiency.

- It reduces cost— members equally share/divide the cost of labor and materials that are needed in maintaining water harvesting irrigation systems.

- It builds internal community unity and camaraderie — fighting among members is lessened.

- It can strengthen efforts to defend their resources in the case of competition from outside the community.

Collective action can lead to more equitable water allocation and lower cost for farmers, because the cost of maintaining WHI systems is shared by the community.

What Hinders Collective Action?

Given the increasing demand for water from the uplands for use by lowland communities, collective action is the best option to achieve the objectives of sustainable water harvesting irrigation. Factors hindering collective action include the following:

- conversion of community-owned farm lands to privately/individually owned farm lands;
- availability of off-farm job opportunities and diversified forms of livelihood;
- increased migration of male members of communities, leaving women as the primary source of labor; and
- reduced community cohesion.

Many off-farm job opportunities can hinder collective action.

Conclusion

Changing property rights over land and water, a growing number of available work opportunities outside farm areas, increasing water scarcity, increasing number of users, increasing migration of male farm workers to other economically lucrative areas, and feminization of the farm labor force are among the many challenges that confront small-scale water harvesting irrigation systems.

Despite water scarcity and crop failures, farmers can still respond collectively to address these problems.

The two case studies illustrate how communities respond to these challenges in the context of collective action. In Trojes de Paul, the community collectively built the water harvesting reservoir. They shared labor and materials and sought external support for the reservoir from the Agriculture and Water Resources Ministry. Their social cohesion and relations, both internally and externally, resulted in improved crop yields for community members.

Case Studies on Water Harvesting Irrigation

The Case of Trojes de Paul

Trojes de Paul is a community in Mexico which practices a more conventional WHI system. The water user group is more formally organized, and members discuss water management issues separately from their regular *ejido* meetings. They clear the canals at the start of irrigation and decide together on the schedule of water distribution. They also work together in managing the use of water.

In 1968, they collectively acted on constructing a water harvesting reservoir. They shared labor and materials and sought external support for the reservoir from the Agriculture and Water Resources Ministry. Their social cohesion and relations, both internally and externally, resulted in higher crop yields.

The Case of Nápoles

Nápoles is another Mexican community, smaller than Trojes de Paul, and water is more scarce. The terrain is more accessible, and members have more contacts with other communities. With more contacts outside, members often engage in diverse livelihoods and in more off-farm work.

Water users of Nápoles are less organized. There is a small number of the water users groups, with few members, and a high degree of absentia from the community in general (due to migration and urban employment). Decisions related to irrigation tend to be made informally.

Lessons from the Case Studies

Collective action for the conventional WHI system in Trojes de Paul contributed to high crop and water productivity. The cohesiveness of the water users group also allowed farmers to take on additional (collective) watershed management tasks, including actions to deal with erosion and sedimentation issues.

Location contributed to the cohesion of water users groups in Trojes de Paul. Geographically, it is not as accessible as Nápoles is to other communities, and its members have less contact with outsiders, and fewer opportunities to engage in off-farm livelihood activities.

In the second, more water-scarce system of Napoles, WHI was subsumed under a broader set of community goals, where sharing water among all members of a group was an important means to ensure solidarity. In this system, WHI supplements rain-fed agriculture, and water management structures are only one part of wider household economic strategies.

So far, both WHI systems studied have continued to receive low but sustainable levels of household labor and financial resources. Despite increased urban and non-agricultural activity, keeping a foot in agriculture is an important form of income diversification, to hedge against the risks involved in other economic activities, and water harvesting plays an important role.

On the other hand, in Nápoles, where water was scarce and there were more crop failures, community members still responded collectively to outsiders claiming water, but also relied more heavily on off-farm income sources.

WHI will remain a subsistence activity. As a result, ensuring productive and equitable benefits to users is critical for their continued viability.

Suggested Readings

Dayton Johnson, J. 1999. *Irrigation Organisation in Mexican Unidades de Riesgo: Results of a Field Study*. Irrigation and Drainage Systems. 13(1): 55-74.

Ostrom, E. 1992. *Crafting Institutions for Self Governing Irrigation Systems.* San Francisco, CA: Institute for Contemporary Studies.

Von Koppen, B. 1998. *More Jobs per Drop: Targeting Irrigation to Poor Women and Men.* Amsterdam: Royal Tropical Institute.

How Institutions and Organizations Contribute to Making Water Accessible to Farmers

SOURCE:

Meizen-Dick, R. 2007. *Institutions, Organizations, and Water Access.* Paper presented at the Agricultural Water Management Strategy Meeting on 26-27 November 2007.

Experience in the past 30 years of irrigation has shown that technology alone is not sufficient to reduce poverty, enhance food security, and increase rural livelihoods. In many cases, farmers have not adopted or maintained the technologies, or the poor, women, and other marginalized groups have not enjoyed the benefits of technologies. In this context, institutions and organizations of collective action can help farmers acquire and adopt the technologies that best fit their needs.

Importance of Key Institutions for Agricultural Water Management

Figure 1 illustrates the importance of two types of key institutions for agricultural water management. The vertical axis illustrates the spatial scale of a technology, from an individual plot, through a whole farm, to one that covers several farms, a village, or a region. All approaches that are above

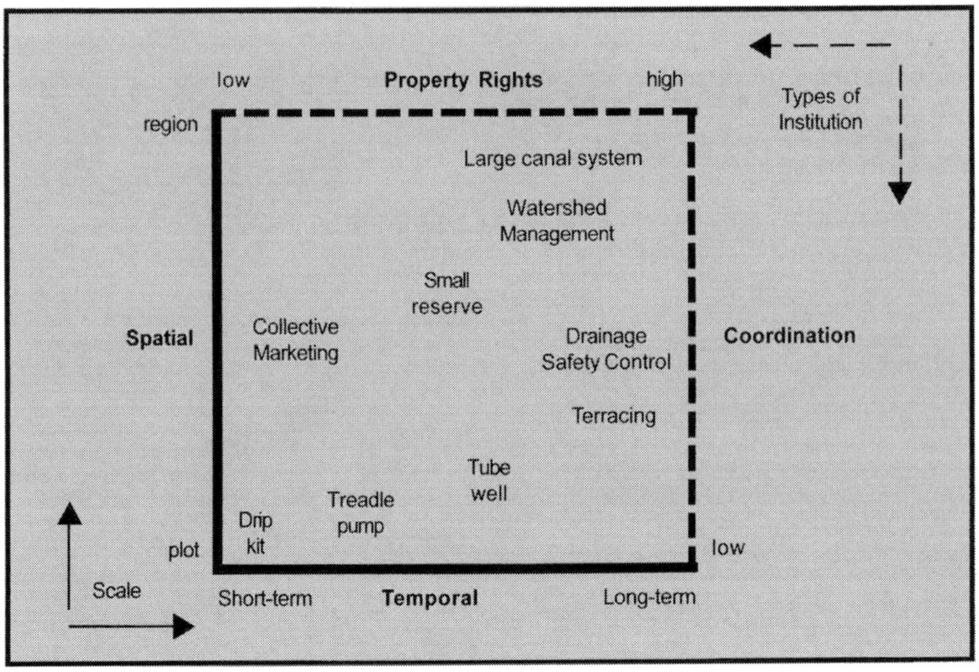

Figure 1. Institutions for Agricultural Water Management.

the scale of the individual farm require some form of coordination—either by local organizations, the state, or the market.

For example, a drip kit may be adopted by an individual small farmer, and even many tubewells serve just one farm. Where holdings are very small and tubewells have large capacity, farmers may join together to buy and operate a tubewell, or the state may install and operate it, or one farmer might install it and sell water to neighbors.

How well each of those institutions functions will determine whether smallholders receive adequate and timely water supplies. Even if a drip kit can be operated independently by one farm household, access to the kit within a farm household will matter. Depending on the water source or the return flow, other farms might be affected and collective institutions come into play.

Similarly, the horizontal axis indicates the permanence of a technology or approach, or the time frame to cover the investment. The longer the temporal scale, the greater the need for property rights to provide authorization and incentive to make the investment.

Even a tenant or a wife without independent land rights can install a drip kit, but may not be allowed to install a treadle pump or tubewell, and may not have the incentive to install and maintain terracing or drainage systems for salinity control. Even if farmers have secure rights to the land, they may not be willing to invest in irrigation systems if they do not also have secure rights to the water. This has been the problem with many irrigation management transfer systems, where farmers are expected to bear the costs, without secure rights to the water from the systems.

While the exact location on this figure would depend on the size and scale of the farms, as well as the cost/return ratio of the particular technology, this provides a useful starting point to ask about which institutions are likely to be critical.

Nevertheless, important institutions is relatively easy compared to ensuring that these are in place. Analogies of "social engineering" have been misplaced, because they imply a mechanistic approach. Rather, institutions are organic and path-dependent — they cannot be simply imported from one context to another. This requires a more nuanced approach, which may require mutual adaptation of the physical and institutional environment.

Coordination Institutions

The example of the tubewell cited above illustrates that coordination functions can be provided by the state (a public tubewell that supplies many farms), collective action (farmer group), or markets (farmer selling water). Which institution is most appropriate depends on the particular conditions — e.g. scale, technical sophistication of the technology and the farmers, and cultural factors (social capital, market orientation). In general, the advantages of the state are greatest at the largest scale; collective action at more localized levels, and markets are highly variable in whether they provide effective coordination among smallholders.

If group-based approaches are selected for water management or technology dissemination, it is important to look beyond formal rules and membership roles to see whether the group is actually acting collectively and who is included and excluded from active membership and decision-making. This means asking about women as well as men, landowners and tenants, farmers and other water users (e.g. fishers, livestock keepers, home gardens, domestic users, other enterprises). There may be formal as well as informal barriers to participation, different motivations and returns to be considered.

There are indications that organizations with the active participation of men and women may be more effective in managing resources like water because they draw upon the skills and resources of both, but the costs of establishing active mixed organizations are also greater than single-sex organizations, especially where there is high gender segregation in the society. All of these factors should be considered when identifying which groups to work with, particularly if that organization will gain stronger control over technology or water itself. Furthermore, just setting up the organizations is not enough for sustainability: they also need to become internalized and 'institutionalized'.

Water Rights and Access

Many poor people do not have formalized rights to the water they depend on for their livelihoods. Strengthening their rights, which may involve getting the government to recognize them as legitimate claimants, will help increase their security and provide incentives for investments — even if very small — in agriculture.

But just passing laws and regulations will not necessarily change water rights, as they do not derive only from government law. A wide range of customary laws and practices, religious law and interpretations, and project regulations also relate to water rights, and people may base their claims on any of these.

A better approach is to start with people's experiences with water—how they access it, what claims they make for their different water uses, etc. This will help to identify the relevant legal frameworks to address. Then an intervention can work to strengthen the claims of poor people for their important water uses. Ensuring that women, smallholders, livestock keepers, or other poor and marginalized water users are represented in those organizations is an important step to strengthening their water rights.

Conclusion

It is not technology alone that contributes to efficient water governance, but an interplay of roles among state, collective, and market institutions. Instead of trying to import new institutions, policies should then seek to identify the strengths of the existing institutions and build from them. The next step is to look for the connections between different types of institutions so they can strengthen each other, for example, by agencies providing financial training to water users groups or user groups creating accountability for government agencies.

To have a real impact on water management, the results of research must be built in to adaptive learning that strengthens the capacity of the state and water users to address evolving challenges: a process that requires going beyond panaceas.

There is a need to start by asking people how they access water, and what claims they make for their different water uses. This will help to identify the relevant legal frameworks to address.

Suggested Reading

Meinzen-Dick, R. 2007. *Beyond Panaceas in Irrigation Institutions.* Proceedings of the National Academy of Sciences 104:15200-15205.

Sourcebook on **Resources, Rights, and Cooperation**, produced by the CGIAR Program on Collective Action and Property Rights (CAPRi)

Improving Agroforestry through Effective Property Rights and Collective Action

Agroforestry is a system that combines agriculture and trees. In this system, trees play a prominent role. Benefits derived from agroforestry include the following:

SOURCE:

Place, F., K. Otsuka and S. Scherr. 2004. *Collective Action and Property Rights for Sustainable Development: Property Rights, Collective Action, and Agroforestry.* 2020 Focus Brief 11, International Food Policy Research Institute, Washington, D.C.

- *Tree products:* fuel wood, timber, poles, medicines, and resins.

- *Services by trees:* shade and soil conservation.

- *Global benefits:* biodiversity, watershed protection, carbon sequestration, and microclimate regulation.

Different agroforestry systems require different periods of time to develop and manage. Over longer time periods, property rights increase in importance; over larger areas, collective action becomes more important. Depending upon what benefits are sought, farmers will adopt various degrees of joint action or coordination within the landscape.

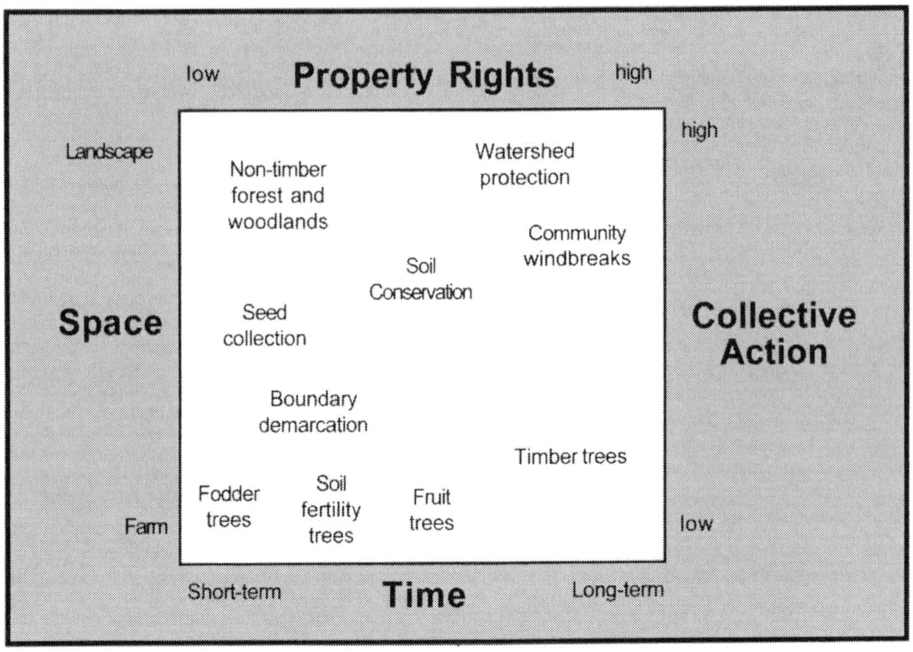

Figure 1. Relative Importance of Property Rights and Collective Action.

Figure 1 shows how different types of agroforestry outputs or activities will demand different levels of property rights or collective action.

Property Rights and Agroforestry

To justify investing in trees, a household or group must have reasonable assurance of receiving the benefits from their investments. Investors must have confidence that tenure will be secure in the future. In much of the world, the rights to plant, harvest, and benefit from trees are linked to underlying land rights.

Permanent Ownership. In many parts of the world, the rights to plant, harvest, and benefit from trees are linked to whether the farmers formally or legally own the lands or not.

Temporary Ownership. Farmers who acquire land on a temporary basis agree on some share-cropping arrangements. This is a situation where rights and incentives to plant trees are weak.

Government Intervention. In some cases, governments complicate the planting and harvesting of trees by issuing regulations that either strengthen or weaken the planting of or investing in trees.

Tree Tenure. The importance of tree tenure must also be considered at a landscape level. Where farmers have unfettered access to trees in woodlands or forests, the incentives to plant on their own land are reduced, even if their rights to plant are unquestioned.

Communal Land Tenure. In strong communal land tenure systems, communities may be encouraged to establish agroforestry systems that provide communal benefits, such as riverine vegetation or common dry season tree fodder reserves.

Customary Tenure System. In customary tenure systems, individual rights to land are often granted to those who invest in the land. Thus, these systems have been associated with both investment in clearing trees from forest to grow crops as well as planting tree specie of choice.

Common Property Rights System. In the case of woodlands, the protection of non-timber products is costly, but tree management is not very important because of relatively low returns to improved management for these lower-value products. In this case, collective protection under a common property regime system often works best.

Collective Action and Agroforestry

Most agroforestry systems can be established on individual plots and managed without explicit collective action. But collective action can increase the effectiveness of agroforestry, either by reducing risks or costs or by enabling positive externalities to occur. Examples include:

- collecting and mixing tree seeds to prevent genetic deterioration;
- managing group nurseries to take advantage of scarce water sources;
- establishing grazing rules to prevent browsing of seedlings; and
- collectively guarding valuable tree stands to reduce protection costs.

For agroforestry systems intended to produce community-wide agricultural or environmental benefits, other types of collective action are essential for establishment and management. Examples include the coordinated planting of trees to reduce soil erosion in a watershed or the establishment of a community-wide windbreak and the joint fencing of lands to restore natural woody vegetation for biodiversity and water management. These examples of collective action for agroforestry are seen throughout the world.

Although non-government organizations (NGOs) or external projects often attempt to create new local organizations to carry out such activities, mobilizing existing local groups can be more effective over the long term. Even if the work is new to these existing groups, they can be successful because social capital (trust and mutual obligations) and organizational systems are already established.

Relevant Lessons for Agroforestry

The importance of property rights or collective action arrangements for management incentives will depend on the particular agroforestry-related task, product, or service being evaluated. Consider the difference between timber and non-timber forest products. In the case of a timber plantation (lower right portion of Figure 1), incentives to invest and manage determine the level of benefits received. Since it is relatively simple to detect harvesting activities and the size of timber area is often limited, it is easy to protect the trees. In such a case, a clear private property rights system leads to an efficient management outcome. In the case of woodlands (upper left portion of Figure 1), the protection of non-timber forest products (NTFPs) is costly, but tree management is not very important because of relatively low returns to improved management for these currently lower-value products. In this case, collective protection under a common property regime system often works best.

In many parts of the world, the rights to plant, harvest, and benefit from trees are linked to whether the farmers formally or legally own the lands or not.

Effective property rights or collective action arrangements need not be formalized. In many examples throughout the world, indigenous systems provide appropriate incentives for the development of agroforestry systems. Social institutions for property rights and collective action clearly shape agroforestry investments. Agroforestry development initiatives must consider these institutions as they work with local people to identify suitable tree species, agroforestry systems, planting sites, and management systems. In the short term, there may be limited scope to modify these institutions but considerable room to work creatively within them. Over the medium to long term, the development of property rights and organizations for collective action will be critical to improved land management, including agroforestry.

In the future, property rights and collective action will play increasingly pivotal roles in defining rights and responsibilities over the externalities of tree management practices. As stakeholders recognize the need for the effective management of, for example, erosion resulting from tree felling or rights to carbon sequestration from tree planting, they will increasingly value and depend on the institutions that protect their property rights.

Suggested Readings

Meinzen-Dick, R., A. Knox, F. Place and B. Swallow (eds.). 2002. *Innovation in Natural Resource Management: The Role of Property Rights and Collective Action in Developing Countries.* Baltimore: Johns Hopkins University Press.

Otsuka, K. and F. Place (eds.). 2001. *Land Tenure and Natural Resource Management: A Comparative Study of Agrarian Communities in Asia and Africa.* Baltimore: Johns Hopkins University Press.

Cashew Agroforestry and Changing Property Rights in Post-War Mozambique

Mozambique was the world's number one producer of cashew nuts in shell in the 1970s. Cashew trees existed largely on smallholder land, in groves and intermixed with cassava, cowpea, maize, and groundnuts. A civil war beginning in the late 1960s and lasting nearly two decades changed the situation. The war dislocated people and stopped the planting and replacing of the old and unproductive cashew trees.

SOURCE:

Unruh, J. D. 2001. *Land Dispute Resolution in Mozambique: Institutions and Evidence of Agroforestry Technology Adoption.* CAPRi Working Paper No. 12. International Food Policy Research Institute, Washington, D.C.

Restoration of peace in the 1990s brought land tenure issues to the fore. Many demobilized and displaced smallholders returned to find their lands occupied by others, resulting in significant numbers of land disputes. Rural households expanded areas under cultivation as farmers brought areas long under fallow due to the war back into cultivation. There were also large-scale recovery efforts to rehabilitate agricultural sectors, such as cashew and livestock production.

Small-scale agricultural producers were given access to land in areas with the most fertile soils, perennial water supplies, infrastructure, markets, relief services, and physical security. As a result, food-insecure migrants came into conflict with long-term customary residents. While this unfolded, commercial interests with capital were formally acquiring pieces of property in these agronomically-favored areas.

At least nine million hectares of land were reported to have been awarded through the formal land tenure system as concessions for farming, hunting, tourism, and mining activities. Practically, all these concessions overlap with lands held by smallholders who were not part of formal land allocation decisions. In an environment of competing and overlapping property rights institutions, the situation generated further conflict between migrants, indigenous communities, and concession holders.

Conflicts have led to the non-adoption of cashew agroforestry because technology is related to land ownership. The presence of cashew and other valuable trees is the single most important piece of evidence for defending or asserting rights to land, regardless of the average number of trees per smallholder. This is true even in situations where institutions regarding property rights are most displaced, in less agronomically endowed areas, and in critical resource areas.

Cashew trees as evidence for property rights are accepted even in areas which are less disrupted, those where migrant numbers are huge, and where there are less investments in cashew natural resource management (NRM) technology.

The War: Its Effects on Land Tenure

1. **Dislocation and disruption created and maintained an age gap in cashew trees. The following interrelated forces worked, in a mutually reinforcing way, to create and maintain a significant age gap in cashew agroforestry trees:**

    - Migrants, then residing on other people's lands, were prevented from planting by their hosts because it would be seen as a land claim.
    - If migrants removed trees from the land, it was seen as challenging the owner's claim.
    - For migrants cultivating land with no clear ownership, the temporary nature of their residence deterred tree planting.
    - For communities not dislocated, tree planting was precluded by the need to produce annual crops to address more urgent food security concerns.

Tree planting is precluded by the need to plant annual crops that address more immediate food security concerns.

- Older cashew trees near the end of production were not removed, as they still provided small amounts of cashew for food-insecure agriculturalists.
- Smallholders in areas with land conflicts were especially reluctant to remove older trees due to their greater evidence value of long-term occupation compared to seedlings and saplings.
- As more smallholders lost land in the course of their displacement, they had to rent out or borrow land from other smallholders, again discouraging planting.

2. Dislocation and disruption have made other forms of evidence of land tenure less available and legitimate.

Population displacement during the war led to many agricultural areas being repeatedly occupied and abandoned at different times and by different groups. This has obscured, confused, and made less accessible many forms of evidence of human occupation of the lands. It has also lessened social interaction regarding power arrangements of various land-related transactions, such as landownership, loaning, renting, purchase, and others. The problematic post-war existence or availability of such forms of evidence have not only an influence on their legitimacy, but also on the comparative importance and legitimacy of other forms of evidence (agroforestry) that remain in place.

Three categories of evidence were used to claim land ownership, namely social, cultural-ecological, and physical evidences, all of which vary considerably in their utility. It is the combination of social evidence with cultural-ecological evidence that is most valuable in constructing an argument for a land claim. This is because social evidence ties individuals to communities, and cultural-ecological evidence corroborated by social evidence constitutes the connection between the physical signs of land occupation due to human pressure, and the social aspects, which are bound up in cultural-ecological evidence (inheritance of land, networks of lending land, etc.).

In Mozambique, reductions in the availability of social evidence for populations with significant numbers of migrants appear to have resulted in a shift that favors forms of evidence that are available — physical evidence and some cultural-ecological evidence — with the relative permanence of older agroforestry trees emerging as one of the most important and durable pieces of evidence available.

Forms of Evidence of Tenure

Social evidence is oral or testimonial evidence provided or confirmed by others in the community. It demonstrates occupation and serves to tie individuals and households to local communities. Social evidence corroborates other social as well as physical and cultural-ecological evidence.

Cultural-ecological evidence consist of physical pieces of evidence that exist due to human activity on the landscape, such as agroforestry trees, current and old field boundaries, cemeteries, and others. It demonstrates occupation and corroborates social evidence and some other forms of cultural-ecological evidence.

Physical evidence involves naturally occurring terrain features that are easily observable. It demonstrates familiarity with an area and corroborates no other category of evidence.

3. Different types of tenure and evidence of tenure.

In post-war Mozambique there are three different general approaches to land tenure: customary, statutory legal, and migrant, or 'displaced.' The migrant or 'displaced' term is characterized by a comparative lack of social connections to the community regarding land, and a higher value placed on naturally occurring physical forms of evidence in claims to land.

Land disputes involving parties from different tenure approaches can involve attempts to bring to bear forms of evidence regarded as legitimate and therefore respected. However, if not respected by the opposing party, such evidence became unworkable, forcing the different parties, particularly the less powerful, to place increased value on evidence that is mutually legitimate evidence.

Different forms of evidence of tenure must be negotiated between migrant and customary owners.

Customary and migrant groups express high preference for only two forms of evidence: soil type and agroforestry trees, with soil type much less important than agroforestry trees. No data exists for the formal groups, but land law at the end of the war acknowledged forms of smallholder evidence that demonstrated occupation and explicitly allowed social evidence.

The strongest evidence that demonstrates "occupation" is agroforestry trees, especially the older trees, which are also accepted in the formal land tenure system. Thus, agroforestry trees serve as evidence under existing customs and rules not only within, but also between groups operating from the three different tenure approaches. As disputes among these three groups become common in certain areas, agroforestry trees as mutually acceptable and respected evidence for defending rights to land receive strong incentives.

The Effect of Technology on Property Rights Institutions

There are two overall effects of cashew agroforestry on property rights in post-war Mozambique. These are:

1. The rules and customs regarding the link between agroforestry trees and land tenure have, in a post-war context, greatly facilitated (at no cost to the state) the coordination of defending and asserting rights to land, and hence land re-access and dispute resolution.

2. The use of agroforestry trees as evidence for property rights affects the adoption and maintenance of cashew agroforestry, as these intersect with the formidable tree age gap. The failure to adopt or re-adopt tree replacement strategies due to the high value placed on older trees as evidence will eventually result in a decrease in this evidence as the older tree dies out, with impacts on the overall technology (loss of agroforestry, as opposed to adoption) and property rights. Along with the decreasing numbers of trees as forms of evidence, so too will the set of customs and norms that pertain to them as evidence disappear.

Very high value will continue to be placed on older trees unless other forms of evidence become available and legitimate and institutions pertaining to these are able to evolve and deliver in terms of tenure security. The derivation of other forms of evidence, possessed by and legitimate to smallholders, and at the same time legitimate in the formal land tenure system and able to complement agroforestry trees, would likely amplify the number and kind of meaningful forms of evidence. It will also highlight some of the comparative importance of agroforestry trees, thus allowing the adoption or re-adoption of practices necessary for agroforestry as a natural resource management technology.

Suggested Reading

Fortmann, L. and J. Bruce. 1988. *Whose Trees? Proprietary Dimensions of Forestry*. Boulder, CO: Westview Press.

Property Rights, Collective Action and Plant Genetic Resources

Conservation of genetic resources contributes to plant genetic diversity, which includes both the combination of species in agricultural ecosystems, as well as the number of different varieties within a species (genetic diversity).

SOURCE:

Eyzaguirre, P., N. Mccarthy, M. Di Gregorio and E. Dennis. 2004. *Collective Action and Property Rights for Sustainable Development: Property Rights, Collective Action, and Plant Genetic Resources.* 2020 Focus Brief 11, International Food Policy Research Institute, Washington, D.C.

Loss of biodiversity in cultivated and wild species can increase plant vulnerability to insect pests and diseases, worsen nutrition through declines in the variety of foods available, reduce the capacity of plant resources to adapt to changing conditions, and lead to loss of local knowledge about diversity. These effects can in turn reduce food security, threaten the sustainability of agricultural production systems, and jeopardize the livelihoods of rural communities today and for generations to come.

Factors that affect the conservation of biodiversity include demographic changes, technological developments, national agricultural policies, and economic, social, and cultural factors. Institutional aspects related to property rights and collective action play a key role in local plant genetic conservation outcomes.

Property Rights to Land-Based Resources

Access to land and water is crucial for the conservation of genetic resources. In particular, land tenure and water rights are likely to affect *in situ* conservation (conservation in natural surroundings) for a variety of reasons:

- The type and strength of property rights arrangements affect farmers' time horizon and investment choices and, as a consequence, crop diversity.

- Stronger land use and management rights for farmers can increase their ability to grow a variety of crops. Where farmers' investments are crop-specific, however, security of property rights might lead to less diversified cropping patterns.

- Property rights, together with available genetic resources, affect people's capacity to manage variability and risk. Many traditional communities present "patchwork landscapes" with various ecological niches that favor the use of unique varieties and plant types adapted to those niches. High genetic diversity reduces risk, and access to a diverse pool of plant genetic resources improves the long-term resilience of the agricultural production system in the face of adverse shocks like drought.

Formal property rights often coexist with and differ from locally exercised property rights. The existence of different overlapping arrangements and regulatory frameworks (legal pluralism) must be taken into account in order to assess their effects on biodiversity conservation. For example, in Ethiopia, sacred groves managed by the Christian Coptic churches not only provide landless people with access to non-timber forest products, but also assure protection to areas with some of the highest amounts of biodiversity in the country.

Positive and Negative Impacts of Property Rights Regimes

Different property rights regimes have different advantages and disadvantages for biodiversity conservation. For example, local forest and pasture resources held as common property enable farmers to avail themselves of a much wider range of resources than they could use if all land were cultivated.

Common property rights provide landless poor in Kenya with access to indigenous fruits and vegetables, and foster their conservation.

State imposition of new property rights regimes that fail to account for traditional rights can also affect the maintenance of local knowledge of specific varieties. For example, in 1975, a forest ecosystem in Uzbekistan was converted to a protected nature reserve. As a consequence, the surrounding communities lost access rights to this land, which contained a wild plant species that had been used locally to cure heart ailments. Having lost access to this wild species, the local people over time lost knowledge about the health properties of this plant, and with that a low-cost health remedy.

Traditional Genetic Resources and Property

In Kenya, indigenous leafy vegetables are an important resource for food security. The genetic resources of these species are found and used in both wild and cultivated landscapes. The plant *Amaranthus graecizans L.* is collected from the wild in communal areas along roadsides and rivers, but seldom is cultivated in gardens. Common property rights provide landless poor with access and foster local conservation of this unique genetic resource. Often, when access to communal areas is restricted, not only are livelihoods affected, but also species lose their value as the traditions associated with them disappear.

The Role of Collective Action

Whereas the state sector can sustain *ex situ* conservation (collection and storage of genetic resources to ensure availability in the future), *in situ* conservation requires coordination by farmers and other actors. Both formal and informal networks can work to increase access to diversity and availability of genetic variation, or they can work in conflicting ways, thus reducing diversity. In marginalized and remote areas where farmers' own seed systems continue to play a major role in meeting their heterogeneous needs for seed supply, collective action is especially important.

Germplasm information is composed of both scientific and local knowledge. Local-level collective action can provide the means to facilitate the maintenance of traditional knowledge. Farmers' organizations for seed management, local seed exchange networks, and seed fairs increase the information available about plant genetic resources, contribute to local capacity to conserve local crop varieties, and increase the possibilities for improving local varieties.

Finally, a group of farmers should be able to maintain more diversity with a higher chance of accessing new populations and a lower probability of loss of populations than any individual. Strengthening local capacity to undertake collective action may thus allow farmers and communities to maintain greater genetic resource diversity.

Intellectual property rights allow local indigenous communities to protect and share in the benefits from local genetic resources.

Farmers' Indigenous Rights to Genetic Resources

Local conservation efforts are also affected by international policies on the development of intellectual property rights for genetic resources. Intellectual property rights, like all other property rights, provide the rights to the stream of benefits (including income) from the resource in question. Article 8 of the Convention on Biological Diversity affirms the rights of local indigenous communities to access and benefit from local genetic resources. The recently signed International Treaty on Plant Genetic Resources for Food and Agriculture also addresses intellectual property rights to allow local communities to access and benefit from local genetic resources.

Public policies have paid significant attention to private ownership, and commercial incentives underpin genetic resource innovation using biotechnology. It has, however, paid less attention to property rights of agrarian communities and cultures for whom genetic resources are essential livelihood assets.

In the case of biotechnology, genetic resource innovations are treated as individual property. On the other hand, farming communities use genetic resources to meet a variety of livelihood, environmental, and cultural needs, and innovations in genetic resources over time are often the product of long-term collective efforts, such that no single individual can claim to be the owner or originator of the innovation process and the resulting genetic resources.

The rules assigning property rights over genetic resources to individuals or groups of users will affect people's livelihoods. One risk of failing to recognize local indigenous rights is that external actors might appropriate exclusive rights over genetic resources they did not in fact, "innovate". Given the neglect of property rights of agrarian communities and cultures, collective action can help empower farmers to demand that government bodies guarantee rights to local genetic diversity to farmers. The other side of the coin is that collective action can also be used to limit use of germplasm by others, thereby worsening access and benefits to society as a whole.

Collective action can help empower farmers to demand that governments recognize farmers' rights to local genetic resources.

Risks and Problems of Exclusive Property Rights to Genetic Resources

Even if local groups have legally-recognized rights to genetic resources, privatization itself can lead to reduced availability of germplasm. In particular, assigning exclusive property rights to germplasm might reduce access to plant genetic material for everyone, and particularly for poorer farmers. Often, less informed, less well educated, and marginalized rural populations are at a disadvantage in claiming ownership.

Policymakers should be aware of the links between property rights, collective action, and local conservation of local plant genetic diversity. In order to avoid eroding genetic diversity and increasing the vulnerability of the poor, it is important to take into account local regulatory frameworks as well as the existence and overlap of multiple legal systems. It is necessary to build on these regulatory frameworks, and avoid policies that might reduce access to genetic diversity for local populations.

Suggested Readings

Brush, S. (ed.). 2000. *Genes in the Field: On-Farm Conservation of Crop Diversity.* Ottawa, Canada: International Development Research Centre.

CIP-UPWARD. 2003. *Conservation and Sustainable Use of Agricultural Biodiversity* International Potato Center (CIP)–Users' Perspectives with Agricultural Research and Development (UPWARD). Manila. (http://www.eseap.cipotato.org/upward/Abstract/Agrobio-sourcebook.htm)

FAO. 1997. *The State of the World's Plant Genetic Resources for Food and Agriculture.* Rome: Food and Agriculture Organisation of the United Nations. (http://www.fao.org/WAICENT/FaoInfo/Agricult/AGP/AGPS/pgrfa/pdf/swrfull.pdf)

Watson, J.W. and P. B. Eyzaguirre (eds.). 2002. *Proceedings of the Second International Home Gardens Workshop: Contribution of Home Gardens to In Situ Conservation of Plant Genetic Resources in Farming Systems.* 17–19 July 2001, Witzenhausen, Germany. (http://www.ipgri.cgiar.org/publications/pdf/753.pdf)

Animal Genetic Resources Management and Property Rights

Approximately 2 billion people depend on livestock for at least part, and in some cases most, of their livelihood. The poorest livestock keepers are the ones that most need animals that are tolerant of high temperatures and resistant to diseases and drought. These genetic characteristics are referred to as animal genetic resources (AnGR).

SOURCE:

Anderson, S. and R. Centonze. 2006. *Property Rights and the Management of Animal Genetic Resources.* CAPRi Working Paper No. 48. International Food Policy Research Institute, Washington, D.C.

While the animals kept by poor livestock keepers in marginal areas have high diversity of adaptive genetic characteristics, it is these AnGR that are most at risk of genetic erosion. One reason for this is the rising demand for animal products in developing countries, leading to changes in how livestock is raised. With population growth and increasing resource constraints, crops and livestock are being managed more intensively than in the past. However, the types of animals bred for the intensive production systems found in the developed world are often not appropriate for the production systems of the poor. Indeed, this shift from grazing-based to industrial livestock production systems brings disadvantages in terms of genetic conservation and environmental impacts.

The value of indigenous breeds of animals that are adapted to local ecosystems may only be recognized in the future when climate change and other pressures mount. The loss of hardy breeds and their corresponding adaptive genetic traits means a reduction in the range of environments that can be utilized by humankind. This suggests that there is a high potential future value to society of AnGR kept by the poor (referred to as the 'option value').

Option Values of Animal Genetic Resources

Option values refer to the benefit derived from safeguarding an asset for the option of using it at a future date. It is a kind of insurance against the occurrence of, for example, a disease or drought. The opportunity provided by locally adapted livestock for the production of manure, meat, wool, and milk, and the provision of work, transport, and social functions in harsh environments, represents an entitlement (endowment) of local people. Furthermore, in the eventuality of a wider market demand for specific traits, the livestock represent an option value for wider society.

Option value can then be projected into the future either on a global scale or on a local scale as part of the entitlements of a given household or population. The option value for a given breed increases with the uniqueness of its characteristics, with the genetic distance of its traits from others', and with the rarity of the breed itself.

Option Values for Species and Breed Diversity in India

For the Raika ethnic group in Rajasthan, NW India, the option value of a breed or of a species is a kind of insurance against the occurrence of, for example, a new disease or drought. Though Raika are specialist sheep breeders, their flocks typically have some goats. Shrinking land area available to these pastoralists is causing a shift towards goat production, and away from sheep, due to the goats' better foraging and browsing ability. Keeping mixed herds of sheep and goats has several advantages due to the ways the Raika manage natural resources. While sheep milk is sold every morning at the dairy collection points, goats' milk is used for household consumption. Goat meat is also preferred by the Raika and is highly valued for religious and ceremonial purposes. Goat meat achieves a higher market price than sheep meat, and sales are an important source of Raika household income, especially during the dry season.

Goats are very well adapted to the ecosystem; they are more resistant to diseases than sheep, and during the dry season they can browse trees and bushes. On the other hand, sheep have the advantage of producing wool, in addition to milk and meat. They are shorn up to three times per year, and sheep dung is considered to be of better quality than that of goats.

Beyond mixing species for optimal natural resource management, the Raika also keep some sheep of a hardy local breed in their herds, which are able to survive deficiencies in fodder and water availability, although they are relatively less productive than other breeds under good conditions. Obviously, they recognize and value the future benefits derived from safeguarding these AnGR assets.

Loss of Animal Genetic Resources from a Property Rights Perspective

If local people and society value AnGR, why are we losing it? One of the main reasons is *poorly defined property regimes* and inefficiencies in markets. Market failures are one of the main causes of (agricultural) biodiversity loss. When genetic resource conservation generates economic values that are not captured in the market place (e.g. less soil erosion, water conservation), the result of this 'failure' is a distortion where the incentives are against genetic resources conservation and in favor of the economic activities that erode such resources (e.g. bigger animals that eat and drink more).

To establish sustainable AnGR management regimes capable of making contributions to improving the livelihoods of poor livestock keepers, a greater understanding is required of the ways local communities organize ownership, access, and management of AnGR; as well as the enabling environment required for local people to best maintain and enhance AnGR.

Once these are better understood, sustainable AnGR management regimes should provide the means whereby local, national, and international property rights systems are integrated to provide security of assets for the poor and processes of benefit sharing from the maintenance and realization of the option values of AnGR managed by the poor.

Local Rules and Institutions for Animal Genetic Resources: *Evidence from India*

Table 1 illustrates a synthesis of the wide range of rules regarding animal ownership and resource use and control in the Raika pastoralist community in Rajasthan. They include rules related to boundaries, access, position (social status), scope, aggregation and payoff, and authority and information.

Property right regimes, land types, and access to each type of property also contribute to AnGR management. The Raika example highlights the importance of the right to make decisions related to the selection of animals, which may involve purchase, loan, exchange, and other means at the moment of breeding.

The right to make and implement husbandry decisions related to the rearing of the animal is also important, as well as the right to prescribe slaughter, which may be religiously and culturally directed. Unfortunately, environmental policies aimed at natural resource conservation and fading reciprocity between farmers and livestock keepers are challenging the sustainability of AnGR management in this harsh environment.

Table 1. Property Rights Rules for the AnGR of Raika Pastoralists in Rajasthan, North West India

Property Rights Rule	Example from Raika AnGR Management Systems in Rajasthan
Boundary rules	Sale of female animals out of the Raika caste is prohibited. The rule governs access and avoids outward flows. Although declared as religious, this norm has political and economic aspects. Members of other communities are prevented from starting the activity of animal breeding, thus not exceeding the use of common property resources. Females are maintained inside the flock as renewable production resources, preventing financial collapse in emergency situations.
Access rules	Being able to gain access to breeding male animals depends on community boundaries and personal relationships.
Position rules	Livestock owner may dedicate the animal to God and define who has access to the animal, including for loan. The owner has to ensure good condition of the *sand* (animals with religious value) until its natural death.
Scope rules	Female small ruminants, holy males, and any cattle cannot be slaughtered. Furthermore, no money can be gained from the *sand* through the provision of breeding services.
Aggregation and payoff rules	Collective access and use of genetic resources require the livestock breeders to contribute to feeding (ghee, oils, sweets, and fodder). Each herder, depending on his access to labor and capital, will adjust the number of animals grazed in the *gochar* (common grazing lands). Periods of resource appropriation with respect to small and large ruminants accessing common land. Small ruminants, more destructive of the available fodder, are allowed in only after the larger ones. Communal mechanisms of solidarity towards herders in need. 'Common bull' and 'buffalo bull' purchased by all the villagers for their religious value.The activity of grazing is also organized in common for all the village cattle and buffaloes. This institution is called 'four legs'; and works during the rainy season when the animals need to be kept out of the agricultural fields. It relies on a 'villager herder' paid by all cow and buffalo owners. A 'Gowsala' is a collective shelter where non-productive and productive cattle are brought at an inter-village level during drought.
Authority and information rules	Selection mechanisms of AnGR vary across species. For small ruminants the choice is personal and may benefit from informal advice. However, the purchase of a bull is a village matter; the best knowledge available in the community is identified and utilized.

Conclusion

Poor people that keep indigenous animal breeds provide a service to society that is unrecognized and unrewarded. These animals and their wider value to society are partly maintained through traditional husbandry and property rights rules and practices, often in very harsh environments.

Collective action for AnGR management by the poor is only possible where the genetic resource is central to livelihoods in cultural and/or socio-economic terms. The way such collective action is organized — in terms of equity of access, exclusivity of benefits, etc. — depends not only on the characteristics of local AnGR ownership rights, but also on who has access rights to the common property resources required for animal production. Traditional practices of animal husbandry central to the management of AnGR are at risk and in some cases are breaking down in the face of external factors that are also marginalizing livestock keepers.

Towards a Sustainable AnGR

Processes for the maintenance of local institutions of AnGR management are required to allow the development of markets and the provision of incentives for the conservation of AnGR option values managed by the poor. Local property right systems need to be taken into account and respected (where possible through integration) in the development of national legislation for AnGR management.

Sustainable AnGR management regimes should provide the means whereby local, national, and international property rights systems are integrated to provide security of assets for the poor. A process of negotiation over AnGR property rights is required between the sets of actors currently involved in managing AnGR of likely high option value (often poor livestock keepers) and those investing in the biotechnology necessary to exploit these option values.

Poor people that keep indigenous animal breed provide a service to society that is unrecognized and unrewarded.

Suggested Reading

Anderson, S. 2004. *Environmental Effects on Animal Genetic Resources.* Review for the FAO AGAP. Rome: FAO. <http://www.fao.org/ag/cgrfa/docs.htm#bspftp://ext-fao.org/ag/cgrfa/BSP/bsp28e.pdf>

Chapter 3

Property Rights and Collective Action for Natural Resource Management

Property Rights and Collective Action for Pro-Poor Watershed Management

SOURCE:

Swallow, B, N Johnson, R Meinzen-Dick, and A Know. 2006. The Challenges of Inclusive Cross-Scale Collective Action in Watersheds, Conceptual Framework of Theme 2 of the CGIAR Challenge Program on Water and Food. (http://gisweb.ciat.cgiar.org/wcp/download/Collective_Action_Swallow.pdf)

Watersheds are simultaneously managed at various social and spatial scales, from micro-catchments to transnational river systems and lake basins. They are also often managed for multiple objectives: environmental conservation and economic development. The flow of water, soil, nutrients, and other materials across a landscape extends the consequences of decisions about resource use well beyond the individual land user or manager, resulting in externalities. Upstream pollution by agricultural chemicals can expose downstream users to economic and health costs. More positively, upstream soil erosion can transport fertile soil that can enrich downstream rice paddies or other fields. Because watersheds have such broad impacts at so many levels, they have special implications for property rights and collective action in the management of resources.

Property Rights and Watersheds

All watersheds share two keystone resources: water and land. Property rights to these two resources are often interrelated, for example, land rights often presume rights to water.

> **Catchments and Watersheds**
>
> A catchment is the land area that drains to a particular body of water, be it a river, lake, wetland, estuary, or ocean. The watershed is the upper area of one or more catchments. In practice, the terms are often used simultaneously, usually to refer to the catchment.

Especially important for watershed management outcomes are property rights to filters — small areas of land that help to check, divert, absorb, or stop an undesirable flow of soil, sediment, or pollutants within a watershed. Some types of filters, such as rice paddies and contour strips, are man-made and privately owned and managed, whereas others are naturally occurring and can range from private to communal to public ownership. Rights to land, water, or other benefits need not be exclusive to be secure; they can be held in common or overlap with different resource users.

Property rights to common or public lands such as wetlands, riverbanks, forests, footpaths, and grazing areas are sometimes insecure and contested. In these situations, community management, public regulation, or co-management by communities and local government agencies may be appropriate to enhance access and operation.

Insecurity or conflict over property rights may encourage extractive use of resources. Experiences from the Sumber Jaya catchment area of Indonesia illustrate the problems arising from ill-defined property rights, as the management of upper watershed areas is still dominated by the state. The Forest Department manages 70 percent of the land where local people, classified as illegal squatters, live. Conflict over property rights generates uncertainty about reaping gains on investments in conserving resources and instead provides incentives for farmers to clear primary forest land and adopt farming practices that generate short-term rather than long-term returns.

> **The Two Keystone Resources of Watersheds**
>
> 1. ***Water Resources.*** Most often, water rights are more dynamic, flexible, and contested than land rights. Whereas the supply of land is relatively fixed and certain, water supplies vary depending on rainfall, hydrologic conditions, and amounts extracted by other users. Economic and urban development increases demand for water for urban and industrial use as well as for agriculture. Water users with conditional, secondary, and insecure rights to water are most vulnerable to dispossession. Markets may increase the value of water and economic incentives for its efficient use, but the more water becomes a commodity, the greater is the potential for dispossession of poor and vulnerable groups.
>
> 2. ***Land Resources.*** Property rights to land resources generally vary across the different types of land that make up watersheds. Insecure property rights to cropland can reduce incentives to invest in land improvements and conservation practices, such as terracing or tree planting, that could reduce soil erosion and sediment flows.

Inclusive Collective Action in Watersheds

Initiatives that seek to foster collective action in watersheds need to account for the very different interests of stakeholders in water and watershed management. While there may be relatively straightforward ways to foster collective action at a local scale, some forms of collective action may, in fact, be detrimental to other stakeholders at higher scales. In the developing world in particular, there are often geographic pockets and social groups that are chronically disadvantaged in collective and public processes. Water users' associations and basin authorities may exacerbate these disparities and further marginalize already poor people. New statutory institutions may intentionally or inadvertently weaken effective customary local institutions.

Given that the relationships between different types of stakeholders, and the links between watershed management and poverty, are likely to vary from one watershed to another, projects and program designers need a systematic framework for assessing the implications of alternative interventions before taking action. Such a framework must integrate concepts drawn from the biophysical and social sciences, including new perspectives on watershed components, poverty and collective action. It should also reflect that collective action for water management at one level of socio-spatial organization can have effects at lower and high levels of social-spatial resolution.

Stakeholders of watersheds include all people who use their keystone resources: land and water.

Cross-Scale Linkages in Watersheds

The watershed is an intricate and complex set of biophysical and social components linked across levels and scales. These multi-scale interactions are presented in the conceptual model in Figure 1. The nodes represent the multiple levels or scales of interaction between and across components in the watershed. Together, these interactions determine the level and distribution of welfare across individuals in the three zones, as well as environmental outcomes in headwater and lowland ecosystems.

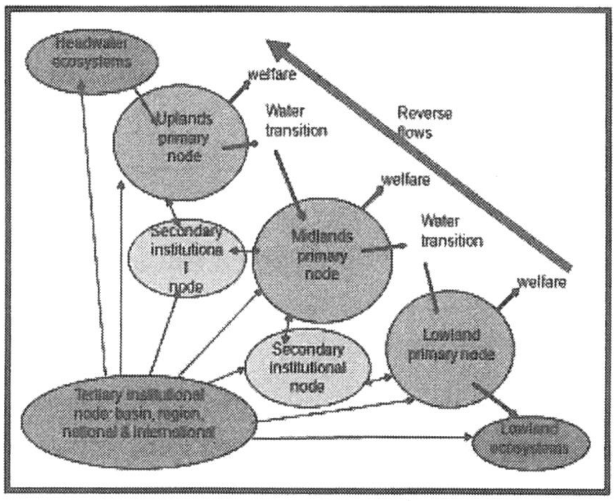

Figure 1. A conceptual model of a multi-scale interactions.

Primary Nodes. People live in the upland, midland and lowland zones. Each node is a locus of individual and collective actions that affect human welfare and the environment, both within and beyond the zone. Social and economic performance in a node is determined by factors such as available resources, policies, institutions, and technologies.

Effective watershed management requires stakeholders to coordinate their use of and investments in these resources.

Secondary and Tertiary Nodes. Unlike primary nodes, these "virtual" nodes represent arenas of negotiation, conflict and/or collective action among adjacent water users. Examples include watershed, basin, national or international level institutions governing water, land and/or forest management. These institutions condition the nature of activity within the node as well as the upward and downward flows between zones.

Welfare and Water Transitions. The way that individuals and groups in a given zone manage water directly affects welfare in that zone. Watershed management within a zone also influences livelihood options in lower zones indirectly through its effect on water transitions. These externalities are called 'water transitions,' defined as changes in the quantity, quality or timing of water flows between primary nodes. They depend on water use and the biophysical characteristics of the catchments, as well as on the technology and management practices of people in upland nodes. Water changes from an upper to a lower node may have positive or negative impacts on downstream water users.

Reverse Flows. If downstream residents are aware of the water transitions, they make take action to either reduce or increase them. These responses may involve 'reverse flows' which can take the form of economic, social or political resources flowing from downstream to upstream. Direct flows can range from cooperation and negotiation among upstream and downstream stakeholders to conflict and use of force. Reverse flows can also be mediated by some public agency as in the case of regulations, subsidies, taxes, or public investments in water infrastructure. Payment for environmental service (PES) schemes are an example of reverse flows, as is lobbying by downstream residents to change land use regulations in upper watersheds.

Where are Watershed Management Decisions Made?

Water transitions and reverse flows reflect the outcomes, intentionally or otherwise, of individual and collective decisions. Understanding the factors that shape those decisions is fundamental for watershed management. These decisions are made in nodes or arenas; however, as the diagram suggests, it is possible that a specific watershed issue might be dealt with in different areas simultaneously. For example, local land use norms based on customary or religious law may coexist with rules of local customs, watershed associations or state environmental regulation. When there are no conflicts, such contradictions may not be important, but when conflicts arise, parties may seek resolution in the arena where they feel they have the best chance of getting a favorable outcome, a phenomenon known as "forum shopping." Similarly, resolving conflicts that involve stakeholders such as mining companies or state agencies, or even people living outside the watershed, may not be able to be resolved locally. Such attempts often result in incomplete and unsustainable solutions, since key stakeholders are left out. What is important is to identify all stakeholders or actors who need to be involved in decisions and find a forum in which they can interact on a level playing field.

Key Links Between Water and Welfare Across Scale in Watersheds

- Improved access to good quality drinking water can improve family health and free up time that can be diverted to more productive, less laborious activities. Small amounts of water put to productive use can greatly enhance livestock production, horticulture and some small-scale industry within the homestead. Outside the homestead, supplemental irrigation and improved water management can contribute to major improvements in crop production over dryland agriculture. *Upland and midland areas are often thought of as suppliers of water; however, small increases in water use in these areas can have significant impacts on poverty because the poor are often, though not always, concentrated in these areas.*

- Quantity of land owned is often used as an indicator of wealth, and wealth is often considered synonymous with power in negotiations. In a watershed context, however, *the extent to which land can be an effective resource in negotiations also depends on where it is located*, either along the upstream-downstream continuum or in relation to the filters that ultimately determine the magnitude of water transitions. Actions of people living in upland areas will affect those downstream far more than those downstream can directly affect those upstream. Where water and power flow in the same direction (i.e. where better off people are located in upstream areas and in areas with high impacts on downstream communities or on watershed function), it may be difficult to reach win-win solutions to watershed problems.

- The nested and overlapping nature of watershed management makes it difficult to sustain investments in water resource management over time. For example, water-poverty traps in Africa often arise because of the high variability of water resources in time and space, and because most of the important river basins cut across national boundaries, thus being subject to numerous political and institutional risks. These factors serve to reduce returns and increase costs associated with water investment at lower scales. Poor credit facilities and low self-financing capacity further constrain investments in water, which in turn translate into low water storage capacity and poor water supply infrastructure. Poor water supplies then lead to limited production and ill health, which constrain development more generally. As such, *poverty traps replicate and reinforce themselves across scales: failure to surmount thresholds at one scale reduces returns on investments at other scales, while success at one scale increases return on investment at other scales.*

- *Knowledge and information shape people's participation in watershed institutions and negotiation processes, and this knowledge may vary widely between stakeholder groups.* Poor people frequently lack knowledge about their rights and the avenues for defending them. Consensus seeking approaches are likely to disadvantage them even further. While these approaches may prevent disagreements, they can prevent contentious but critical issues from being addressed. Negotiation, however, requires a high degree of participation and collaboration among interest groups as well as trust in one's representatives.

Conclusion

Watershed management is a complex issue that draws its many stakeholders — from the forest, the upland and lowland farms, management and conservation bodies, down to urban areas — in an intricate social and ecological relationship. Such complexities mean that simple win-win situations are rare; decisions about alternative intervention scenarios about (re-)allocating rights or (re-)organizing stakeholders need to evaluated to determine the potential trade-offs involved. A common framework and key principles can facilitate such assessments by policymakers and practitioners.

Suggested Readings

2002. *Water Policy* 3(6). Special Issue on Property Rights and Collective Action in Watershed Management.

FAO (Food and Agriculture Organization of the United Nations). 2006. *The New Generation of Watershed Management Programmes and Projects*: A Resource Book for Practitioners and Local Decision-Makers based on the Findings and Recommendations of a FAO Review, FAO Forestry Paper 150. www.fao.org/docrep/009/a0644e/a0644e00.htm

Ostrom, E., 2005. *Understanding Institutional Diversity*. Princeton University Press New Haven, CT, USA

Sadoff, C.W. and D. Grey. 2002. Beyond the River: *The Benefits of Cooperation on International Rivers.* Water Policy 4(5): 389-403.

Managing Mobility in African Rangelands

SOURCE:

Niamir-Fuller, M. 2005. *Managing Mobility in African Rangelands. In:* Mwangi, E. *(ed). Collective Action and Property Rights for Sustainable Rangeland Management.* CAPRi Research Brief, International Food Policy Research Institute, Washington, D.C.

In arid and semi-arid lands in Africa, pastoralists manage uncertainty and risk and access a range of markets through livestock mobility. Mobility enables opportunistic use of resources and helps minimize the effects of droughts. Benefits include lower-cost fodder at minimal labor cost, and increased resistance of animals to diseases. Mobility also impacts on the ecological condition: continuous, sedentary grazing in the wet season may result in lower pasture palatability and productivity, higher soil compaction and lower water infiltration, ultimately leading to pasture degradation.

Undergrazing of remote pastures or in protected areas can lead to the invasion of unpalatable plants, lower vegetation cover, and lower diversity of plants, and can sometimes be a more serious problem than overgrazing. Many areas used by pastoralists over millennia are now considered "grazing dependent," and mobile pastoralism can therefore be bio-friendly.

The scale and magnitude of persistent environmental decline in dryland Africa — and how livestock grazing has affected such changes — appear to have been overestimated. Indeed, the pattern of anthropogenic land degradation is much more severe around permanent settlement sites than in open rangelands. Mobility can contribute to pasture sustainability and improvement, since mobile pastoralists can modify herds and access alternative areas while waiting for degraded pastures to regenerate.

Mobility and Sedentarization in Pastoral Systems

Transhumance

Transhumance is the seasonal movement of people and livestock between well-defined pasture areas. It is a key survival strategy of pastoralists, and is dependent on both collective action and flexible property rights.

Mobile pastoral systems also appear to be more economically efficient than their sedentary counterparts or commercial ranching. If flexible access to different habitats and resources is ensured, higher populations of herbivores can be maintained in any given area. The mobile system involves common property regimes that share the risk and spread the burden in arid lands, where uncertainty is high and the risks to production and survival are higher. Though sedentarization has positive results — such as access to education and health — benefits are not evident for all.

High rates of sedentarization and declining mobility have been driven by a combination of factors, such as:

- major droughts;
- increased individualization and disruption of political structures within pastoral societies;
- growing economic vulnerability of transhumant groups;
- increased competition and conflicts over land; and
- increased land ownership by investors outside the pastoral sector.

Government policies have upset the economic balance between crops and livestock by favoring crops and agricultural encroachment onto rangelands. Governments have discouraged investments in the range and livestock sector and claimed "vacant" pastoral land for national parks and government-owned farms.

Impact of Development Assistance Projects

Projects in Africa have long sought to develop livestock productivity rather than enhance livelihoods. Drawing on the classical ranching model from the United States, interventions encouraged sedentarization, destocking, and water development. However, they did not increase livestock productivity, and some were very destructive.

In Francophone West Africa, failed, underfunded efforts were made to create official transhumance routes, with permits, supervised cross-border movements, watering points, and quarantine stations. The early 1980s saw the advent of integrated rural development projects, which were less coercive, more service-oriented, and had a nodding appreciation for local perspectives. However, this approach continued an implicit sedentarization agenda. It gave way eventually to natural resource management projects that addressed land degradation. However, the blueprint approach persisted, and land use "guidelines" were discussed with land users only after their creation.

There were attempts to modify institutional structures for natural resource management. Legally registered pastoral associations were created and given the responsibility of managing (but not owning) a defined land area. However, because the new institutions had undefined relationships to customary ones, ineffectiveness or further breakdown of customary institutions resulted.

Development assistance projects then pursued natural resource management at a more localized scale, and were strongly influenced by common property theory. Such projects were partially successful in building local-level institutions for natural resource management, but they have been critiqued for overlooking informal local institutions and ignoring differences between the interests of leaders and non-leaders. The approach also ignored mobile pastoralists, or saw them in a secondary, receptive position. The focus on the village (or groups of villages) seemed spatially myopic, and the promotion of exclusionary mechanisms in land tenure systems evidenced under-appreciation of the variability of resource endowment in dryland areas.

In the 1990s, community-based natural resource management projects attempted to allocate common property tenure to local institutions and facilitate more participatory forms of development, though very few included mobile pastoralists. Mobility was still seen as a problem to be eliminated, not a trump card to be strengthened.

Recommended Remedies

Livestock needs to be seen as an integral part of conservation and development in Africa, since transhumance may even be a necessary precondition to sustainable development in arid lands.

- Mobile pastoralism is not a "backward" means of livelihood — laws, policies and procedures should be considered backward, since they do not recognize the ecological and economic value of mobile pastoralism.

- A clearer understanding of common property regimes and a holistic analytical framework for pastoral development activities are also required — to build capacity, develop and strengthen rules and regulations for common property management, manage key sites, and develop socio-economic safety nets and drought contingency measures.

- The fundamental design principles related to managing institutions for mobility are nested property rights, fluid boundaries, inclusivity, flexibility, reciprocity, negotiation, and priority of use. This means that the pitfall of most projects must be avoided: rigidly and arbitrarily defining the boundaries of a community and then ignoring the participation by surrounding people. There is a need for definitions that classify people into an agreed upon set of socio-geographical communities. A nested hierarchy of sociogeographical units — reflecting the nested nature of communal property — would ensure that a series of institutional structures are in place to accommodate the needs of mobility. Exclusive and inclusive land tenure can then be assigned accordingly. Reform that increases the security of transhumant claims to land is also needed, along with serious consideration for livestock mobility, common property management, and the roles more informal institutions have played in providing controllable but flexible resource access in arid rangelands.

- Resource holders need to retain authority to grant temporary use rights to secondary and tertiary users. Flexibility can be maintained by the legal recognition and development of appropriate legal language, which entails developing local administrative and judicial institutions to manage common property and recognize temporary rights of usage, establish — through local dialogue and participation — the principles and guidelines for judging claims, create the means and procedures for enforcing rules, and develop appropriate conflict resolution mechanisms that fill gaps left by disintegrating customary systems and inappropriate western systems.

- There has been strong momentum toward "co-management," or systems of common property regimes that combine government decentralization with community participation. Though the approach is far better suited than any other to mobile pastoralism, it needs to deal with large-scale management of contiguous land.

- Management of livestock mobility also requires multiple institutions working at multiple spatial scales, authorities, and functions. To modify or create the institutional structure for a legitimate, locally controllable transhumance, the function — not just the structure — of new institutions must be addressed.

Suggested Readings

McCarthy, N., C. Dutilly-Diane, B. Drabo, A. Kamara, and J. Vanderlinden. 2004. *Managing Resources in Erratic Environments: An Analysis of Pastoral Systems in Burkina Faso, Niger and Ethiopia.* IFPRI Research Report 35. CGIAR Systemwide Program on Collective Action and Property Rights for Poverty Reduction (CAPRi). International Food Policy Research Institute: Washington, D.C. [online] http://www.ifpri.org/pubs/abstract/135/rr135cover.pdf.

Niamir-Fuller, M. (ed.) 1999. *Managing Mobility in African Rangelands: The Legitimization of Transhumance.* London: Intermediate Technology Publications.

Scoones, I. (ed.) 1994. *Living with Uncertainty: New Directions in Pastoral Development in Africa.* London: Intermediate Technology Publications.

Vetter, S. (ed.) 2004. *Rangelands at Equilibrium and Nonequilibrium: Recent Developments in the Debate Around Rangeland Ecology and Management.* Cape Town: Programme for Land and Agrarian Studies, University of the Western Cape.

UNDP. 2003. *Pastoralism and Mobility in the Drylands.* The Global Drylands Imperative, Second Challenge Paper Series. (www.undp.org/drylands/docs/cpapers)

Institutional Options for Managing Rangelands

SOURCE:

Ngaido, T. and N. McCarthy. 2005. *Institutional Options for Managing Rangelands.* Collective Action and Property Rights for Sustainable Rangeland Management, CAPRi Research Brief, International Food Policy Research Institute, Washington, D.C.

Rangelands occupy nearly one-half of the Earth's land area or around 16 billion acres. About one-half of this area is used for grazing livestock. Rangelands have been subject to a wide range of tenure arrangements, with different structures for regulating access to, use of, and management of rangelands. These include many customary and tribal institutional arrangements that have functioned for long periods.

Each of these property rights regimes and institutional options is associated with different costs for achieving various goals, such as poverty reduction, equitable access to resources, and sustainable use and management of those resources. The benefits and costs of alternative tenure and institutional arrangements and the impact of existing legal and policy frameworks on the sustainability and equity of pastoral production systems vary depending on the category of land ownership: state ownership; individual ownership; or common property.

State Ownership

Proponents of state involvement maintain that only an external authority can enforce the best use of, and investment in, common pool natural resources as the state has greater financial resources

with which to make large-scale investments and can bear the risk associated with such investments better than community members can.

State ownership often fails to promote community stewardship and thus limits collective action and incentives for members to manage their resources effectively and make long-term investments. Competing claims between pastoral communities and states have created situations of confusion and open access, leading many pastoralists to challenge both state and traditional range management rules and activities and, in some cases, to illegally appropriate common rangelands.

Other problems that arise with state ownership include:

- Optimum utilization requires good local knowledge, which government agencies often lack particularly on agroecological conditions and local rules of use and management. These information problems increase the costs of enforcing management decisions by government agents.

- In the arid and semi-arid regions, flexibility and mobility are valuable strategies for managing spatial and temporal variation in climate. But centralized government decision-making and enforcement structures severely reduce this flexibility.

- Collective action is likely to be lower under state tenure because pastoralists may fear that claims on returns to investments on state land will not be recognized in the future.

Nonetheless, a number of different institutional arrangements have been introduced to manage some of these costs, including the granting of common use rights to communities or cooperatives, grazing licenses, and leaseholds.

Pastoral Cooperatives

In most West Asian countries, pastoral cooperatives have mainly been involved in distributing subsidized feeds. In Jordan, however, the new herder-driven cooperatives, which have management rights granted by the state on their traditional pastures, are getting better range productivity results than state-managed reserves, without requiring expensive fencing and guarding. This type of cooperative fosters collective action because members are certain to reap the benefits of their investments and control access to improved pastures. There remain, however, concerns about potential conflicts between cooperative members and non-members.

Common Use Rights for Pastoral Communities

Some governments provide tacit recognition of pastoral communities' use rights and their potential for informally operating grazing networks. This tacit recognition, however, gives pastoralists only a limited role in management and investment decisions and an even smaller role in deciding on the evolution of property rights. Often users do not have the right to reallocate common land to alternative activities like cropping or reserves, a situation that limits the capacity of pastoralists to respond to local conditions. By appropriating pastoral resources and limiting the role of local-level pastoral institutions, state ownership has often fostered land use conflicts and the breakdown of collective action within and across pastoral groups. In particular, where the state claimed ownership but expended limited resources to manage rangelands or relied on bureaucrats to implement management schemes without knowledge of local resources and institutions, many land use conflicts have arisen and resources have become degraded.

Common Use Rights for Pastoral Organizations

Theoretically, state and local organizations could work together to create and enforce use rules and investment activities. But in practice, the costs of negotiating such rules have often been prohibitive. Numerous projects have attempted to reorganize pastoralists into cooperatives with the aim of improving rangeland resources and promoting collective action, but the cooperatives have rarely been effective managers of rangelands.

Grazing Licenses

To reverse rangeland degradation, government-managed grazing reserves grant licenses determined by a well-defined and well-funded investment strategy. These areas are then opened for grazing during specific periods of the year, and any herder can buy a license, whether or not he or she is a member of the tribe or community with traditional claim to the reserve area.

Since pastoral communities contribute little to the management of these reserves, the main collective action of community members has often been to hinder state licensing policies. With high costs of fencing and guarding reserves, community participation in improving and managing these reserves has been lacking.

Individual Leaseholds

The practice of granting long-term individual leaseholds on range resources remains limited. In some cases such as Botswana, individual leaseholds have contributed to increasing livestock production and improving rangeland conditions. However, some issues that arise with individual leaseholds are:

- The policy has been strongly criticized on equity grounds.
- People with previous claims to resources have been dispossessed or denied further access without compensation leading to additional pressures on the now smaller common pool resource base, increasing range degradation, and conflicts between large and small herd owners.
- Widespread individual leaseholds increase the vulnerability of pastoral communities during droughts by limiting their capacity to move and negotiate access to neighboring pastures.
- There is very little collective action under this system.

Individual Ownership

In pastoral areas of central Tunisia, individual private property rights fostered the transformation of pastoral and nomadic systems into agro-pastoralist systems. Privatization led to the wide-scale adoption of fodder crop production, including cacti and shrubs. The efficiency of this option depends on the performance of land, purchased input, credit and output markets, and legal and institutional provisions to reduce land fragmentation.

Some concerns that arise with individual ownership include:

- There is potential for misappropriation of land by the politically-powerful, thus raising equity concerns.
- This system is likely to reduce herd size, mobility, and collective action within and between pastoral groups, and consequently pastoralist households may become more vulnerable to drought.

Common Property

Common property rights for communities make tenure more secure, but the communities must bear all costs of making, monitoring, and enforcing rules regarding rangeland management. Managing access to and use of resources can be difficult, particularly when benefits and costs are not equally distributed among community members.

In this system, local institutions may keep their traditional roles of managing the resources, deciding how to allocate resources between pastures and croplands, and deciding on the nature of the rights to be allocated to members and non-members. These opportunities may empower local institutions and provide them with the capacity to mobilize collection action and sustain the livelihoods of their communities.

Because land-owning communities may have difficulties mobilizing financial resources and technical expertise, they may enter contractual arrangements for improving their resources. Under such contracts, as in central Tunisia and Morocco, state institutions, generally forest services, are entrusted with the responsibility for improving and managing the resource. After the improvement of the resource, rights holders purchase grazing or cutting licenses, and the revenues generated from the licenses are used to pay off improvement costs. Theoretically, these ranges will revert to communities once improvement costs are recuperated; in practice, however, such transfers have often not taken place.

Since common property rights are generally granted to a fixed and well-defined group for rangelands with well-defined boundaries, it can lead to limiting flexibility and herd mobility.

Conclusion

Achieving efficient, equitable, and sustainable rangeland management depends on the costs and benefits of alternative systems. These costs and benefits, in turn, depend on agro-ecological, socio-cultural, and economic characteristics. The conservation and management of rangelands require not only tenure security, but also an understanding of local livestock production and risk management strategies and factors that promote collective action, which can then be integrated into national policy formulation strategies and project designs.

Suggested Readings

McCarthy, N., B. Swallow, M. Kirk and P. Hazell. 2000. *Property Rights, Risk, and Livestock Development in Africa.* International Food Policy Research Institute: Washington, D.C. (http://www.capri.cgiar.org/proprights.asp)

Ngaido, T. 2002. *Pastoral Land Rights.* Paper prepared for the World Bank's Regional Workshop on Land Issues in Africa. Kampala, Uganda, April 2002. (http://lnweb18.worldbank.org/ESSD/ardext.nsf/24ByDocName/PapersPastoral/$FILE/Pastoral+Land+Rights_Ngaido.pdf)

Ngaido, T., N. McCarthy and M. Di Gregorio. 2002. *International Conference on Policy and Institutional Options for the Management of Rangelands in Dry Areas: Workshop Summary Paper.* Working Paper 23. CGIAR Systemwide Program on Collective Action and Property Rights for Poverty Reduction (CAPRi). International Food Policy Research Institute: Washington, D.C. (http://www.capri.cgiar.org/wp/capriwp23.asp)

Collective Action and Collaborative Management of Forests

SOURCE:

Wollenberg, E., B. Campbell, S. Shackleton, D. Edmunds and P. Shanley. 2004. *Collaborative Management of Forests.* 2020 Focus Brief 11, International Food Policy Research Institute, Washington, D.C.

Governments around the world increasingly seek to manage their forests with the collaboration of the people living nearby. Forestry Ministries or their equivalents usually do this by offering local people access to selected forest products or forest land, income from forest resources, or opportunities for communicating with government forestry officials. In return, the agency obliges local people to cooperate in managing the forests around them by protecting existing forest or by planting trees.

Governments claim that the programs devolve control over forests to local people and provide more secure livelihoods, as well as help maintain and regenerate forests. By sharing rights among local groups and the state, the programs also help to reconcile the resource claims of local people with those of the national government. Everybody supposedly wins.

Millions of the rural poor now participate in collaborative forest management schemes under a variety of tenurial and organizational arrangements. These arrangements were examined to find out whether local people have indeed gained more access to benefits from and control over forests. Some of the findings suggest the following:

- Most co-management projects actually maintain and even extend central government control. Where communities had already managed forests in Orissa and Uttarakhand in India, for example, the government required that they share their incomes with the state forest department.

- Governments in many countries typically predetermine which species can be planted in reforestation or agroforestry schemes and what types of organizations can be given rights to manage forests.

- Whereas local people have gained greater legal access to forests and some might have increased their incomes, many have also lost out. For example, game areas and plantations have been frequently established on land used by poorer members of communities for grazing or cultivation.

- Local people have also not shown a consistent interest in forest management.

The Collaborative Management Model

Collaborative management, or "co-management", forest programs have had a huge impact. These programs have generally helped to protect forests and improve access rights of the rural poor to forest resources, but have often fallen short of their potential to improve significantly the livelihoods of the poor.

Collective action has been a key feature of organizational arrangements for co-management. These arrangements have included the following:

- corporate, legal organizations of rights holders such as rubber tappers' organizations in Brazil, ejidos in Mexico, or trusts in Botswana;

- village committees facilitated by government departments such as Forest Protection Committees in India;

- local government organizations such as Rural District Councils in Zimbabwe; and

- multi-stakeholder district structures aligned to line departments such as the Wildlife Management Authorities in Zambia.

Impact of Collaborative Management

- In India, more than 63,000 groups have enrolled in joint forest management programs to regenerate 14 million hectares.
- In Nepal, 9,000 forest user groups are trying to regenerate 700,000 hectares of forest.
- In Brazil, farmers help to manage 2.2 million hectares as extractive reserves.
- Half the districts in Zimbabwe participate in CAMPFIRE schemes, in which local communities can share revenues gained from tourist use of wildlife areas.

Collective action assists in co-management by reducing the number of people that forest agencies must deal with and by bringing together different groups to play complementary roles in forest management. Even when governments contract directly with households or individuals, community organizations usually help with the programs, as in the case of Integrated Social Forestry in the Philippines.

State Control

The organizational arrangements for co-management strongly influence how much government agencies can control forest management and outcomes for local people. Forestry agencies exert more control over decisions about species selection, harvesting practices, sales, consumption, and the distribution of benefits where they have devolved management to local governments or larger-scale organizations. In such cases, the agency's interests in timber production, revenue generation, and environmental conservation have often overridden villagers' interests in livelihoods.

Forestry agencies exercise control over individuals and village groups by making local organizations accountable to the agencies rather than to local stakeholders. The agencies use standardized contractual agreements and regulations that limit local people's self-determination. Local people who organize collectively are better able to mobilize resources and negotiate for desired benefits. They are able to exert more influence when they have the direct support of non-government organizations (NGOs), donors, federations, and other external actors. Collective action, both within communities and together with outside groups, thus helps local people become more influential stakeholders in co-management arrangements. Where local groups have managed their own forests without state intervention, however, they have not necessarily been better off. Without government support, they often have had difficulty implementing or enforcing their decisions.

Addressing Poverty

Collaborative management has improved formal access to forests for rural people. Harvesting forest resources helps them meet subsistence needs and offers a safety net in times of shortage. Nonetheless, local people's rights to valuable commercial products such as timber or game remain restricted. Where forests yield financial benefits, governments often fail to deliver local people's promised share of incomes, or instead deliver them primarily to local elites. For the poor to benefit substantially from forest access, they need more secure property rights over valuable resources. Only rarely have poor communities received substantial financial benefits, such as in Botswana, where 45 families shared about US$125,000 annually from the Chobe Trust.

Local knowledge and capacities are ideal enablers in co-management, given the strong internal harmony and leadership.

Focusing too narrowly on organizing collective action around managing a single resource such as a forest may divert potentially productive efforts. Converting forests to agriculture or other uses or initiating land reform, may bring local people greater economic benefits in many areas. Forest co-management programs alone are not sufficient to address poverty.

Organizing Collective Action: Challenges for the Future

Co-management has revealed the difficulty of dividing roles, rights, and responsibilities, especially where the groups involved have highly divergent interests. Forest agencies have had varying experiences in organizing collective action. Romantic ideals about harmonious communities and the local knowledge and capacities of "traditional peoples" have been counterbalanced by internal conflict and lack of leadership in many communities and the difficulty of organizing collective action where local social capital is weak.

Increasing competition and fragmentation of forests have led to more *de facto* privatization of land, making it difficult for communities to organize together around a common resource.

Many co-management efforts rely on outside agents to facilitate collective action, but sustaining that action has proved difficult. Other stakeholders, such as local governments or NGOs, often create their own sets of incentives or pressures for local people that work against co-management initiatives.

Forest co-management has created a useful institutional entry point. It now seems time to build more actively on the lessons learned. State officials and local people have had different expectations about the process and goals of co-management. Forest departments have controlled the terms of co-management and been reluctant to share their benefits. People in forest areas now must achieve the rights and power to bring about a fair division of control, responsibility, and benefits between themselves and the government.

Checks and balances need to be in place to ensure that local elites or other groups do not monopolize benefits and decision-making. The process should acknowledge the multiple interests found among different groups and give special attention to the livelihood needs of the poor. Initiatives need to build better on existing management practices and enhance local livelihood options.

Addressing the Interests of the Poor

In the past, it has been difficult for large centralized forestry agencies to accommodate local interests, and local groups have had little voice in agency decision-making. This is changing as governments decentralize and as the role of NGOs increases. Choosing the right facilitators and settings for these negotiations is critical for ensuring that the interests of the poor are met.

The current bureaucratic approaches to co-management do not address the complexity of these different needs. Frameworks for natural resource management that are developed locally by stakeholders and then linked to national objectives are more flexible and responsive to local interests.

Local responsiveness will be higher when institutional arrangements facilitate good communication and learning among stakeholders. The learning process should include both local interest groups and national policymakers to reflect different interests.

Where forestry incomes are limited and less attractive than incomes from other sustainable land uses and other activities, the rural poor should be encouraged to pursue economic options other than forestry, to better meet their needs.

Triggered by past experiences and by the increasing complexity of demands from different interest groups, the co-management paradigm is shifting. Management increasingly involves not just a local group and the government, but a range of stakeholders, and acknowledges overlapping systems of management and diverse interests. The actors involved have recognized that more emphasis is needed on the institutional and political aspects of management design.

Thus, forest management efforts are focusing on negotiation and on frameworks that emphasize local people's right to self-determination and allow for effective representation of rural poor people in negotiations. The rural poor and their federations and advocates are bringing a new sophistication to negotiations and demanding that their voices be heard.

Suggested Readings

Baland, J.M. and J.P. Platteau. 1996. *Halting Degradation of Natural Resources: Is There a Role for Rural Communities?* Oxford: Clarendon Press.

Ribot, J. 2002. *Democratic Decentralization of Natural Resources.* Washington, D.C.: World Resources Institute.

Shackleton, S., B. Campbell, E.Wollenberg and D. Edmunds. 2002. *Devolution and Community-Based Natural Resource Management: Creating Space for Local People to Participate and Benefit.* Natural Resource Perspective. Overseas Development Institute.

Property Rights, Collective Action and Pro-Poor Payment for Environmental Service (PES) Options

SOURCE:

Swallow, B., R. S. Meinzen-Dick, and M.V. Noordwijk. 2005. Localizing demand and supply of environmental services: Interaction with property rights, collective action, and the welfare of the poor. CAPRi Working Paper 42. International Food Policy Research Institute, Washington D.C.

Interest in the potential of payments for environmental services (PES) schemes to improve incentives for sustainable land management is increasing in the face of global climate change and environmental degradation. A range of schemes have been set up to reward people and land users that provide environmental services (ES) related to carbon sequestration, biodiversity conservation, and watershed management, all aiming to match the demand for services with the incentives of land users.

While there has been considerable attention given to formal mechanisms for PES programs, there has been less interest in looking at how PES fits into the broader institutional context in rural communities. In many cases, the interactions between PES schemes and existing property rights and collective action institutions will be important determinants of their impacts on the poor.

Payment for Environmental Services

PES include a range of voluntary transactions in which farmers or other land managers are rewarded — directly or indirectly — for practices that will continue or increase the provision of environmental services. Cash payments to individuals or communities are one form of reward; others include strengthened rights to land or other resources, better prices for products produced on sustainably managed land, income from eco-tourism enterprises, etc.

While the largest PES programs are government-initiated (e.g. the large Sloping Lands Conversion program in China), there are also a growing number of private transactions, many with startup financing from private foundations (e.g. Shell Foundation, FACE Foundation, Mercedes-Benz, Dow Company Foundation) and support from multilateral or bilateral development agencies such as the UK Department for International Development, the International Fund for Agricultural Development, and the United States Agency for International Development. Some programs are also funded directly by the users of the services, especially for biodiversity conservation or watershed functions that benefit downstream water systems.

Key Linkages Between Property Rights, Collective Action, and PES

Of the 10 main factors that affect, either positively or negatively, the development and functioning of PES markets, nine relate to property rights and collective action. Some examples of key linkages are:

Linkages Between Property Rights and PES

Legal restrictions associated with PES market development. Secure property rights are often a necessary pre-condition for ES markets. In most cases, PES contracts require that ES providers have clear and secure rights to perform agreed upon actions on the land. While secure property rights do not necessarily have to be in the form of individual titles, for simplicity the possession of such a title often becomes a pre-condition for participation in PES. As a consequence, many people and even regions and countries are left out because their land tenure regimes consist of common property, customary tenure, or other alternatives to individual, private tenure. PES mechanisms can even cause the poor to lose their existing access to resources if their rights are not secure and there is a push to formalize rights to be able to enter PES schemes.

ES production and payment timeline. ES demands that are satisfied through one-off purchases of services already rendered or to be rendered in the near future, such as energy projects that replace non-renewable with renewable energy sources, do not require secure property rights as much as ES demands, which must be met through periodic and indefinite payments such as carbon sequestration projects.

Partner resources for ES supply. In situations where the production of environmental services requires long-term commitment of land resources, land tenure security may be a very important determinant of the production of environmental services. In such cases, stronger and more secure rights over land and access to other partner resources such as water can be used, instead of or in addition to other payments, as a reward for environmental service provision.

Functional relation between investment and supply of ES. There is large variation among ES, and the knowledge base on the factors that affect how much ES is actually supplied from a given land use or land management practice is limited and context-specific. This is particularly the case where important threshold effects and non-linear cause-effect relations are present, for example, relating to the amount of land conserved and the species diversity on that land. Among the three environmental services, carbon sequestration has the most certain and linear functional relationships with resource use. Furthermore, the form of property rights can shape opportunities for different types of ES and ES mechanisms. For example, community-based environmental tourism may do better under communal tenure than where land has been privatized.

Spatial specificity in ES supply. Some environmental services, particularly watershed functions and biodiversity conservation, are heavily dependent on key resources such as wetlands, riparian areas, corridors, and buffer zones. One of the dilemmas of ES supply is that this high environmental value also justifies public ownership of those resources. If public resources are well managed and regulations enforced, then this might lead to high levels of ES supply. On the other hand, if such public resources are poorly managed, then the resources may be overused and poor levels of ES produced. In such circumstances, it becomes very important that the public sector concentrates on key resources, where it has comparative advantage, and encourages collective and private management of other resources.

PES and the creation of new property rights to environmental services. The creation of PES institutions itself represents the creation of new forms of property, with all of the tensions and trade-offs associated with the process. For example, watershed protection payments create a new benefit stream related to land use. How should rights over this benefit stream be allocated? This not only has equity implications, but also affects the structure of PES mechanisms. Where does one draw the line, for example, between those who should be rewarded for providing clean water and those who have a duty not to pollute?

Even if laws are passed to define property rights over ES, these rights will not be effective unless they are accompanied by effective enforcement. Experience with forest, water, and rangeland management indicates that neither state nor local bodies are likely to be able to enforce such property rights alone, and that some type of co-management regime will be most effective. Cultural or religious norms can also come into play as enforcement institutions.

Linkages Between Collective Action and PES

Functional relation between investment and supply of ES. The relationship between effort and the supply of ES affects the potential benefits of collective action. Carbon sequestration benefits are approximately proportional to the amount of land involved; the contribution of one farmer growing trees on one hectare is approximately the same, whether or not neighboring farmers grow trees. By contrast, species counts have often been observed to increase as the area targeted in an ecosystem grows larger. When not adopted on a sufficiently large area, the benefits may not be realized at all.

Transaction costs of market function/entry. Even where the provision of ES is not "lumpy" due to critical thresholds in supply, collective action offers an important means of reducing the costs of verification and payment for PES systems. Experience from around the developing world has shown that smallholder land users often are both important and efficient producers of valuable environmental services to larger social groups; however, international and national institutions that govern PES are often designed in ways that entail transaction costs which cannot be feasibly met by individual smallholders. Economies of scale in contracting, monitoring, and making payments favor larger suppliers such as plantation owners over many individual smallholders. When smallholders group together in cooperatives or other forms of user groups, they can achieve some of these economies of scale. In some cases, the PES may even be channeled through producer cooperatives as a premium price of output for "certified" producers.

Small numbers of ES buyers and sellers. Concentration in the supply or demand for ES could hinder or enhance markets for ES. Collective action could strengthen the bargaining power of smallholders relative to other producers of environmental services and buyers of environmental services. In the Sumber Jaya area of Sumatra, farmers' groups have been very important for providing a voice for upland farmers previously considered squatters on public land. In negotiations for new social forestry agreements, the farmers' groups have been effective in convincing local officials that they are concerned about the environment and are willing to adopt land use practices that have been documented to produce high levels of environmental services. Farmers' groups often need assistance with such negotiations, however, since they normally are formed for other purposes and are unfamiliar with the concept of producing environmental services through their farming activities.

PES schemes affecting collective action. The nature of environmental service payments can also influence collective action. Conventional regulatory approaches stress enforcement and negative penalties. Demanders have a feeling of entitlement and expect public agencies to assume the responsibility to deliver services or protect against negative impacts. Under a regulatory regime, collective action among suppliers may even be to evade rules and enforcement, rather than collective action to enforce the rules, especially if these rules do not have local legitimacy. By contrast, PES offer positive economic and other incentives for ES provision. These in turn provide greater potential for collective action to enforce the rules and provide a service.

Some Conclusions on Pro-Poor PES

While there will clearly be differences from site to site, even within a broad category of ES, some key tendencies can be identified regarding the potential of certain types of PES to contribute to poverty alleviation.

Carbon sequestration. Because of the long carbon sequestration timeframe and the preference for one-time payments, secure property rights over land resources are likely to be very important for carbon PES mechanisms. However, this can be a two-way relationship: land rights are required as a condition for participating in PES, but secure tenure also is a potential incentive mechanism for ES in itself. Since both land and tree resources are relatively immobile, defining property rights is easier than is the case when the key resources are mobile or fluctuating. The linear and observable nature of carbon sequestration means that collective action is not required for provision, though it can reduce transaction costs for payment. Although smallholders are very appropriate suppliers of carbon sequestration, the lack of differentiation among suppliers means that any purchasers can go to many alternative suppliers; hence, the bargaining power of any particular smallholder or group is likely to be low.

Biodiversity. The fluctuating nature of genetic resources (particularly animals, but also plants), the generation of current and future values, and the need for recurrent investment lead to a combination of one-time and recurrent payments. Long-term property rights over land are not as essential; rewarding tenants might be just as important as rewarding land owners. On the other hand, because of important threshold effects, collective action is likely to be much more important for provision than in the case of carbon. Smallholders occupy many of the global biodiversity hotspots, but this does not automatically give them bargaining power. In many cases, smallholders' livelihoods are perceived as in conflict with biodiversity, and public agencies are viewed as an alternative supplier.

Watershed function. Like biodiversity, watershed functions produce current and fluctuating future values. While land is certainly a key resource, vegetation and water itself play a key role, but fluctuate considerably. This combination of factors often leads to recurrent payments, which means that long-term property rights over land may not be as essential as decision-making rights over land, vegetation, and water flows. The supply of watershed ES is non-linear — it doesn't increase proportionally with the area of land being managed. In addition, there are important scale effects as well as differentiation in the importance of different types of land within a watershed. Thus, collective action is important, but not all land or farmers are equally important in the sense that not all land contributes equally to the provision of services. Nor do all watersheds generate equal value; those upstream of major cities, industries, hydroelectric facilities, or other critical water users are more likely to receive attention. Smallholders may be able to benefit from watershed PES if they live in such critical areas, but public agencies are important alternative sources of supply, and regulation is more common than rewards.

As with many other "new" resources (i.e. those which have suddenly become more valuable and do not yet have clearly established claims), PES has generated considerable enthusiasm on the part of those who hope that it might provide income streams or other benefits to poor people. Nevertheless, experience to date indicates that this is far from assured. In general, the poverty impact of PES will depend on whether poor people are potential suppliers of ES and whether they will be empowered or excluded by PES mechanisms.

Suggested Readings

Balmford, A., A. Bruner, P. Cooper, E. Constanza, S. Farber, R.E. Green, M. Jenkins, P. Jefferiss, V. Jessamy, J. Madden, K. Munro, N. Myers, S. Naeem, J. Paavola, M. Rayment, S. Rosendo, J. Roughgarden, K. Trumper, R.K. Turner. 2002. *Economic Reasons for Conserving Wild Nature.* Science 297: 950-953.

FAO. 2007. *The State of Food and Agriculture: Paying Farmers for Environmental Services.* Rome: Food and Agriculture Organization of the United Nations.

Miranda, M., I. Porres and M.L. Moreno. 2003. *The Social Impacts of Payments for Environmental Services in Costa Rica.* Environmental Economics Programme. International Institute for Environment and Development, London.

Pagioala, S., A. Arcenas, and G. Platais. 2005. *Can Payments for Environmental Services Reduce Poverty? An Exploration of the Issues and Evidence to Date from Latin America.* World Development 33(2): 237-253.

Turpie, J. K., C. Marais and J.N. Blignaut. 2008. *The Working for Water Programme: Evolution of a Payments for Ecosystem Services Mechanism that Addresses both Poverty and Ecosystem Service Delivery in South Africa.* Ecological Economics 65: 788–798.

Co-Managing Fishery Resources

> **SOURCE:**
>
> Ahmed, M., K. Kuperan Viswanathan and R.A. Valmonte-Santos. 2004, 2020 Focus Brief 11, International Food Policy Research Institute. Washington, D.C.

Fisheries are complex and interdependent ecological and social systems that require integrated management approaches. The actions of one person or group of users affect the availability of the resource for others. Managing such common pool resources requires conscious efforts by a broad range of stakeholders to organize and craft rules enabling equitable and sustainable use of the resources for everyone's benefit. Collective action is often a prerequisite for the development of community-based institutions and the devolution of authority that is required from central to local authorities.

Collective Action in Fisheries: Examples from the Philippines and Bangladesh

There is extensive evidence that communities can improve the conditions of the shared resources on which they depend. Over the past decade, the community of San Salvador in the Philippines has organized and established, with the help of government intervention, a marine sanctuary and reserve. An arrangement for community-based management of coastal resources fostered collective action by forming and strengthening local organizations. These organizations became responsible for marine resource management and income-generating projects, and they reduced overfishing and other destructive practices.

A local ordinance banned fishing within the sanctuary and allowed only non-destructive fishing methods in the marine reserve. The local municipal council passed an ordinance providing legal

Co-management. The approach ensures sustainable management of fishery resources.

protection for the sanctuary. From 1988 to 1996, the average fish catch increased, and living coral cover and the number of coral species doubled.

But not all efforts to establish collective action in fisheries are successful. Research in Bangladesh suggests that the boundaries of the bodies of water, the scale of the resource, and the type of fishery all play a significant role in determining whether efforts to foster collective action succeed. Existing property rights also influenced the types of new institutions for collective action that could be established. One community in Bangladesh was unable to regulate access to the closed fishing grounds where leaseholders had historically controlled access to and stocking of carp, even after community-based fisheries management was introduced and individual leasing was discontinued. Only through successful collective action was it possible to protect group rights over individual ones.

Property Rights Arrangements

Private, state, or community control each has its own limitations in fisheries management. Private ownership often has prohibitively expensive enforcement costs and unequal distributional outcomes. Direct state control has high information costs and often lacks monitoring mechanisms, trained personnel, or financial resources. In some cases, community control excludes the poorest people from access to a common property resource, thus increasing inequality. Combining state, private, and community control over fisheries in imaginative ways can offer more efficient, equitable, and sustainable management. This combination is often referred to as co-management.

Co-management in fisheries involves the active participation and cooperation of government, non-governmental organizations (NGOs), organized fishers' groups, and other stakeholders in management decisions. It can help build cross-institutional collective action, and represents a more democratic governance system than state management because users are more involved in determining rights over the fishery and in sharing decision-making authority. It improves management efficacy by drawing on local knowledge and securing higher compliance with rules.

An Example of Successful Co-Management

Fisheries management involves multiple natural and human settings. San Miguel Bay in the Philippines is a multi-species, multi-gear bay surrounded by three cities and 74 coastal villages whose major livelihood is fishing. Since the 1980s, conventional fisheries management problems—overfishing, distributional inequity, and limited economic opportunities—and negative impacts from various coastal and land-based sectors have been evident.

In the 1990s, the World Fish Center conducted an issue-based, multi-sectoral, and multidisciplinary analysis (including ecological, economic, social, political, and administrative perspectives) that led to the production of a coastal environmental profile. The technical report detailed the status of fisheries, and included an integrated fisheries management plan describing financing and monitoring schemes, participatory implementation plans involving diverse organizations and institutional levels, and the establishment of the San Miguel Bay Fisheries Management Council.

San Miguel's experience highlights:

- the critical role of an appropriate human perception of the situation;
- the importance of collective action and stakeholder participation at key stages of research, planning, and implementation;
- the usefulness of structured decision methods for research, planning, and associated debates; and
- the efficacy of research combined with planning efforts to ensure its utilization and relevance on one hand and to provide a scientific basis for management planning on the other.

Empowering Communities

Unfortunately, governments rarely undertake co-management as a means of empowering fishing communities and increasing democracy. Instead, governments often consider co-management an instrument to achieve their objectives more efficiently by involving fishing communities in the implementation process. Part of the problem is that the organizational structures of government departments have not adapted to the new co-management concept. Most fisheries departments are still staffed with natural scientists and are almost exclusively focused on resource conservation rather than on fishing communities' livelihoods.

Collective action can help to empower poor communities, as the example of San Salvador Island shows. However, effective co-management requires government to devolve real and substantial rights and responsibilities to representatives of fishing industry organizations or groups of harvesters in order to achieve sustainable resource management. Moreover, devolution of rights is generally not successful without collective action.

For collective action to succeed, governments and fishers should meet to discuss problems and their possible solutions and to develop arrangements for management. Fishers should be asked to express their concerns and ideas and be given an opportunity to develop their own organizations, networks, and coalitions.

The government's role is to provide legitimacy and accountability for local organizations and help develop collective action institutions such as community-based and co-management organizations. Successful long-standing arrangements for marine fishery co-management, such as in Japan and Norway, all have a legal foundation.

Where authorities do not devolve some of their powers, governments can abuse co-management arrangements to extend control where it was previously absent. Government agencies need to supplement department staffing with new professional skills and develop enough capacity to deal with co-management processes in several communities simultaneously. Such changes may require reorienting mindsets both in government organizations and in communities.

The Challenges Ahead

Despite progress in achieving collective action and co-management for fisheries, a number of challenges remain:

- ***Developing co-management institutions on a larger scale.*** Many of the problems and issues facing fisheries can be solved only on provincial, national, or even international levels, as fishery resources are generally too large to be entirely within the control of a few communities. In these cases, it is imperative to provide for representation of fishery groups at different levels.
- ***Reconciling local and global agendas.*** Often international agreements on fisheries and local environmental management contradict each other. The government needs to meet its double obligation of attending to international agreements while sharing decision-making power for fisheries management with communities.
- ***Identifying a management knowledge base acceptable to stakeholders.*** To maintain scientific validity and achieve wide acceptance, co-management systems need to reconcile both formal scientific knowledge and fishers' knowledge. One approach may be to identify science-based indicators of the status of the resource system that also reflect fishers' observations.
- ***Developing approaches to manage conflicts.*** Management arrangements may require access rights to be limited to some resource users and to exclude others, often resulting in conflicts. Participatory approaches for managing such conflicts are crucial for successful co-management.
- ***Reforming existing institutions to empower local communities to participate in determining management objectives.*** This step may require substantial changes in governmental fisheries management agencies and in stakeholders' perceptions of their respective roles.

These issues must be addressed in practical experiments with collective action and co-management. The results need to be documented and the experiences communicated to others who may be in the process of establishing or developing collective action capacity among fishers.

Suggested Readings

Ahmed, A., A.D. Capistrano and M. Hossain. 2004. *Experiences of Partnership Models for the Co-Management of Bangladesh Fisheries.* Fisheries Management and Ecology 4 (3): 233–248.

Katon, B., R. S. Pomeroy and A. Salamanca. 1997. *The Marine Conservation Project for San Salvador: A Case Study of Fisheries Co-Management in the Philippines.* Working Paper No. 23. Manila: International Center for Living Aquatic Resources Management.

Kuperan Viswanathan, K. and M. Ahmed. 2002. *Communities and Institutions for Common Property. Fisheries Co-Management News.* No. 10. Penang, Malaysia: World Fish Center.

Kuperan Viswanathan, K., J. Raakjaer Nielsen, P. Degnbol, M. Ahmed, M. Hara, and N. Mustapha Raja Abdullah. 2003. *Fisheries Co-Management—Findings from a Worldwide Study: A Policy Brief.* Manila: World Fish Center.

Silvestre, G.T. 1996. *Integrated Management of Coastal Fisheries: Lessons from Initiatives in San Miguel Bay, Philippines.* Manila: International Center for Living Aquatic Resources Management.

Collective Action for Equitable Natural Resource Management in Eastern African Highlands

SOURCE:

German, L., W. Mazengia, W. Tirwomwe, S. Ayele, J. Tanui, S. Nyangas, L. Begashaw, H. Taye, Z. Admassu, M. Tsegaye, F. Alinyo, A. Mekonnen, K. Aberra, A. Chemangei, W. Cheptegei, T. Tolera, Z. Jote and K. Bedane. 2008. *Enabling Equitable Collective Action and Policy Change for Poverty Reduction and Improved Natural Resource Management in the Eastern African Highlands.* CAPRi Working Paper No. 86. International Food Policy Research Institute, Washington, D.C.

Despite an increased awareness of the institutional foundations of development and natural resource management, development interventions continue to have a strong technological bias. Development and conservation interventions continue to be carried out with an uncritical view to equity or the possible negative repercussions on certain social groups, or on environmental sustainability. Local institutions (rules and structures) remain largely invisible to outside actors. However, the shortcomings lie not only with practitioners, but also within research which, on the institutional dimensions of development and NRM, continues to emphasize problems rather than solutions. One way of addressing these shortcomings is by integrating institutional analysis for problem identification and targeting of interventions with action research in the form of institutional interventions for development of good practice.

Findings from Institutional and Action Research in the Highlands of Ethiopia and Uganda

Local communities were found to have a rich array of collective action institutions, which in turn provided a variety of economic and social support functions. While some of these were seen to support some groups more than others, most forms of collective action were found to have played largely positive roles in livelihoods. Practices of formal support agencies were found to be biased by wealth, gender, and levels of political influence, exacerbating inequities over time. Action research on methodological innovations to overcome these biases and to build upon the strengths of local institutions was needed.

> **Action Research**
>
> In action research, hypotheses are tested through a real-time experiment, with research designed to test and assess the actions or interventions. This involves putting ideas into action, analyzing process and outcomes, and adapting the program as the research unfolds. As with other research approaches, there are many techniques used in action research, but process documentation is a fundamental element, that provides continuous reflection on what is happening.

Local forms of collective action seldom emphasized common solutions to felt NRM problems other than provision of inputs (land, labor, capital). Efforts are needed to strengthen the institutional foundations for community-based NRM. Action research findings have illustrated the potential for improving livelihoods and fostering the more sustainable use of natural resources by catalyzing collective action on NRM where it is absent. Effective collective action seems to require use of both informal negotiation support processes and formal by-law reforms and enforcement. Participatory by-law reforms create stakeholder buy-in, which reduces ambiguity and makes people feel more accountable to other parties for their actions.

The combination of formal and informal mechanisms seems to be needed to revitalize natural resource governance and related livelihood and environmental service outcomes. External agents, be they non-government organizations (NGOs), community-based organizations, or local government, have also been instrumental in bearing the transaction costs of organizing collective action.

Involving people in situation analysis is recommended over a top-down approach in determining interventions.

These roles included information provision, community mobilization, facilitation, advocacy, monitoring, and negotiation support.

Strategies to improve NRM at farm and landscape levels were more effective when more equitable decision-making processes were used to explicitly acknowledge diverse stakes. However, given the diversity of these stakes, by-laws also played a fundamental role in holding each party accountable to resolutions reached through negotiations.

Adapting by-laws to local conditions and stakeholder priorities also induced marked livelihood improvements by enabling collective action and technology adoption. However, participatory by-law negotiations did not reduce the need for by-law enforcement. Rather, participation made people more responsible for agreements, increasing the effectiveness of informal efforts to increase compliance. Improved governance of natural resources is, therefore, a process that involves overcoming past expectations and behaviors, and gradually learning the value of trust.

Implications for Practitioners

- Collective action serves critical development and social support functions in local communities. External institutions should seek ways to build upon local institutions that are highly valued or contribute most to livelihood goals, in particular, for women and poorer households. Part of this effort should be oriented toward finding ways to minimize the effect of

Co-Management of Mt. Elgon National Park

Through a series of government declarations, the Benets (Ndorobo) of Uganda lost legal rights to own and use the land that they had inhabited for 200 years inside Mount Elgon. The livelihood changes induced by resettlement and other factors only increased pressure on Mt. Elgon's resources, compromising both livelihood and conservation objectives.

Benet elders, with the support of Action Aid and Land Alliance, formed a legal entity, the Benet Lobby Group. With the help of the Benet Settlers Association, they worked at all levels to raise awareness of their situation, and won a court case against the government in 2005.

The Kapchorwa District Landcare Chapter (KADLACC) worked to bring an intervention that would end the impasse between the two parties. The intervention strategy included:

- a participatory action research methodology to identify interest groups;
- focus group discussions with the stakeholder groups;
- stakeholder meetings;
- communicating to the authorities to acquire technologies;
- district-level meetings on livelihood and conservation issues;
- development of an action plan around agreements; and
- informal discussions with community members, and multi-stakeholder meetings.

The reconciliation process was jump-started through technology sharing between the Benets and the authorities. A trust-building process enabled both parties to understand that conservation of biodiversity was a bottom line that would not be compromised.

Though still in its early stages, a number of lessons have emerged to shape further interventions. These include the following:

- KADLACC has provided a forum for both parties to engage positively, despite a history of conflict. Support for local champions to facilitate multi-stakeholder NRM processes has been instrumental in managing conflict.
- Dialogue has created opportunities for rapprochement and greater mutual understanding despite a tense situation.
- Collective action among diverse stakeholders to address NRM issues has promoted dialogue and fostered greater access by communities to the natural resources in contention.
- Parallel multi-stakeholder processes at diverse levels have helped bridge the gap between policy intent and realities on the ground by creating dialogue among diverse interest groups at each level.

wealth on the potential for wealth accumulation by linking technology dissemination with low-risk forms of credit and diversification of assets of the poor.

- External development institutions often unintentionally increase existing inequities (based on gender, wealth, age, or ethnicity) by working only with active community members and failing to establish mechanisms for equitable access to project benefits. Methodological innovations to overcome these biases and socially disaggregated monitoring of interventions (by gender and stake, and including non-participants of any activity) are needed to capture such biases early on and identify ways in which they can be overcome.

- Local forms of collective action emphasize enhancing buying power and safety net functions, leaving many common NRM problems unaddressed. External support for horizontal negotiations among local resource users is needed to support collective solutions to NRM problems that remain unaddressed, despite their negative livelihood consequences.

- Extension and development organizations must consider the political dimensions of NRM in terms of winners and losers from any given development intervention, as well as the existence of diverse interests and stakes on any given issue. They must then learn to work explicitly with these political dynamics to foster more equitable solutions to development and NRM challenges through stakeholder identification, negotiation support (to identify socially optimal NRM solutions and mechanisms for equitable benefits capture), and socially disaggregated monitoring of interventions.

- There is also an urgent need for NGOs, local government and other development actors to get involved in natural resource policy formulation and implementation processes. This is due to the intimate association between negotiation support, technological innovation, rules and regulations on NRM, and the urgent need to engage their facilitation skills in fostering more equitable and participatory natural resource governance processes.

There is an urgent need for NGOs, local government, and other development actors to get involved in natural resource policy formulation and implementation processes.

- Fostering collective action where it is absent in addressing felt community needs requires informal negotiation support, formal by-law reforms, and forms of enforcement adapted to local social realities. Participatory by-law reforms create stakeholder buy-in, which reduces the cost of enforcement and reduces ambiguity. Neither formal nor informal mechanisms would be fully effective without the other.

- The external agent, whether an NGO, community-based organization or local government, often bears the transaction costs of organizing collective action. The role of these actors involves both information provision and time spent in organizing and facilitating community events.

Policy Implications

- Policymakers must seek ways to build upon the strengths of local institutions and the crucial social support functions they provide, in particular for women, the poor, and other marginalized groups. They must also seek ways to facilitate the participation of poorer households by assisting them in bridging the assets gap that hinders their ability to invest.

- Many national natural resource policies exist, although a good deal is not followed. Participatory by-law reforms suggest an interest in improved natural resource governance among local residents. More attention should be paid to building the "soft skills" and processes required to create community buy-in to good governance, and to enforcement mechanisms that are effective, while providing alternatives (technologies, cost sharing among stakeholders) where policies restrict livelihoods options.

- The partitioning of mandates between research, extension, and law enforcement agencies causes these issues to be treated separately and important synergies to be lost. Mechanisms and incentives for institutional cooperation toward more equitable and negotiated solutions to NRM are needed to harvest the potential of technology-governance synergies.

- Local residents can formulate NRM by-laws that address their own felt needs, but by-law enforcement by communities themselves is more of a challenge. Communities want local government to play a role in the enforcement of by-laws which should be taken into account in the process of local government reforms in the region so that participatory governance processes can be institutionalized.

- Empirical research on the institutional aspects of development has advanced understanding of the pitfalls of development practice and the characteristics of local institutions. Nonetheless, two fundamental gaps remain. The first is ensuring widespread access to lessons learned among development practitioners to improve their practice. The second is the need to move beyond the identification of problems to the identification of viable solutions ("good practice") through the coupling of empirical and action-oriented research.

Suggested Readings

German, L. and A. Stroud. 2007. *A Framework for the Integration of Diverse Learning Approaches: Operationalizing Agricultural Research and Development (R&D) Linkages in Eastern Africa.* World Development 35 (5): 792-814.

Grootaert, C. 2002. *Does Social Capital Help the Poor? A Synthesis of Findings from Local Level Institutions Studies in Bolivia, Burkina Faso, and Indonesia.* Local Level Institutions Working Paper No 10. Washington, D.C.: The World Bank.

Lubell, M., M. Schneider, J.T. Scholz and M. Mete. 2002. *Watershed Partnerships and the Emergence of Collective Action Institutions.* American Journal of Political Science 46(1):148-163.

Sustainable Forest Management and Stewardship in Mexico: Gains, Challenges and Lessons

Mexico, one of the world's 10 mega-diverse countries, has 56.5 million hectares of forest of high global value. Biodiversity occurs in a wide variety of forest ecosystems: humid and dry tropical forests and various types of temperate forests. Together with richness in terms of number of species, Mexican forests also host very high genetic diversity, as it appears to be one of the centers of origin of *pinus* and *quercus*. High biological productivity is another key feature of these forest areas, as pine forests in Central Mexico enjoy growth rates of 15 square meters of timber per hectare per year, three to five times higher than those found in natural forests in the United States and Canada.

SOURCES:

David, B., L. Merino and D. Barry. 2006. *The Community Forests of Mexico.* Managing for Sustainable Landscapes. University of Texas Press, Austin.

David, B. and L. Merino. 2004. *La Experiencia de Las Comunidades Forestales de México.* Instituto Nacional de Ecologia, México. (http://www.ine.gob.mx).

For centuries, Mexico's forests have been inhabited, managed, and used. As many as 14 million people, many from indigenous groups, live today in 8,500 forest communities. Despite this biological and cultural richness, 50 percent of the inhabitants of these forest communities are extremely poor.

Community Forestry in Mexico: Potentials and Achievements

As a result of an extensive land tenure reform (1930-1980), 70 percent of the country's forest land is owned by local communities. This land tenure pattern has created opportunities as well as challenges for sustainability. In many forest communities, collective property, together with undesired impacts of different public policies, have contributed to repeated "tragedies of unmanaged commons." In a meaningful number of cases, however, property rights have enabled forest dwellers to take a long-term perspective on forest use, while collective property has created incentives and restrictions that favor social capital and collective action around the use and protection of forest commons.

The Tragedy of the Commons

In 1968, Garret Hardin published "The Tragedy of the Commons", a brief paper that quickly had enormous policy impacts. Hardin argued that collectively-owned lands, which he defined as "open access," were inevitably subject to uncontrolled overuse. In a much later work, published in 1994, Hardin himself acknowledged that the "tragedy" was limited to unmanaged collective goods. Unfortunately, however, his original paper continues to influence thinking on the performance of common property resources.

Mexico has the largest share of forests under community management in the world; 18 percent are directly managed by local communities. This is an outcome of different community forestry programs and forest laws that have, at different times since the early 1980s, sought to provide responses to the vast deforestation experienced mainly during the 1970s and 1980s. Community forestry became an alternative to either closing forests or giving concessions to outsiders, two strategies that had been previously applied with poor social and ecological outcomes.

Community forest programs have provided economic incentives for local communities to engage in forest protection, mainly through the development of community commercial logging operations. Over time, these programs also became engaged in the development of local technical and administrative capacities, conservation and management of forest biodiversity, diversification of forest use — including the harvest of non-timber forest products and marketing of environmental services — and fostering communities' collective action and forest governance. NGOs have been actively involved in community forestry and have been key facilitators for the success and sustainability of these efforts.

Community forestry has worked as an important local development driver. As in other developing countries, in Mexico forests provide households with fuel, food, fodder and traditional medicines. In addition, where commercial community forestry has developed forest assets, these are the base of community enterprises that provide local employment and income.

In 2006, 80 percent of the country's timber production was provided by forest communities. Non-timber forest products make a similar contribution to local economies. Tourism and marketing of environmental services have appeared in an increasing number of cases. The profits of communities' enterprises are frequently invested in the development of communities' infrastructure and services, schools, clinics, and roads. Even libraries and internet facilities have been funded with the profits of communities' forest business. These investments are particularly important in remote regions where government investment tends to be scarce.

Community Forest Conservation: A Success Story

In the *Ejido El Balcón* on Mexico's Pacific coast, the local community has sustainably managed its 15,000 hectare temperate forest for more than 20 years. In the late 1980s, it acquired forest industry facilities and in the mid-1990s, *El Balcón* became certified. Since then it has been exporting timber products to the United States. In 2009, it started selling furniture to the European Union. This collective business provides employment to all *ejido* members, their children, and to some members of neighboring communities. Young people who want to study in the local university can be funded by the *ejido*, in exchange for two years of community work when they finish studying.

The 300 hectare forest of *Ejido El Paso* is the best preserved area in the buffer zone of the Biosphere of the Monarch Butterfly in the mountains of Central Mexico. *Ejido* members have sustainably logged and protected their forest for more than 60 years, providing important contributions to local livelihoods. Achievements of *El Paso* sharply contrast with the conditions of most of the 104 communities of the Reserve, where poverty and deforestation are widespread.

Through community forestry, local societies have achieved other less tangible, though no less important, gains. In most cases, sustainable management of common forests is largely based on previous social capital, defined as relations of trust and cooperation within communities. Where community forestry has been successful, social capital has grown and expanded and local institutions developed and strengthened. In this sense, community forestry also contributes to a key public good: the possibility of local governance, an especially important "good" in the context of increasing violence that Mexico is currently facing. Finally, collective management of common forests also requires and promotes human capital.

Community forestry has made important contributions to biodiversity conservation: the largest and best preserved area of cloud forest, the most endangered type of forest in the country, is located in various community-protected areas in the southern state of Oaxaca. Nearly half of the communities in the five main forest states of Mexico have created areas devoted solely to conservation. A million hectares of community-managed forests have been certified as well managed by the Forest Stewardship Council (FSC).

Mexico's pioneering experience is being successfully adapted and adopted in other Latin American countries like Guatemala and Bolivia.

Old and New Challenges to Sustainable Forest Management

In spite of these achievements, it has to be acknowledged that these areas still face important economic, political and environmental challenges. Mexican forest areas are going through a process of change: traditional challenges remain while new threats for sustainability have emerged.

Traditional Challenges

> **Collective and Participatory Management**
>
> Members of forest communities meet regularly to discuss collective forest management and forest business. With the support of NGOs, many of them have developed participatory land-use planning that often includes the segregation of areas devoted to forest and water source protection, and even for biodiversity conservation. Community assemblies have also developed local by-laws regarding forest management, where community members' rights and responsibilities are defined and agreed upon.

- Successful cases are largely constrained to temperate forests with a higher density of tree species with commercial value; regional markets for most tropical timber species are non-existent.

- Forest production is over-regulated (by central government), which results in additional costs.

- Illegal logging is widespread and, there are no market instruments that enable consumers to identify legally produced timber, and the capacity of the government to monitor and sanction is extremely low.

- Over-grazing occurs in forest areas with few resources of commercial value, largely promoted by long-time subsidies.

- There is a lack of public understanding of both current contributions and future potential of community forestry.

Emerging Challenges

- Community businesses have to compete in global markets without access to proper funding and adequate macro-economic policies, while market prices do not always pay for all the costs involved in sustainable timber production.

- Out-migration is an increasing phenomenon, the impacts of which on forest management and local governance are not yet fully understood. Due to out-migration of the young, community rights holders are aging, often without generational replacement. Population loss may reach a point at which social capital and local institutions weaken and forest resources lose social value.

The main social and ecological challenges are faced by communities without management schemes in the majority of the forests of the country. The most endangered forest types are cloud forests and dry forests, rich in biodiversity, but poor in resources with market value. In these regions, the contributions of forests to local employment and income are very low or non-existent.

Experience shows that there is a strong relation between successful collective forest management, high levels of social capital, and strong local institutions. The opposite is also true — as a general trend, deforestation, uncontrolled forest fires, and illegal cutting occur mostly in contexts of poor social capital and scare opportunities of economically-viable legal forest use.

Conclusions and Lessons Learned

More than 20 years of experience of community forestry in Mexico has produced important social learning:

- Local communities can be viable local stewards of resources and ecosystems of high public value.

- The development of economic incentives, the empowerment of collectives and local rule are imperatives for forest sustainability in the context of inhabited forest regions. Forest conservation requires the development of local capacities for forest management, forest economy, and local governance.

- Ecological knowledge — local and academic — has an important role to play. As commercial extractive uses develop, and management evolves towards sustainable harvest and landscapes, it provides fundamental inputs for rule making and decision-taking processes.

- The sustainability of community forestry in Mexico requires the support of both well-crafted policies and markets able to recognize and value its environmental and social costs.

- The creation of new types of markets requires a coordinated intervention of the state and the civil society.

Suggested Readings

Garrett, H. 1994. *The Tragedy of the Unmanaged Commons.* Trends in Ecology and Evolution, Volume 9, Issue 5, Page 199.

Rudel, T.K., O. T. Coomes, E. Morán, F. Achard, A. Angelsen, J. Xu and E. Lambin. 2005. *Forests Transitions: Towards a Global Understanding of Land Use Change.* Global Environmental Change, pp 23-31.

White, A. and A. Martín. 2002. *Who Owns the World's Forests? Forest Tenure and Public Forests in Transition.* Forest Trends. Washington, D.C.

Chapter 4

Changing Market Relations

Enabling Collective Action for Smallholder Market Access

Discussions about poverty reduction inevitably include the need to increase small landholders' ability to participate successfully in market exchanges. However, smallholders must be aware of new opportunities and challenges brought about by changes in the global agricultural economy. Prominent among these changes is the growing demand for higher value and for processed foods, as well as the increasing number of supermarkets as outlets for farm products that have in turn altered procurement systems and made quality and safety standards more stringent.

SOURCE:

Markelova, H., R. Meinzen-Dick, J. Hellin, and S. Dohrn. 2009. *Collective Action for Smallholder Market Access.* CAPRi Policy Brief No. 5. International Food Policy Research Institute, Washington, D.C.

Markets in developing countries are characterized by pervasive imperfections such as lack of information on prices and technologies, high transaction costs, and credit constraints. New challenges

include the rise of procurement systems that expect larger supply volumes, favoring large landholders, and free trade agreements that have imposed on farmers the need to compete not only nationally, but also internationally.

How can smallholders overcome these constraints and challenges? One way is to organize into farmer groups or producers' associations. By acting collectively, farmers will be in a better position to reduce transaction costs for market exchanges, obtain necessary market information, secure access to new technologies, and tap into high-value markets.

Cooperation is recognized as crucial for the poor to overcome challenges posed by unfavorable policy and market context, and to create sustainable livelihood options. However, collective action is not automatic and requires specific enabling conditions that are important for the formation and functioning of farmers' groups. What are these factors? These are types of markets, types of products, group characteristics, and institutional arrangements.

Types of Markets, Smallholder Access, and Potential for Collective Action

Smallholders will find certain markets more difficult to access. Theoretically, these are the "long" marketing chains that require costly transport and storage, and demand stringent quality and scale standards. However, collective action can facilitate smallholder access to the markets that promise better returns.

Table 1. Enabling Factors for Collective Action.

Types of Markets	Smallholder Access	Potential for Collective Action
Local	Easier to reach — fewer logistical differences, less competition from larger producers.	Offers relatively low gains because farmers can sell individually.
Emerging urban	Relatively difficult because of transport and storage issues, acquisition of technologies and certificates to comply with quality standards, need to reach economies of scale to supply desired quantity, and quality of product.	Collective action can allow smallholders to reach larger markets. It can enable them to deal with various issues and requirements such as storage, certificates, quality, and quantity standards.
Regional		
Export market	More challenging in terms of transport and market risks. Smallholders may be unable to compete with agribusiness and meet international quality and food safety standards.	Collective action can enable smallholders to meet necessary quality requirements through certification.

Farm Product Types and their Implications for Collective Action

Table 2. Incentives for Collective Action.

Product Types	Characteristics and Choice of Output Markets	Incentives for Collective Action
Staples	Relatively easy to store and transport; usually destined for the local market.	Few.
Perishables	Carry higher risks; require more sophisticated and costly storage and transport facilities.	Producer organizations can be effective in marketing horticultural products to quality conscious markets by allowing smallholders to deal with quality requirements.
Cash crops	Require processing, thus smallholders usually sell to agribusiness which can afford processing equipment.	Collective action can enable smallholders to acquire processing equipment and market to domestic and international markets.

Group Characteristics

Group Size. Small groups often have higher internal cohesion because it is easier to know and monitor other members. However, larger groups can achieve economies of scale, a particular advantage in marketing. Federated organizations that build up from smaller groups offer a way to combine small base groups with economies of scale, but as with the viability of collective action at the local level, the viability of federations should not be assumed.

Group Membership. Clearly defined group boundaries facilitate collective action. However, there are trade-offs between inclusiveness and tighter membership rules that may exclude the poorest farmers but lead to greater group effectiveness.

Shared Norms, Social Capital, and Past Successes. These facilitate collective action in new areas. Marketing organizations that build upon pre-existing social groups have an advantage because they can build on local norms and trust. However, external programs should not push marketing activities on existing groups unless the members want to undertake joint marketing.

Group Relationship. Interdependence among members generally facilitates collective action. There is a debate on whether heterogeneity constrains or enables collective action; some argue that homogeneity of socio-economic status and values is necessary, while others cite cases where internal differentiation allows necessary leadership to evolve.

Leadership. Leaders should be trusted, able to motivate the members, and have necessary skills for the collective enterprise. They should also have linkages to outsiders and key business skills.

Institutional Arrangements

Simple and understandable rules increase compliance, establish accountability, and serve as an enforcement mechanism. Rules crafted by group members have a higher likelihood of being followed, contributing to the effectiveness and sustainability of collective marketing efforts.

Various sizes of groups ranging from small groups and federated structures to multiple linkages and networks along the commodity value chain, may be appropriate for collective commercial activities. Public-private partnerships have also helped in linking smallholder groups with other actors in the marketing chains, who enable these groups to upgrade their facilities, skills, and production techniques.

External Environment

Relations with the markets and the state are two major aspects of the external environment that studies of collective resource management have identified as important. Strong market linkages are often reported as reducing collective action for managing resources, partly because in communities with less market integration, people are more interdependent.

Group formation cannot happen in a context of state hostility or macro-economic instability. Good governance that ensures legal and credit systems in favor of the poor will undoubtedly increase economic opportunities for smallholders and provide incentives to join with others.

Key Recommendations for Collective Action

Create Incentives for Cooperation. The state should improve rural infrastructure, provide extension services, make credit markets accessible, and make available relevant information. These measures should enable farmers' groups to effectively compete in markets. In addition, the state should make group registration processes simpler. Specialized training for members can impart the required expertise in technical and marketing skills.

Provide Enabling Facilitation. To enable farmers' groups to access profitable markets, they need a facilitator or a "chain champion" to aid in the processes by which farmer groups overcome barriers to entry, such as low technical and organizational capacity, informational asymmetries, and often financial constraints.

Outsiders can help groups that organize themselves to get access to microcredit.

Facilitation can be provided by the state and its agencies, by members of civil society and non-government organizations (NGOs), donors, or even by private firms. Facilitators can help farmers' groups to obtain access to business development services such as inputs, supplies, micro-credit, market information, transportation services, technical expertise, quality assurance, and product development assistance.

Participation of all three sectors, the private sector, and state and civil society represented by NGOs may be necessary for a group of smallholders to effectively participate in markets. This calls for innovative institutional arrangements between state agencies, companies, NGOs, and producer groups that would take care of various relationships along a commodity value chain and ensure the timely provision of funding and business development services.

Address Equity and Sustainability Issues. To address equity considerations, policies and programs aiming to enhance marketing access for the poorest need to carefully consider their target beneficiaries.

Sustainability of collective marketing is important for long-term, pro-poor development. It involves both business and marketing sustainability and longevity of collective action, which must work parallel to each other. Market development and social development agendas must be reconciled. Extreme care must be taken so that public sector financing in the form of subsidies does not create perverse incentives for collective action, thus creating the need for careful planning and timing. The facilitating agent must carefully assess its role, capacity (both financial and human), and level of participation at the onset of the project, and design a viable exit strategy.

Have Realistic Expectations. It is important to remember that the success and effectiveness of collective action groups depend on many factors and, in most cases, facilitation by an outside agent from the public, private or civil society sectors to catalyze both collective action and market development. Without these factors in place, collective marketing may not be a realistic goal for a group of smallholders.

Collective marketing as an approach to pro-poor development is not a "silver bullet" that is applicable and replicable in all situations. There is a need to remember that market development is not always going to help the poorest, since they may not have the minimum asset threshold needed to participate in market exchanges.

Conclusion

Smallholders are excluded from successfully participating in market exchanges because of changes in the global agricultural economy and market imperfections in the developing world.

Organizing farmers into groups or producers' associations can help smallholders overcome constraints caused by these imperfections, as well as deal with emerging challenges and take advantage of new opportunities. However, collective action is not automatic and requires specific enabling conditions for the effective formation and functioning of farmers' groups. These factors are types of markets, types of products, group characteristics, and institutional arrangements. Moreover, farmers' or producer groups need enabling facilitation to make collective action happen.

Suggested Readings

Agrawal, A. 2001. *Common Property Institutions and Sustainable Governance of Resources.* World Development 29(10): 1649-1672.

Bebbington, A. 1996. *Organizations and Intensifications: Campesino Federations, Rural Livelihoods and Agricultural Technology in the Andes and Amazonia.* World Development 24(7): 1161-1177.

Meinzen-Dick, R., H. Markelova, J. Hellin and S. Dohrn (eds). 2009. *Collective Action for Smallholder Market Access.* Special Section of *Food Policy* 34 (1): 1-59.

Weatherspoon, D. and T. Reardon. 2003. *The Rise of Supermarkets in Africa: Implications for Agrifood Systems and the Rural Poor.* Development Policy Review 21(3): 333-355.

Collective Action and Agroindustries

SOURCE:

Johnson, N. and J. A. Berdegué. 2004. *Collective Action and Property Rights for Sustainable Development: Property Rights, Collective Action, and Agribusiness.* 2020 Focus Brief 11, International Food Policy Research Institute, Washington, D.C.

Two fundamental global economic tendencies have caused a shift in interest towards promoting rural agroenterprises and agroindustrialization to combat rural poverty. Increasing income levels and demographic changes, i.e. increased female labor force participation, has fueled demand for high-value and processed products. Structural adjustment and liberalization policies have reduced barriers to trade globally and allowed markets to reach even the most isolated rural areas.

Together, these trends are fueling a process of agroindustrialization that is transforming agriculture in the developing world, most visibly in Asia and Latin America, with Africa beginning to show similar effects. Agroindustrialization brings major opportunities but also many challenges, especially to poor farmers and small agroenterprise entrepreneurs, most notable of which is equitable distribution of benefits.

The agroindustrialization process has three main characteristics.

1. Growth in off-farm agriculture-related activities, such as the supply of farm inputs or the processing, distribution, and sale of farm products. The suppliers, farmers, and distributors form supply or product chains.

2. Increased level of integration among actors in the supply chain, ranging from loose coordination to contracting, and even outright ownership.

3. Changes in products, technologies, and market structures accompany these shifts in number and integration of actors.

Implications of Market Orientation and the Importance of Collective Action

Market orientation means adjusting production processes and products to respond to *specific* consumer demands and market signals and trends. Although many small farmers in developing countries will continue to grow subsistence crops, increased production for the market is the trend in many countries. What small farmers grow and how they grow them are increasingly determined by what urban consumers want.

Agroindustrialization processes are often accompanied and stimulated by liberalization of economic policy. This means that agroindustries — and the producers supplying them — must be competitive internationally to survive. To be competitive, agroindustries typically work only with farmers who produce the best quality products at the lowest possible cost. Often, the competitiveness of the agroindustry is strengthened through strict grades and standards, imposed on their farmer-suppliers through contracts. In negotiating and enforcing those contracts, power relationships between agroindustries and farmers — especially small and poor farmers — tend to be highly asymmetric, favoring industry.

Agroindustrialization processes are often accompanied by privatization of land and other natural resources. The rationale is to facilitate the development of markets that permit transfers of assets toward the highest productivity uses. Typically, this situation has meant a net transfer of productive assets from small farmers and poor rural communities to commercial growers and large-scale corporations, both domestic and multinational.

Where customary rights and communal ownership are important, the shift to private property may disadvantage those whose access rights are not recognized under the new regime. To the extent that these people are more marginalized in a society, there is the risk of widening existing inequalities. Similar patterns can be observed with shifts away from traditional labor exchanges toward wage labor.

Where the costs of accessing markets are high due to poor infrastructure, inadequate technology, or information barriers, collective action can help small producers be more competitive. A study of Associative Peasant Businesses in Chile found that cooperation benefited producers in markets where transaction costs were high and where product differentiation was important. In traditional markets for undifferentiated crops, no benefits to association were found. Associations were also found to be good vehicles for introducing new managerial and farming practices that enhanced farm profitability. Only about a fifth of these small farmer associations achieved their objective of helping their members participate in new markets, despite extensive government support.

The reasons for their many failures included, among others, their inability to:

- develop and enforce adequate systems of rules to direct relations among the members and between each of them and the organization;
- establish effective networks with public and market agents; and
- become competitive in the market in which they operate.

Cooperation can enable farmers to be more competitive.

Implications of Integration for Small Farms and Firms

More striking than the changes in agricultural products and practices is the integration that has occurred in agroindustry over the past decade. The rise of mega-processors and retailers has resulted in very little produce being traded on the open market. A striking example is the rise of supermarkets in Latin America, which in a decade moved from 10–20 percent to 50–60 percent of the retail food sector. Collective action can sometimes allow producers to re-balance market power relationships and gain bargaining power in negotiations with big buyers.

A driving force behind this integration is the need to coordinate the timing and quality of purchases, and deliveries along the supply chain. Perishability was behind early integration, but other factors relating to economies of scale in the management of information about consumers and their preferences, for example, reinforced the trend.

In agricultural production, the increasing use of contracts by processors reflects this integration. Contracting can be positive for many farmers, but the small farmers are often bypassed because the transaction costs associated with managing the contract outweigh any productivity advantage the small farmer might offer. Since contracting is characterized by economies of scale, collective action among farmers, such as producers' associations, can make them competitive in an integrated supply chain. Collective action among farmers is, however, difficult to organize, coordinate, and manage.

A similar situation faces small agroenterprises. Even where farms and firms do not operate under contract, cooperating can help them negotiate better prices for inputs and outputs, manage crises, or improve local infrastructure.

Well-organized farmers have competitive advantages, but collective action at the local level is not likely to be enough to allow small rural enterprises to exploit new market opportunities fully. Whether they are acting individually or collectively, farms and firms need to stay informed about technological and managerial innovations, as well as emerging market opportunities in broader networks. A growing array of service providers — formal and informal, public and private — now exists to offer technical assistance, from quality control to marketing to financial planning. Firms that identify and take advantage of these services are more competitive. A study in Colombia found that a 10 percent increase in the number of relationships that an agroenterprise maintained with other actors was associated with increases in income per worker of up to 18 percent. This means that for farms and firms that participate in technically demanding, information-intensive supply chains, managing their relationships can be as important as managing their production processes.

Collective action can sometimes allow producers to re-balance market power relationships and gain bargaining power in negotiations with big buyers.

External contacts are important, but internal relationships are also key to business performance and survival. Increased attention to promoting small enterprises is often accompanied by a push to form and legalize businesses. Decisions about how businesses should organize themselves are often made on the basis of legal costs and potential access to government subsidies for certain types of businesses.

Different organizational structures, however, have fundamental differences that firms need to consider.

- ***Cooperative forms of organization*** are based on economic and social objectives and require high levels of commitment and collective action to function. In practice, these levels of commitment are often hard to maintain, even if the groups are subsidized.

- ***Partnerships*** have lower legal and administrative costs, but they assume high levels of trust among the partners, a condition reflected in the shared, unlimited liability for the firm's obligations.

- ***Corporations*** have the highest administrative costs, but they may be the best structure for firms where investors do not share high levels of trust and are likely to change frequently.

Evidence from Colombia shows that no one organizational structure is best for either economic performance or social impact. The appropriate structure depends on the individual characteristics and objectives of the members.

Conclusion

Agroindustrialization is transforming agriculture and rural communities in developing countries. As a result, farmers and entrepreneurs need to change the way they do business. Part of the solution is precisely that: to think about and organize themselves as a business and to be more attentive to market signals and opportunities. Because they are in markets that are not perfect, investment in collective action and networking can bring high returns.

The reality of agroindustrialization also means that the public and private sector research and development organizations that support agriculture and rural development must re-evaluate how best to support agroenterprise development through policy, technology, and institutional innovations. High-value products and opportunities for adding value should complement the focus on productivity improvement in undifferentiated commodities. Capacity building in business skills, accompanied by more and higher quality business development services, can improve the competitiveness of small rural businesses.

A better understanding of how to develop and support networks, and innovative forms of organization beyond traditional agricultural cooperatives is also needed. On a more fundamental level, organizational and institutional innovations often arise in response to high transaction costs associated with market failures. Ameliorating these market failures, especially in the area of information and communication, will contribute to a more efficient and equitable agribusiness sector.

Suggested Readings

Berdegué, J.A. and G. Escobar. 2001. *Agricultural Knowledge and Information Systems and Poverty Reduction*. AKIS Discussion Paper. Washington, D.C.:World Bank.

Johnson, N., R. Suarez and M. Lundy. 2002. *The Importance of Social Capital in Colombian Rural Agroenterprises.* CAPRi Working Paper No. 26. Washington, D.C.: International Food Policy Research Institute.

Reardon, T. and J.A. Berdegué. 2002. *The Rapid Rise of Supermarkets in Latin America: Challenges and Opportunities for Development.* Development Policy Review, 20(4): 371-388.

Participatory Market Chains and Stakeholder Platforms: The Papa Andina Strategy

Native potatoes grow better in the highest altitude of the Andes, where small, semi-commercial farmers predominate. These farmers possess a deep knowledge of native potatoes and the most suitable cultivation methods for them in their native environment. Native potatoes do not grow as well at lower altitudes, where more commercially-oriented farmers grow modern varieties and employ more industrial inputs.

SOURCE:

Devaux, A., C. Velasco, G. López, T. Bernet, M. Ordinola, H. Pico, G. Thiele and D. Horton. 2008. *Collective Action for Innovation and Small Farmer Market Access: The Papa Andina Experience*. CAPRi Working Paper No. 68. International Food Policy Research Institute, Washington, D.C.

Papa Andina is a regional initiative hosted by the International Potato Center that promotes pro-poor innovation for development in Andean potato-based production and marketing systems in Bolivia, Ecuador, and Peru. With its national partners, Papa Andina seeks to contribute to poverty reduction by strengthening the capacity of small farmers to participate more effectively in markets for potatoes and potato-based products and by facilitating the creation of new market opportunities for their potatoes.

Papa Andina Strategy

Through action research in Peru, Bolivia, and Ecuador, Papa Andina and its research and development partners have developed two complementary approaches to enhance small-scale farmers' market access through collective action.

The Participatory Market Chain Approach (PMCA)

The PMCA was developed as an approach for identifying and exploiting new business opportunities that benefit small-scale farmers by stimulating market-driven innovation of different types. It engages market chain actors, researchers, and other service providers in identifying and analyzing potential business opportunities. In addition, it helps to build trust among market actors and research and development organizations and to empower small farmers.

Stakeholder Platforms

Stakeholder platforms provide opportunities to bring small potato producers together with market agents and agricultural service providers to identify common interests, share market knowledge and carry out joint activities to develop new business opportunities.

Three Phases of PMCA

The PMCA involves three phases, each of which has specific objectives, core activities, and tangible outputs. The entire process is usually implemented over a period varying from several months to a year.

Innovations Using the PMCA

- ***Commercial Innovation*** involves the development of new products or services for specific market niches, to add value to potato production. In Bolivia, for example, new colored potato chip products made from native potatoes have been introduced into the market. In Peru, selected and washed fresh potatoes in plastic sacks of uniform variety and weight have been introduced.
- ***Technological Innovation*** involves improvements in the way commodities are produced or transformed. The interaction of researchers, development professionals, potato producers, and other groups has improved the dissemination of technological innovations and helped research organizations to align their research agendas to better contribute to innovation in the region.
- ***Institutional Innovation*** relates to changes in attitudes, habits, or relationships among stakeholders, in order to create more favorable conditions for pro-poor innovation. New institutional arrangements such as stakeholder platforms have helped deal with the lack of trust that is common in market chain interactions.

Figure 1. Structure and Objectives of the Three Phases of PMCA

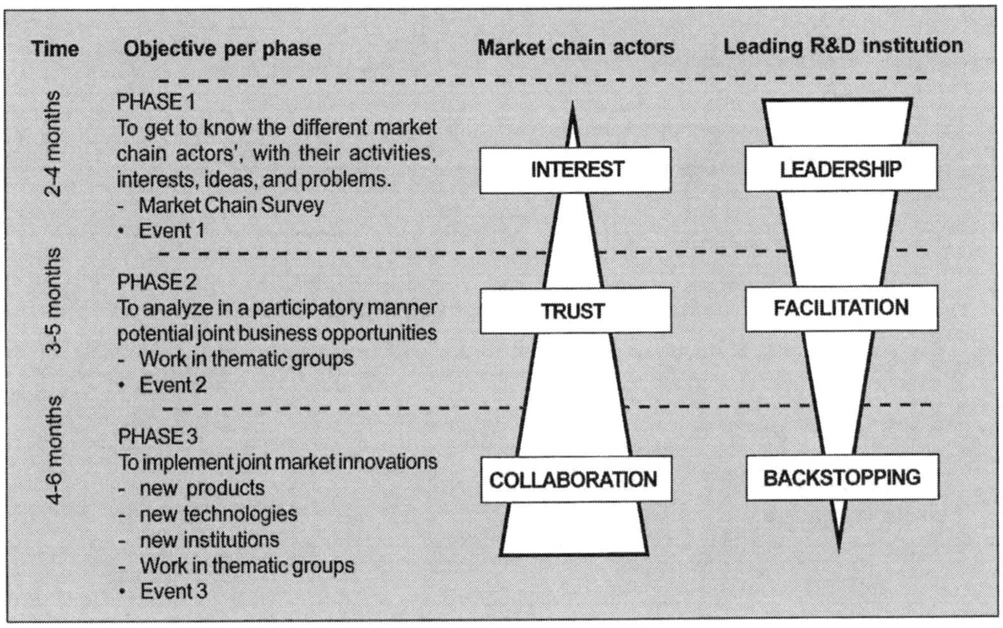

A multi-stakeholder platform is a space for interaction that aims to reduce conflict, build trust, and lead to coordination and joint action. Through a platform, things that none of its members could achieve on their own can be accomplished.

Stakeholder platforms promote collaboration between a diverse range of market actors.

Papa Andina has applied the "stakeholder platform" concept to promote interaction, social learning, and collaboration between the diverse range of actors who may contribute to the innovation process. Platforms are a means to promote collective action through utilization of the following functions:

- Help stakeholders understand the interests and perspectives of other market chain actors and help small farmers take advantage of market opportunities.
- Facilitate the process of social learning, discovery, and utilization of ideas, which contribute to empower the participants, especially small-scale farmers.

Role of Collective Action in Papa Andina Strategy

Collective action has been defined as voluntary action taken by a group to pursue common interests or achieve common objectives. In pursuing its objectives, Papa Andina has promoted collective action at various levels.

Local Level. Papa Andina and its partners have promoted the organization of potato producers, in order to empower small farmers, reduce marketing costs, and increase efficiency in the delivery of technical assistance.

Market Chain Level. Papa Andina has fostered the creation of platforms that bring farmers together with transporters, traders, processors, managers of supermarkets, researchers, extension agents, chefs, and others with a stake in the production and marketing of potatoes.

National Level. Papa Andina and its partners have supported the formation of farmers' organizations such as the Consortium of Small Potato Producers in Ecuador and multi-stakeholder platforms such as "Quality Agricultural Market Chains in Peru" for CAPAC.

Regional Andean Level. The Papa Andina initiative itself represents a form of collective action among research and development partners.

Pursuing Common Objectives

Within Papa Andina, different groups operating in different contexts at different levels have pursued different specific objectives. However, a few broad objectives have been common to all the groups:

- ***Empowerment and Capacity Development*** of group members at the different levels — from farmers to research organizations — by strengthening the capacities they need to participate in innovation processes.

- ***Knowledge Sharing and Social Learning*** to build mutual understanding and trust for collaboration and joint actions among R&D partners.

- ***Building Networks and Relationships*** *to* encourage partners to go beyond their traditional alliances and experiment with new partners and new forms of collaboration.

- ***Pro-poor Innovations*** that benefit poor potato producers by identifying and developing commercial opportunities for native potatoes grown by small farmers in the Andean highlands.

Challenges in Linking Smallholders with Markets

In the work of Papa Andina with the PMCA and stakeholder platforms in Bolivia, Ecuador and Peru, there have been five main challenges:

1) *Providing adequate facilitation for group work.* Effective facilitation of groups implementing the PMCA and developing stakeholder platforms requires well-trained facilitators who understand the complexity of developing business opportunities with small-scale farmers, without being paternalistic.

2) *Ensuring the sustainability of collective action.* Smallholders generally face higher marketing costs than larger farmers because of their small volume of marketable surplus, their lack of business skills, and lack of access to information and technology.

3) *Scaling up.* Factors such as lack of business tools and skills needed to adequately evaluate business opportunities, as well as limited time, market size, and financial resources, have prevented the expansion of markets and limited the number of farmers and businesses involved.

4) *Costs of participation.* The PMCA and development of stakeholder platforms involve participatory processes that are, or seem to be, time consuming, especially in the beginning, before tangible results have been produced.

5) *Gender equity.* Women have participated in the work carried out in the three countries; however, much remains to be done to significantly impact gender equity.

Smallholders generally face higher marketing costs because of their small volume of marketable surplus.

Papa Andina intends to address these issues through the following approaches:

- Capacity building of partners in the areas of market analysis, chain development, participatory approaches, product development, social responsibility and areas where women can play more significant roles in collective action.

- Particular attention will be paid to strengthening their capacity to access and effectively manage resources for promoting private-sector development.

- Monitoring, evaluation, documentation of Papa Andina cases in order to draw lessons from its work and to scale up use of the PMCA and stakeholder platforms.

- Knowledge-sharing measures such as development of guidelines for approaches that have potentially broad applications. Training materials have been developed on participatory methods for collective action at different levels, such as the PMCA User Guide prepared in Spanish and English and a Trainer Guide.

Lessons Learned

The experience of Papa Andina and its partners demonstrates how different forms of collective action involving different stakeholders can stimulate commercial, technical, and institutional innovations that contribute to market integration and poverty reduction. Some of the key lessons identified are as follows:

Lesson 1: Collective action can stimulate innovation in ways that contribute to smallholder market integration and poverty reduction.
The interaction of people participating in group activities strengthened business contacts, social networks, knowledge sharing, and interpersonal trust. In Bolivia, Ecuador, and Peru, collective action led to technical, commercial, or institutional innovation that in turn contributed to improved market participation of smallholders and improved livelihoods of the poor.

Lesson 2: Diversity within multi-stakeholder platforms can be a valuable source of commercial, technical and institutional innovation.
Diversity promoted learning and innovation and resulted in new products, processes, norms, and behaviors. Multi-stakeholder initiatives directly benefit those participating in these platforms as they gain important insights, make new and interesting contacts, and possibly access new business opportunities.

Lesson 3: Commercial innovation can drive subsequent technological and institutional innovation.
Experiences with the PMCA in Peru, Bolivia, and Ecuador have shown that commercial innovations (i.e. development of new products) can stimulate the use of new production technologies as well as new institutions. The launching of native potato products, for example, has stimulated the formation and strengthening of farmers' organizations to facilitate marketing and improvements in production and post-harvest practices.

Lesson 4: Collective action at different levels can produce valuable synergies.
Stakeholder platforms and the PMCA have proven to be highly complementary. Producer associations and stakeholder platforms at the local level have benefited from market chain development work that identified new market opportunities and built social and commercial networks to link producers with market actors.

Lesson 5: Collective action does not just happen — it needs good facilitation.
Opportunities for information exchange and collective action need to be actively created. This is especially true for bringing together actors along the market chain who compete in their daily business and whose time has a high opportunity cost. To guarantee active participation

The launching of a new product based on native potatoes can stimulate further innovations that benefit small farmers.

of key actors in a participatory setting, good process facilitation is needed to generate tangible benefits for actors who get involved.

Lesson 6: Biodiversity and cultural identity can add value to collective action for market access.

In Bolivia and Peru, where there is greater potato biodiversity than in Ecuador, commercial innovation with native potatoes has been a key element in linking small farmers to markets. The products have a good potential to do well in external markets because they are seen as exotic and coming from a well-recognized region, the Andes.

Suggested Readings

Antezana, I., T. Bernet, G. López y R. Oros (2008). *Enfoque Participativo de Cadenas Productivas (EPCP): Guía para Capacitadores.* Papa Andina/Centro Internacional de la Papa, Lima, Perú.

Bernet, T., G. Thiele and T. Zschocke. 2006. *Participatory Market Chain Approach (PMCA) User Guide.* Lima: International Potato Center (CIP) – Papa Andina.

Bernet, T., Devaux, A., Thiele, G., López, G., Velasco, C., Manrique, K., Ordinola, M. 2008. *The Participatory Market Chain Approach: Stimulating Pro-Poor Market-Chain Innovation.* ILAC Brief 21, ILAC-CGIAR.

Thiele, T., Devaux, A., Velasco, C., and Horton, D. (2007). *Horizontal Evaluation - Fostering Knowledge Sharing and Program Improvement within a Network.* American Journal of Evaluation, 28: 493-508.

Creating Market Linkages Through Collective Action

Supplying formal markets such as multinational supermarket chains and fast food restaurants offers both higher income and improved business relations for farmers. However, accessing these markets requires higher product quality, securer supply chains, and more efficient marketing and business management. To meet these conditions and engage with these higher value markets in the long term, farmers need increased levels of bonding social capital and strengthened bridging social capital through partnerships with service providers and market chain actors.

SOURCE:

Kaganzi, E., S. Ferris, J. Barham, A. Abenakyo, P. Sangiga and J. Njuki. 2008. *Sustaining Linkages to High Value Markets through Collective Action in Uganda: The Case of the Nyabyumba Potato Farmers*. CAPRi Working Paper No. 75. International Food Policy Research Institute, Washington, D.C.

The use of collective action, combined with strong leadership and an iterative, market-led learning process, has enabled a smallholder farmers' association in Uganda to supply a perishable crop (potato) to a modern food outlet market with stringent quality parameters. Success in this market linkage was possible through effective support from both development and research providers and the strong entrepreneurial drive from the farmers' association.

This farmers' association in a remote rural area in Southwestern Uganda has successfully sustained market links through sales of high-quality Irish potatoes to a fast food outlet in Kampala. To meet the volumes, frequency of supply, and quality parameters demanded by their client, the farmers had to learn a series of new skills and integrate multiple innovations at the technical, organizational, financial, and marketing levels, and meet many of the classical conditions associated with collective action based on empowerment through social and human capital development.

CIAT's Participatory Learning Approach: Participatory and Area-based Agro-enterprise Development	
Step 1.	Group development and partnership formation.
Step 2.	Product identification and market analysis.
Step 3.	Business planning and enterprise development.
Step 4.	Identifying and strengthening relevant business development services.

The International Centre for Tropical Agriculture (CIAT)'s participatory learning approach was used to build the "market facilitation capacity" of service providers so that they could in turn support the entrepreneurial needs of farmers' organizations and local business development services operating within a defined project area. This investment empowers local organizations to increase their market performance in selected market chains and be more responsive to dynamic market conditions.

Key Factors Supporting a Collective Response to an Identified Market Opportunity

A cluster of social factors enables farmers to make the many changes required to increase their market performance. The following key factors supported a collective response to an identified market opportunity.

1. **The ability of farmers to organize, learn new skills, and innovate is highly dependent upon effective and long-term support from service providers.** "Learning by doing" empowered the farmers' group in developing skills and management capacity, and helped them to strengthen shared norms, interdependence, and trust. The farmers' social capital and technical skills allowed them to rapidly link new organizational structures, technologies, and market opportunities together in their business planning process.

2. **Lack of training in basic marketing limits farmers' ability to capitalize on their social strengths and to use these to focus their investments and innovations.** Long-standing groups usually have improved technology or production skills but lack basic marketing training. Nevertheless, these groups have the characteristics to enable successful collective action such as being clustered in small groups, having shared norms, past successful experiences, appropriate leadership, interdependence among group members, and homogenous interests.

These factors are interrelated but hierarchical in improving the prospects of market success. Strong leadership within the group is the most important factor in identifying and maintaining market links, followed by quality of service provision and then the collective purpose of the group members. Ownership of projects and decision-making capacity are fundamental requirements when investment of work, time, money or trust (social capital) are required.

3. High levels of participation in product selection are required to confirm support for the product and to build the basis for a common purpose. Identifying the product requires the participation of all members of the group or community in offering ideas and confirming the selection of a product. This decision must be based on the information generated from a market analysis. Farmers must feel that they have ownership of this decision, as subsequent investments by the group will be based on this collective decision.

4. Supplying a high-value, high-risk market often requires the innovation of existing production and marketing systems. The new market channel required a fundamental change in the focus of the group, from supplying an input market to supplying an output market. The stringent quality and supply requirements of the preferred market in the case study necessitated the shift from one harvest a year to a consistent supply of a specific quality. These, in turn, required a series of changes in the production system and a familiarization with quality standards. To offset this risk, the farmers identified alternative market channels to receive the produce that failed to meet the requirements of the preferred market.

Challenges for the farmers' group were resolved systematically based on basic business and operational plans. Wider adoption of new methods, as well as the acceptance of the quality standards, was essentially driven by profit. Farmers were encouraged to produce as individuals but to sell collectively. They were rewarded for volume and quality supplied. Rewards were not given simply for being a group member.

5. Financial investment is critical for any enterprise plans. In the short term, the only option to kick-start a new business is to gather the required working capital through a combination of savings, borrowing from family and friends, and taking a loan from the local money lender. In the case study, in order to address the financial issue over the longer term, the members of the group established a savings and credit co-operative (SACCO), which enabled members to save and receive loans to invest in potato production or to cover essential short-term needs as they awaited payments from the preferred buyer.

6. Innovation and market responsiveness require organization to monitor market conditions, identify problems, and find rapid, practical solutions. The organization made changes at critical points in the development of the business model, and decision-making was helped to a large degree by the group's ability to access advice from a number of specialized service providers in their vicinity.

The combination of rapid assessments and access to services accelerated the innovation process. However, it required strong leadership and specialists within the farmers' group to recognize what type of help was needed, test options, and then engage others to take on new ideas.

Market performance of farmer groups may be improved by a combination of strong social cohesion within the group, supported by specialized roles to interact with partners beyond the group. An example of this is a position devoted to marketing that could be located within a farmers' group or a position that serves as an information cluster at the group or association level.

Keys to Maintaining Market Links

Success of the farmers in identifying and maintaining market links was based on a combination of effective service provision, their strong social base, collective learning, sequenced skills development, access to new technology and development of social networks acquired though long-term support.

To overcome the need for investment capital, an interesting alternative is to adopt a savings-led approach to building capital through mechanisms such as SACCOs, saving and internal loan clubs (SILCs), self-help groups (SHGs) and internal savings and loan groups (ISLs). Savings-led interventions mean that group members learn practical financial skills and build social bonding and trust. This type of financial approach allows service providers to focus their interventions on analysis and training or advice, rather than investing in capital items.

The usefulness of new ideas and their performance was based on profit. In this case, there was no need for a sophisticated monitoring and evaluation processes, as profit was a sufficient stimulus to focus the group on finding their own solutions and networking effectively with partners to introduce new ideas and put them into practice.

This outcome highlights the importance of marketing strategies and the value of market linkage through collective action approaches. In the future, as markets become more competitive and product quality more exacting, it is likely that many more market opportunities, particularly higher value options, will only be accessible through disciplined collective efforts.

Suggested Readings

Agrawal, A. 2001. *Common Property Institutions and Sustainable Governance of Resources.* World Development 29(10): 1649-1672.

Ferris, S., E. Kaganzi, R. Best, C. Ostertag, M. Lundy and T. Wandschneider. 2006. A *Market Facilitator's Guide to Participatory Agro-enterprise Development.* CIAT Publication 348.

Collective Action, Social Capital and Group Lending

For low-income households with meager assets, financial services that could potentially augment their income are of extreme importance. Financial mechanisms that could facilitate asset build-up, protect against risks, and sustain livelihoods of poor people would go a long way in improving their living conditions and social status. Microfinance is one such financial mechanism that caters to poorer and marginal households and communities.

SOURCE:

Armendariz, B., and J. Morduch. 2010. Chapter 4 (*Group Lending*) and Chapter 5 (*Beyond Group Lending*). In *Microfinance Beyond Group Lending*. The Economics of Microfinance, 2nd edition. Cambridge, MA: MIT Press.

One of the best known innovations in microfinance is group lending, pioneered by the Grameen Bank of Bangladesh. This has been adapted by the Banco Sol of Bolivia, FINCA of El Salvador, and many other organizations around the world. Group size can vary from as few as three members to as many as 50. What is common across the approach is the concept of group responsibility — sometimes called joint liability — coupled with regular group meetings.

Group lending has succeeded where traditional banks have failed, bringing credit to the poor and to earning Grameen-Bank founder Muhammad Yunus a Nobel Peace Prize in 2006. Notwithstanding these achievements, it is important to note that there are also risks associated with group lending, both for the lender and the borrower, and it is not appropriate for every context. Many recent microcredit schemes are not based on joint liability. Even so, collective action and social pressure can have a positive influence on the performance of microcredit institutions.

What Makes Group Lending Successful

When the Grameen Bank first got started as an experimental bank in the village of Jobra, near Chittagong University in Bangladesh, the first loans were made to individuals without a group responsibility clause. Economies of scale motivated the first use of groups; however, it was quickly discovered that organizing the borrowers in groups not only reduced the bank's administrative costs, it also improved the performance of loans.

> **Group Lending and Joint Liability**
>
> ***Group lending*** refers specifically to arrangements through which individuals without collateral get together and form groups with the aim of obtaining loans from a lender. Loans are made to individual group members but the whole group faces consequences if any member runs into serious repayment difficulties, a practice known as ***joint liability***.

Joint liability means that group members have the incentive to monitor each other and use social pressure to ensure that borrowed money is invested wisely and repaid. In an extreme case, group members may even take responsibility for payment of their co-members' delinquent loans to ensure their own future supply of credit.

Another reason why groups can make lending more attractive for both lenders and borrowers is that when groups form on their own, safe borrowers who are likely to repay can form groups with other safe borrowers, thereby reducing their risk of having to repay someone else's loan. Risky borrowers are left to group with others who are also more likely to default. It has been shown that this "assortative matching" of borrowers into two types of homogenous groups can improve the efficiency of lending, reduce defaults, and allow banks to charge lower interest rates to all borrowers.

Even when groups are formed randomly or by people who do not know each other well, as often happens in big cities or in areas where people are highly mobile, group lending can still improve performance if risky borrowers, when lucky, get higher returns for their investments than safe borrowers who invest more conservatively.

Many empirical studies have, in fact, shown that self-formed groups do not necessarily perform better than randomly formed groups. Similarly, groups made up of people with close social ties do not always do better than groups of strangers. While this may sound counterintuitive, family, and

friendship ties are unlikely to correlate strongly with whether people are both risky or safe borrowers, and friends are more likely to understand and forgive when friends default due to difficulties beyond their control.

While there is no doubt that group lending can bring benefits to both borrowers and lenders in certain contexts, it is important to keep in mind that there are costs and risks involved. Group lending often relies on the fact that it is easy for group members to monitor each other's behavior and to meet regularly. This is often not the case, especially for the poor.

Group Lending: Moral Hazard and Adverse Selection

Moral hazard is the incentive a borrower has to use a loan for unproductive or risky projects or to not repay even if she is able. It is reduced in group lending through peer monitoring. Members of the group and the broader community can easily observe whether borrowers are using their loans appropriately.

Adverse selection occurs when banks cannot distinguish between safe and risky borrowers and offer the same high interest terms to each type of borrower, discouraging safe borrowers from applying. This is reduced in group lending when the members of the group know this information about each other and self-organize into groups accordingly.

In addition, using social pressure to encourage good behavior is risky if it leads vulnerable borrowers to take extreme measures to avoid default, or results in social exclusion and marginalization when default becomes inevitable. Given that group lending is most attractive for the very poor, the risk of furthering the vulnerability and marginalization through such processes should be taken seriously. In fact, some microlenders are exploring ways to support troubled borrowers without jeopardizing the standing of the entire group, which can lead to better outcomes, both economically and socially.

Beyond Joint Liability

While the number of cases in which joint liability is optimal may be limited, there are other ways in which groups and social pressure can improve efficiency and performance of microlending even to individuals.

- Where borrowers know each other well, lenders can use groups as a way to find out information about individual potential borrowers. This practice, known as cross-reporting, is an efficient way for banks to get information about their clients' reliability. Borrowers have the incentive to provide reliable information to ensure their own future credit access.

- Repayment in groups can increase repayment rates because requiring borrowers to repay publicly can provide the incentive to pay and avoid social stigma (as well as reduce the possibility of financial irregularities on the side of the lender).

- Meeting borrowers in clusters in scheduled locations and at scheduled times reduces transaction costs, though it could add to borrower costs.

- Group meetings can facilitate education and training, which may be particularly helpful for clients with little business experience and/or low literacy levels. Education may aid financial performance or it might be valued intrinsically as a way to improve levels of health and knowledge.

- Clients who have no prior experience with commercial banks may feel more comfortable approaching a microfinance institution as part of a group.

Conclusions

Group lending can reach people who lack the assets to make them clients for traditional banks. Successful group lending schemes do not necessarily require that people know and trust each other but that they can monitor each other's behavior relatively easily. Where this is not true, group lending may not work.

Joint liability lending can provide powerful incentives for borrowers to use their loans wisely and repay. However, there is always a risk that constructive social pressure becomes destructive social domination or social exclusion, in which case lenders need to be conscious of the risks that borrowers could face. Even without joint liability, there can be benefits to micro-lending through groups.

Suggested Readings

Armendáriz de Aghion, B. and J. Morduch. 2000. *Microfinance Beyond Group Lending*. Economics of Transition 8 (2): 401-420.

Besley, T. and S. Coate. 1995. *Group Lending, Repayment Incentives, and Social Collateral.* Journal of Development Economics 46 (1): 1-18.

Ito, S. 2003. *Microfinance and Social Capital: Does Social Capital Help Create Good Practice?* Development and Practice 13 (4): 322-332.

Karlan, D. 2005. *Using Experimental Economics to Measure Social Capital and Predict Real Financial Decisions.* American Economic Review 95(5): 1688-1699.

Toward a Code of Conduct in Foreign Land Deals

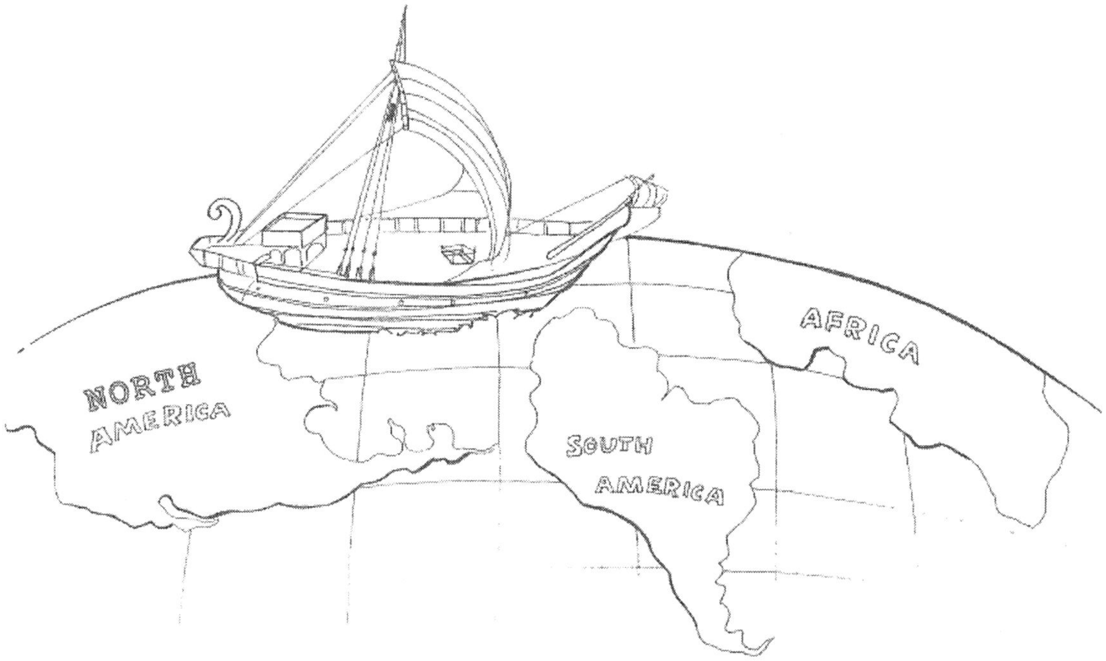

SOURCE:

Meinzen-Dick, R. and H. Markelova. 2009. *Necessary Nuance: Toward a Code of Conduct in Foreign Land Deals.* In *Land Grab? The Race for the World's Farmland*, Kugelman, M. and S. Levenstein, eds. Washington, D.C.: Woodrow Wilson Center.

The foreign acquisition of agricultural land is a trend that is driven by the food and biofuel needs of wealthy nations that have the capital to invest but have sparse land and water resources to produce enough for their own needs. These deals, whether in the form of purchases or leases, have many economic, social, and political implications for both the investor and host countries.

Foreign investment and acquisition of agricultural land in other countries have historical precedent, but this recent wave of land acquisitions has a different scale, new drivers, and a new set of players. In the post-colonial era, the private sector was the main actor, generally buying land from private land owners in the host countries. While private investors remain major actors today, many of the new deals are between governments, or involve governments backing private investments. While the private sector has traditionally invested to maximize profit, food and energy security concerns are the drivers of these recent land deals.

Proponents of these land deals claim that there is an abundance of arable land to be used for agriculture and "unused" or "unproductive" lands to be used for agrofuel cultivation. However, in many cases, these lands are already being used or claimed. This is especially the case in Africa, where up to 90 percent of land is under customary tenure: formally held as state land but used by communities, often for generations. In addition, even though the amount of land that is potentially available for expanded rain-fed crop production is estimated to be about 1.5 billion hectares, half of these reserves are found in just seven developing countries: Angola, DRC, Sudan, Argentina, Bolivia, Colombia, and Brazil.

These estimates also do not take into account population growth, which in the last 40 years has reduced per capita land availability. The availability of marginal and abandoned lands may be higher, but there are often reasons behind their availability and limitations for crop or agrofuel cultivation: lack of adequate water resources, inaccessibility to markets, and ecological unsuitability. Many of these lands are also being used by rural communities for important livelihood activities such as animal grazing, collection of fuel wood, biomass, and fruit production, and access to water sources.

Table 1. Post-Colonial vs. Present-Day Foreign Land Deals

	Post-Colonial Era	Present
Who sells? Who buys?	Private investors buy from private land owners.	Private investors backed by government or government-to-government deals.
How much?	Limited scale.	Large scale.
What?	Tropical commodities, e.g. bananas.	Basic staple crops and biofuel crops.
Why?	Profit.	Food and energy security of foreign interests.

Opportunities and Threats

Proponents of foreign investment in agricultural land point to a number of potential opportunities through which both investors and host country can benefit. However, there are concerns that this "win-win" outlook is unfounded and may not lead to agricultural development or benefit the host countries and their poorest citizens. They present opportunities but also pose threats to the livelihoods of the communities where the land deals are happening. Opportunities may include:

- increased investment in rural areas;
- generation of new farm and of farm employment and livelihood diversification opportunities;
- making new agricultural technologies available in rural areas;
- rehabilitation and upgrades of rural infrastructures (roads, bridges, etc.);
- construction of new health posts and schools;
- local capacity building.

On the other hand, there are plenty of warnings that large-scale land acquisitions may also be detrimental to the socio-economic development of the host countries.

Many of the major benefits, especially payments and infrastructure investments, go to the domestic economies at large, and even these are often subsidized through investor companies being granted general subsidies and tax breaks.

The benefits to local people in terms of employment or increased output prices must be weighed against the number of people who are deriving their livelihoods from the land, in order to assess the net benefits or losses of livelihoods for resource-dependent communities.

Many of the possible benefits for local populations actually depend on their security of land tenure. If the existing land users have secure land tenure and can negotiate with outside investors, there is at least some compensation. Even in these cases, there are concerns over whether the local land owners are adequately informed of fair prices or the full implications of selling their land, or are subjected to undue pressure to transfer their land. In Latin America, in particular, such sales are leading to high levels of land concentration in some countries. The experience in Central America during the coffee boom of the late 19th century, when privatization of customary lands led to the concentration of lands in a few hands, provides a cautionary tale.

Increased investment in food and agrofuel production can have important benefits for the economies of developing countries.

However, if the land is officially designated as state land and existing land users have only customary land rights, negotiations are between the state and the investors, and local people may have little say in the deals and receive little compensation if they are forced off their lands. This lack of attention to existing users who do not necessarily have formally recognized claims to land has already resulted in a number of evictions and contributed to landlessness and impoverishment. This has been especially acute in land acquisitions for agrofuel production. Moreover, the lands often allocated for such use are those designated as "underutilized," but of crucial importance for mobile populations and women. Without formally recognized rights, these groups face a higher risk of displacement.

In addition to the unrecognized rights to resources, local resource users have low bargaining power and virtually no presence in the negotiations over land deals. Even if some form of compensation is agreed upon, it becomes difficult to monitor investor compliance with the agreed terms of compensation and other proposed benefits for the communities. The rapid pace with which many of these deals are being made does not allow the time necessary to establish sound governance mechanisms, especially because of international forces at play.

The ecological sustainability of land and water resources is another important concern, especially considering the relatively short-term orientation of foreign investors versus the long-term outlook needed in considering the environmental impacts of land uses. Large-scale intensive agricultural production can threaten biodiversity, carbon stocks, and the availability of land and water resources. Land that is perceived as "unused" is often in long-fallow cultivation cycles because some tropical soils may be unsuitable for intensive cultivation. If the land is already marginal, further cultivation may lead to further degradation. Moreover, irrigation on these large plantations may divert water from the local users or from environmental flows.

Lastly, large-scale land acquisitions may have a negative effect on the wider socio-political and economic contexts of the host country. These deals touch on the already politically contentious issue of land allocation and land rights, so they carry a possibility of exacerbating existing tensions. Besides, many of these developing countries are already net importers of food and receive large amounts of food aid. For example, Sudan is the site of the largest operations of the World Food Programme; however, it is also the site of some of the larger land deals and is letting investors export 70 percent of the crops grown in the country. This raises concerns about the implications of the foreign land acquisitions on the internal food security of host countries, as high-quality land may be diverted from local food production, livestock grazing, and other livelihood activities of the local communities.

The state does not usually involve customary claimants of lands in negotiations with investors. Without formally recognized rights, formally recognized land users face a higher risk of displacement.

Evaluating Foreign Land Deals

Asking the following questions can help in assessing the extent and distribution of benefits from land deals, and can possibly provide the key to long-term sustainability of investment.

Current Land Use. How is the land being used currently (agricultural production, pastoralism, or biodiversity conservation)? Who are the current users? Are they communities or individuals? What other vital resources (water and forests) are being used in conjunction with the land? If the land is fallow, what are the reasons for this (unsuitable for agriculture, conservation purposes, etc.)? Are these unused lands being used for purposes other than agriculture? These questions will pinpoint who will be affected and will help determine the real value of net benefits of the land deal.

Land Tenure Arrangements. What property rights do current users have? Are these individual or communal rights? Are these recognized by the state and the outside investors? Are there any indigenous groups using the land under customary tenure, and what are their livelihood sources?

Lands under customary tenure are especially prone to expropriation in a manner that is considered legal under statutory law but not legitimate by local people. If the land is under private owner-

Situations of customary land tenure are especially prone to expropriation of the land in a manner that is legal under statutory law but not legitimate by the local people.

ship, the existing users are more likely to have a say in the arrangements and derive a benefit, unless tenancy is widespread. In some cases, indigenous people are especially disadvantaged; in other cases they may be better organized and have stronger land rights than other poor households.

Proposed Land Use and Livelihood. A realistic assessment of the proposed investment patterns on the land is needed to assess the likely scale of benefits and how the benefits from foreign land acquisitions will be shared. It is important to ask if there are opportunities for smallholders to participate (e.g. through smallholder contract farming) and whether improved technologies will be shared with local farmers. Will the new land uses generate more and better livelihoods (through employment, contract farming, and increased local agricultural output prices) and generate more income than from previous sources?

Food Security. It is critical to look at the food security situation in the host country and the region. Will the food produced on the land be exported (all or in part) or sold domestically? What happens if there are food shortages in the host country, and especially in the food producing region? Exporting food while there is hunger not only harms local people, but is likely to cause unrest, undermining the sustainability of the land deals.

Toward a Code of Conduct

A code of conduct for international acquisitions of agricultural land would provide a mechanism to ensure that these projects are economically, socially, and ecologically sustainable. Elements of such a code should include:

- Transparency in negotiations
- Respect for existing land rights, including customary and common property rights
- Sharing of benefits
- Environmental sustainability
- Adherence to national trade policies

Irrigation is one of many issues that need to be settled when evaluating foreign land deals. If it is brought in, will it take water away from others?

Ecological Conditions. Are the proposed productivity increases achievable and sustainable? Will they impose positive or negative externalities? Why is the land currently not under intensive cultivation? What are the production constraints? Can an injection of capital and knowledge really result in sustainable production increases? Will there be land degradation over time, as when most tropical forests are cut for cultivation? If irrigation is brought in, will it take water away from others? Is the irrigation likely to be sustainable or will it lead to salinization over the long term? Will these farming practices reduce biodiversity? Environmental costs need to be weighed against any projected productivity increases, as they not only undermine the long-term sustainability of the foreign farms, but also can harm others.

Transparency. To what extent are existing land users informed and involved in the negotiations over land deals? What compensation or share of benefits do they get? Free, prior and informed consent will create greater legitimacy for foreign land deals.

Terms of Agreement. The nature of the contracts and agreements will shape the distribution of benefits between the investors, the host government, and local people. Is the land sold or leased to the foreign investors? Compared to sales, leases offer reversibility of the arrangements and a revenue stream each year, instead of a lump-sum payment, but short-term leases, in particular, may not create a strong incentive for investors to consider long-term environmental sustainability. Are there other investments such as infrastructure development (roads, bridges) in the terms of the agreement? What revenue do the state and local people receive from sale, rental, or other infrastructure investment, and what tax relief or other incentives are they offering to investors?

Enforceability. Agreements are one thing, delivering on them is another. Therefore, it is important to consider what provisions for enforcement of the terms of the deal are included in the contract. Who will monitor compliance and enforcement? What measures will be used as enforcement mechanisms? Are there arbitration or conflict management institutions that are accessible to local people (who often lack the resources to challenge large companies in court)? Enforcement is especially problematic when there are large power asymmetries between the investors, the host government, and local people, so credible measures are needed to improve confidence in the arrangements.

Not only would such a code provide guidelines to develop land projects, but also its widespread dissemination would help to equip local people, host governments, and investors for constructive negotiations. It may be naïve to think that a code of conduct would level power asymmetries, but even having such a code to appeal to could help in the negotiations. Further, institutional require-

ments to deliver on this include an international system to enforce the code on the investor as well as host country, and host governments that monitor and safeguard local people's rights.

Nevertheless, the international and national government structures alone are not sufficient. There will remain an important role for the media to increase transparency on land deals, and civil society to keep pressure against unjust expropriation. Just as we need to look beyond blanket pronouncements about foreign land acquisitions, we also need to look beyond simple prescriptions for their governance, and engage with multiple types of institutions to forge sustainable, mutually beneficial increases in agricultural productivity.

Conclusion

Examining land deals can help to move beyond blanket pronouncements about foreign investments. Showcasing those cases that are relatively beneficial—and shaming those that are not—can help show investors that it is in their long-run interests to ensure that their investments are not just legal, but also legitimate, by attending to the impacts on local people and the environment. The next step beyond stopping bad cases is to try to ensure that all future foreign investments in agricultural land take into account cost and benefits for all stakeholders and the environment.

Suggested readings

Cotula, L., Vermeulen, S., Leonard, R., and Keeley. 2009. *Land Grab or Development Opportunity? Agricultural Investment and International Land Deals in Africa.* London and Rome: International Institute for Environment and Development, UN Food and Agriculture Organization, and International Fund for Agricultural Development. Available from ftp://ftp.fao.org/docrep/fao/011/ak241e/ak241e.pdf.

von Braun, J. and R. Meinzen-Dick. 2009. *'Land Grabbing' by Foreign Investors in Developing Countries: Risks and Opportunities.* IFPRI Policy Brief 13. Washington, D.C.: International Food Policy Research Institute. Available from http://www.ifpri.org/pubs/bp/bp013.pdf.

Chapter 5

The Role of Collective Action and Property Rights in Mitigating Risk

Collective Action, Property Rights and Risk

Poverty or well-being is determined not only by the assets and income of a household, but also by its degree of vulnerability to risks and shocks. Risks can be characterized by their frequency and probability; some occur frequently (rainfall variation), some with less frequency (elections resulting in change in government), and others rarely (revolutions, earthquakes). The more frequent the occurrence, the more likely that people know the distribution of possible outcomes and, thus, the probabilities of specific outcomes.

SOURCES:

Di Gregorio, M., K. Hagedorn, M. Kirk, B. Korf, N. McCarthy, R. Meinzen-Dick and B. Swallow. 2008. *Property Rights, Collective Action and Poverty: The Role of Institutions for Poverty Reduction.* CAPRi Working Paper No. 81. International Food Policy Research Institute, Washington, D.C.

Mwangi, E. and H. Markelova. 2008. *Collective Action and Property Rights for Poverty Reduction: A Review of Methods and Approaches.* CAPRi Working Paper No. 82. International Food Policy Research Institute, Washington, D.C.

The impact of risk is affected by spatial scale. Poor rainfall in a small area will have quite different effects from low rainfall over an entire region. Prices for agricultural produce in an isolated community will tend to vary with local weather events, whereas price fluctuations due to local weather events should be much lower in the wider economy. Conversely, shocks to national or international markets will affect integrated local markets, but not those that are insulated.

Classes of Risks

Individuals and households are vulnerable to three broad classes of risks: natural, economic or market, social or political (Table 1).

Table 1. Types of Risks and their Occurrence.

Type of Risks	Frequency and Probability of Occurrence		
	Frequent, Well-Known Probability	**Less Frequent, Imprecise Knowledge of Probability**	**Rare Events, Probability Unknown**
Natural	Seasonal Rainfall Hail Endemic Pest Infestations Frost	Drought Floods Morbidity/Mortality	Earthquake Forest Fires Epidemic/Disease Outbreaks Global Climate Change
Economic	Seasonal Prices Input Availability Informal Loan Rates Elections	Formal Sector Interest Rates Inflation Real Estate Values	Asset Bubbles/Stock Market Crashes Introduction of "Revolutionary" Technologies (electricity, computers)
Socio-Political	Petty Theft	Personal Security Property Security Ethnic Discrimination	Changing Regulatory Frameworks Warfare, Revolutions Genocide

Natural Risks. Natural risks differ substantially across regions and can affect all people differently. For instance, the poor might be disproportionately affected by natural shocks because they have fewer options with which to manage or cope. In contrast, the rich may have access to plots that receive more regular rainfall or are less prone to hail or frost; they may have access to a wider range of plots to spread these risks. However, like the poor, even the relatively wealthy farmers are unlikely to avoid exposure to natural disasters. Here, the ability to cope with a shock is more important — the rich having a clear advantage because they have a higher asset base with which to cope.

Economic Risks. Economic risks can occur with the same range of probability as natural risks. Unlike natural risks, however, fluctuations in many economic variables, for example, prices often follow both trends and deviations around a trend. Price fluctuations can occur regularly, e.g., seasonal price patterns, and prices can also fluctuate with local output, where these prices are a function of local climate conditions. In both of the latter cases, people may well be able to form expectations over these relatively short-term fluctuations. Discrete changes in government policies on import taxes or input subsidies might cause a sudden change in input or output prices — changes that do not occur regularly and are difficult to foresee.

Social or Political Risks. Political risks are closely related to the type of political regime and its practice of law and order. Political risks can be quite regular, as in countries with regular election cycles. However, knowing the changes that will occur and their impacts is much less possible than with rainfall or seasonal prices. Political risk is often linked to the actions of political actors at higher policy levels. To some extent, it is socially produced in the particular political regime as with corruption, nepotism or clientelism. Social factors such as an influx of migrants or ethnic tensions may also increase risks such as theft or violence.

Often, people face multiple and overlapping risks. Natural, economic and political risks may reinforce each other. For example, natural disasters can cause price distortion and thus create further economic risks, or economic shocks precipitate political unrest. In this respect, risks that are predictable and calculable may coincide with uncertain, sudden events, resulting in changes in livelihood strategies.

Managing Risks

Given the risks and uncertainties, people can act in one of two ways. They can either move to mitigate exposure to various risks (*ex ante* risk management), or they can act after a negative shock has occurred (*ex post* risk coping).

Risk management includes any activities/choices that affect the exposure of the household to different risks. These strategies usually include income smoothing activities through income diversification (combining several sources of income, usually on-farm and off-farm) or income skewing (allocating resources to low-risk, but low-return activities). For instance, in areas where rainfall patterns tend to differ dramatically across even very short distances, farmers can acquire plots in different locations or they might choose to plant different species and varieties.

Risk coping strategies are things that people can do after an event has occurred. These mechanisms involve self-insurance through assets, savings, and informal group-based risk sharing, which usually consists of informal credit and gift transactions. Some coping strategies such as borrowing money or relying on family and friends can be sustainable; others such as withdrawing children from school or reducing food consumption reduce welfare in the long run.

Implications for Property Rights and Collective Action

Risks and uncertainties shape the benefits and costs to various property rights regimes and collective activities. They also provide opportunities for property rights or collective action to manage and/or cope with the impacts of the risks/uncertainties themselves.

Property Rights. Various types of assets such as land, livestock, and access to other natural resources are widely used for shock mitigation. However, access to an asset is not enough: its real value during a shock depends on the ability to manage it or transform it into income. Therefore, property rights become an asset to use during shocks and a mechanism to access other assets for dealing with uncertainty.

However, risk and uncertainty can reduce tenure security. In conflict situations, for example, farmers or herders may not be able to access their lands, lowering productivity in the short term and possibly also land value.

In times of political turmoil and weak governance, property rights may be unclear or subject to dramatic change. They may become part of the political game of who is excluded or included in specific social or political groups. Similarly, property rights may be part of political class struggles, and the quest for secure property rights may expose households to a higher political risk.

Collective Action. Collective action is an important mechanism for dealing with shocks, especially among the poor, who may lack other assets. Social institutions based on cooperation are among the most used tools in the risk management portfolio of the poor. In times of uncertainty, mutual insurance schemes are often used for transfers such as gifts and loans.

> **Advantages and Disadvantages of Collective Action**
>
> Collective action may result in conflicting situations. It may lead to stronger, more cohesive, and more stable communities. On the other hand, it may divide a community or group. It is therefore essential not to assume that collective action has positive effects per se on buffering risk.

Since formal credit and insurance mechanisms are often absent, the poor establish informal networks for risk smoothing, which they can call upon in time of need. Most of such informal transactions are done between families (first tier) and neighbors or friends within the same village (second tier) for easier monitoring of reciprocity and repayment. For example, in Nigeria, such exchanges serve as a risk pooling mechanism on the village level, and repayment depends on who is affected: when there is a shock to the borrower, the rate of repayment decreases; when the shock occurs to the lender, the rate of repayment increases. Nevertheless, localized collective insurance mechanisms will not be enough to deal with widespread shocks that affect everyone in a community. In such cases, outside help from the state, NGOs, or other mechanisms is needed.

Networks of trust and mutual accountability linking individuals in communities are critical in helping the poor to diversify households' livelihood portfolios to cope with shortages of labor and inputs, and to protect themselves against unexpected expenditures in times of shock. Since collective action usually increases social interaction, participating in risk sharing networks and mutual insurance groups may also lead to stronger, more cohesive, and more stable communities, thereby diminishing risks of devastating socio-political upheavals and even reducing conflicts.

Shocks may also divide a community or group. This is true if collective action involves only part of the community or social group and results in the exclusion of others from the activities and benefit streams of the action. Hence, while collective action can be an effective mechanism for some individuals and groups to deal with risks, it may also create new political risks for others. Thus, efficiency (how effectively natural resources are managed) and equity (who profits from such policies) must be considered.

Conclusion

Both rich and poor rural people are exposed to many risks, but the poor are more vulnerable to the negative effects of shocks on their livelihoods. The poor often are unable to build up stocks of assets and/or to use formal credit and insurance institutions. For them, informal group-based insurance schemes are invaluable in times of uncertainty. Secure rights to resources enable people to use existing assets as a buffer during shocks. However, risks and shocks may also negatively affect the functioning of existing property rights structures and collective action institutions, and external insurance mechanisms are also needed for widespread shocks.

Suggested Readings

Dercon, S. 2002. *Income Risk, Coping Strategies, and Safety Nets.* The World Bank Economic Observer 17(2): 141-166.

Fafchamps, M. and S. Lund. 2003. *Risk Sharing Networks in Rural Philippines.* Journal of Development Economics 71:261-287.

Little, P., K. Smith, B. Cellarius, D.L. Coppock and C. Barrett. 2001. *Avoiding Disaster: Diversification and Risk Management among East African Herders.* Development and Change 32 (2001): 401-433.

Collective Action and Vulnerability: Burial Societies in Rural Ethiopia

Collective action has intrinsic value. Being part of a group and participating in meeting common objectives provide direct benefits to individuals. In addition, collective action has an instrumental value; it can help individuals, groups, and communities achieve common goals.

In Ethiopia, a study found that one form of collective action, *iddir*, or burial societies, helped households in the study areas attenuate the impact of illness.

SOURCE:

Dercon, S., J. Hoddinott, P. Krishnan and T. Woldehanna. 2008. *Collective Action and Vulnerability: Burial Societies in Rural Ethiopia.* In: Mwangi, E., H. Markelova and R. Meinzen-Dick, Collective Action and Property Rights for Poverty Reduction: Lessons from a Global Research Project. International Food Policy Research Institute, Washington, D.C.

Shocks in Rural Ethiopia

Shocks are adverse events that lead to a loss of household income or productive assets or a reduction in consumption. They may be climatic, economic, political/social/legal, criminal, or health-related. Virtually all households experience shocks, the most common of which are drought, death, and illness. Analysis within the study showed that experiencing drought at least once in the previous five years and experiencing illness were the only shocks that had a statistically significant effect on consumption. Disaggregating the data reveals that drought shocks have more severe effects on female-headed and poorer households, and illness shocks matter much more where malaria is common.

Networks, Groups and Collective Action

To better understand social networks and collective action, in 2004, households were asked about the five most important people they could rely on for support in time of need, within the village and elsewhere, as well as other people they could rely on in time of need. Over 90 percent of households reported that there was at least one person they could rely on for assistance, and the median number of people in households' networks was five. There was evidence that households do indeed call on these networks, and there was also evidence of reciprocity.

Study Method

The data in this paper are from the Ethiopia Rural Household Survey (ERHS), a unique longitudinal household data set covering households in 15 areas of rural Ethiopia. Data collection began in 1989 and was expanded and re-randomized in 1994 to yield a sample of 1,477 households broadly representative of the population shares in Ethiopia's three main sedentary farming systems. Survey rounds continued through 2004 and were supplemented with qualitative data gathered separately.

The surveys revealed that these households are very poor, with mean incomes about 36 percent below the poverty line, and that agriculture provides the dominant source (about two-thirds) of income.

Most network relationships were neighbors, fellow villagers, relatives, and people holding adjacent properties. Only 12 percent of network members were neither relatives nor members of the same *iddir* (burial society). Network members were often individuals fromwhom previously the household had borrowed or lent to.

Poorer households have relatively better-off households in their networks, while richer households tend to have relatively poorer households in their networks. However, when the number of oxen was used as the wealth measure, households typically had as network partners other households with the same numbers of oxen.

Networks tended to be quite variable when looked at by age; the difference in age between the household head and other individuals in the network, who were either relatives or members of the same *iddir*, was considerable.

Households with more landholdings have larger networks. The same is true for larger households and households where the head has any formal schooling. Family background also plays a role: having a parent or relative with important social or political positions in the village, or a father who belongs to an *Iddir*, increase the number of persons in a household's network.

Iddir and Their Role in Mitigating Shocks

- **Membership Benefits.** Members of *Iddir* typically meet once or twice a month, making a small payment into a group fund. When a member dies, the *Iddir* makes a payment to surviving family members. *Iddir* membership is widespread: nearly 90 percent of households in the study reported belonged to at least one. Most *Iddir* have no restrictions on membership beyond paying dues and fees. In addition to the death benefit, a third of *Iddir* provide cash payouts to members when they have experienced other types of adverse shocks, such as drought and illness, and a quarter offer loans. *Iddir* that provide health insurance allow households to fare better during a health-related shock. However, the groups cannot insure households against shocks that affect the whole community.

- **Approach to Group Insurance.** Similar to other mutual insurance schemes, *Iddir* has to deal with problems of moral hazard and adverse selection. To deal with moral hazard, most *Iddir* impose some sort of restriction, the most common of which is that geographic members must live in the same peasant association (PA). Other common restrictions include belonging to the same church or mosque, or being a woman. Restricting members geographically makes it easier to learn about members and monitor their behavior. The same is true about the requirement for common church or mosque membership. Direct medical costs are observable. For example, one *Iddir* reported that "If a member takes the money for medication and does not go to the clinic or hospital, he will be asked to return the money." About a third of the *Iddir* in the study had formal checks in place to make sure funds were spent on medical costs. In addition, a considerable number conducted background checks prior to approving a grant or loan, visiting the member at home or asking neighbors to confirm that assistance was needed. Adverse selection was dealt with by imposing a membership fee, which discourages members who anticipate having to incur medical expenses and accessing *Iddir* funds in near future from joining.

- **Avoiding Financial Difficulty.** *Iddir* take a number of steps to reduce the likelihood that the provision of health insurance will lead to financial difficulties for the group.

1. *Age:* The considerable variation in ages members, which will affect spreads risk across generations — young members contribute while older members are more likely to have age-related illnesses. Youth-only *Iddir* are less likely to provide health-related assistance.

2. *Size:* Groups of larger size are less likely to provide health-related assistance.

3. *Funding:* The amount of money provided to members is tied fairly tightly to the amount collected. The average cash grant provides an amount equal to one month's income and the maximum cash grant is slightly more than two months' income. Loans as a ratio of monthly income tend to be higher than cash grants, but about 75 percent require repayment within three months. In addition, most impose sanctions if members do not repay.

Conclusions and Policy Implications

Local collective action, as exemplified by the Iddir, enables rural communities to deal with health-related and other shocks that occur to individual households. Public action and policy that support forms of collective action in this area must recognize that successful collective action is based on norms of trust and reciprocity. As trust is easier to destroy than create, the principle of "do no harm" is important here, particularly when government actions are aimed toward existing collective action institutions.

As wealthier and better educated households tend to participate more in groups and have larger networks, more attention needs to be paid to identifying barriers that prevent other segments of the population from participating in collective action. Realism is also needed in terms of the ability of collective action to respond to shocks. Specifically, where households have limited ability to develop spatial networks, collective action may have limited ability to respond to widespread shocks such as drought. Direct public action is more appropriate in this area.

Suggested Readings

Dercon, S. 2002. *Income Risk, Coping Strategies and Safety Nets.* World Bank Research Observer 17 (2): 141 166.

Dercon, S., J. De Weerdt, T. Bold and A. Pankhurst. 2006. *Group-Based Funeral Insurance in Ethiopia and Tanzania.* World Development 34 (4): 685 703.

Grootaert, C. 2001. *Does Social Capital Help the Poor? A Synthesis of Findings and Recommendations from the Social Capital Initiative.* Social Capital Initiative Working Paper 24. Washington, D.C.: Social Development Department, World Bank.

Collective Action and Vulnerability: Local and Migrant Networks in Bukidnon, Philippines

SOURCE:

Quisumbing, A. S. McNiven, and M. Godquin. 2008. Shocks, Groups, and Networks in Bukidnon, Philippines. CAPRi Working Paper 84. IFPRI: Washington D.C.

Belonging to a group is highly valued in Filipino society. Values supportive of harmonious relationships, and an individual's personal network of selected relatives and other allies, affect how Filipinos function in organizations. This study examines the role of groups and networks in helping the poor manage their exposure to risks and cope with shocks to their livelihoods. Two types of groups are considered: local formal groups and informal networks, and migrant networks composed of family members.

Groups and Networks in Bukidnon, Philippines

Households in the study reported belonging to many groups, which were classified into production, credit, burial, religious, and civic groups. Membership in groups is widespread, with religious groups being mentioned most frequently and civic groups being the least common. Households also belong to diverse trust-based networks. Seventy-five percent reported having a network to turn to in case of economic loss, with the highest asset quartile being the best insured in this way. Households belonging to the lower asset quartiles belong to fewer groups. Households that experienced more negative shocks in the past belong to more groups.

Wealthier households are more likely to take part in productive groups. Households engaged in agricultural or non-agricultural production are more likely to be members of productive groups, with being an agricultural producer having a greater marginal impact. The household's relative asset position has a significant impact on the probability of joining a credit group, with the second and third asset quartiles significantly less likely to join relative to the wealthiest quartile. Both ethnic and educational heterogeneity have a negative impact on participation in credit groups.

Shocks in Bukidnon, Philippines

Drought shocks have the greatest impact on households whose landholdings are below the median land size, households with below median net worth of assets, and (surprisingly) households with greater than median levels of schooling. Short- and longer-term impacts also differ across household types. For example, the impact of the 1987/88 drought was felt most strongly by households with smaller landholdings. However, more recent drought shocks no longer had significant impacts on consumption, indicating that mechanisms to cope with common shocks have improved over time. Sudden increases in input prices, however, significantly reduced per capita consumption in both the later and earlier periods. Not surprisingly, the burden of input price shocks in both periods was felt by households with more land and assets whose exposure to input shock risk is greater.

Burial groups are found in almost all Filipino communities. In comparison to production and credit groups, being less wealthy does not pose a significant barrier to participation. Participation in burial groups also crosses occupational categories, although ethnic and economic heterogeneity in villages reduces participation in burial groups. Compared to production, credit, or burial groups, religious and civic groups do not focus on economic motives. Nevertheless, households with more human capital are more likely to participate in such groups.

The total number of groups to which a household belongs does not affect the density of its networks, but households with more human and physical capital have larger social networks. Networks appear to perform a risk smoothing function, since the number of shocks experienced increases the number of persons that one can turn to for help. Interestingly, the number of daughters living outside the villages exerts a strong negative influence on the size of one's local trust-based networks. This result stems from differences in expectations of parental support from sons and daughters. Daughters, who are more educated than sons, typically migrate and send remittances to support their parents.

Economic Returns to Groups and Networks

The total number of groups to which a household belongs has a positive and significant impact on per capita expenditures — and this is true for membership in burial, religious, and civic groups as well.

Households that have experienced common and individual shocks suggest that local networks have only a limited ability to help households cope, especially in the case of a common shock. For example, several respondents said they feel embarrassed to ask for help from friends and neighbors. When faced with negative shocks, households use a variety of coping mechanisms, including working harder, relying on help from children who have left home, and borrowing money from informal sources.

Remittances perform an important consumption smoothing function for parents, with households experiencing more shocks being more likely to receive remittances and in larger amounts. Schooling attainment of daughters, but not sons, increases both the probability of receipt and amounts received. While unexpected increases in migrant incomes increase both the probability of receipt and amounts received, unexpected increases experienced by daughters result in much bigger remittances to parents than increases experienced by sons.

Conclusions and Policy Implications

The finding that accumulation of social capital comes easier to the wealthy is sobering news for development agencies that encourage the poor to invest in "social capital", because they assume that it is easier to acquire than physical assets. However, participation in less economically oriented groups such as religious, civic, and insurance groups is less closely associated with initial wealth than participation in production and credit groups. Whether or not group members are very much alike matters in the formation and conduct of collective action institutions. Disparities in ethnicity, assets, and education at the village level are likely to discourage the formation of trust-based networks. Thus, external differences are not necessarily "good" for social capital formation. However, having network members located in different places may be important in insurance against covariate shocks. For example, networks of spatially-diversified children — especially daughters — perform an important insurance function against covariate shocks that may not be achievable by local networks.

Implications for policy include:

- Identifying barriers that prevent the poor from participating in collective action is an important task because accumulating social capital does not come easily to the poor.
- Covariate shocks are the appropriate arena for public policy because local networks and other forms of collective action have limited effectiveness in dealing with such shocks.
- Certain types of groups and networks may be more effective in providing insurance against some types of idiosyncratic shocks. These tend to be the sort of shocks where, because of differential access to information between insurers and the insured, public action may be less effective.
- Policies to help poor households cope with shocks must take into account Filipino social and organizational culture and discourage displacement of already existing indigenous networks.

Suggested Readings

Dercon, S., J. Hoddinott, P. Krishnan, and T. Woldehanna. 2008. Collective Action and vulnerability: Burial Societies in Rural Ethiopia. CAPRi Working Paper 83. IFPRI: Washington, D.C.

Fafchamps, M., and S. Lund. 2003. Risk Sharing Networks in Rural Philippines. *Journal of Development Economics* 71: 261"287.

Haddad, L., and J. Maluccio. 2003. Trust, Membership in Groups, and Household Welfare: Evidence from KwaZulu-Natal, South Africa. *Economic Development and Cultural Change* 51 (3): 573 601.

The Transformation of Commons in the Afar Region in Ethiopia

> **SOURCE:**
>
> Bekele Hundie and Martina Padmanabhan, 2008, *The Transformation of the Commons: Coercive and Non-Coercive Ways,* In Mwangi, E., H. Markelova and R. Meinzen-Dick, Collective and Property Rights for Poverty Reduction: Lessons from a Global Research Project, IFPRI: Washington D.C.

Traditional communal landholding has long been prevalent in the Afar region of Ethiopia, accommodating the interests of different user groups for many generations. This form of land ownership, which entails use of pastoral resources scattered over a wide area to produce livestock, is attributable to ecological conditions characterized by frequent drought. The harsh environment in which herders raise their livestock requires constant mobility to regulate resource use via a common property regime. In contrast to the mobile way of life characterizing pastoralism, agriculture as a sedentary activity is only marginally present in the lowlands of the Afar region. However, the traditional land use system is changing because of pressures from both governmental policy and natural events such as drought. Communal land ownership in Afar is under pressure as a result of state intervention (political risks) and natural challenges (natural risks).

Coercive and Non-Coercive Property Rights Changes in the Afar Region

State intervention in the Afar region, mainly since the early 1960s, has produced detrimental effects on pastoralist livelihoods.

1. The state expropriated large areas of dry season rangeland, exacerbating feed scarcity in the area.

2. The state enforced the transformation of pastoralism into sedentary farming, without taking into account pastoral households' capacities to produce crops. Development schemes initiated and financed by the state couldn't enhance the capabilities of pastoral households to derive the full benefits of their land.

3. State intervention created a window of opportunity for some pastoralists, while others, such as women and the poor, were deprived of the benefits of the new arrangements.

Risks to Pastoralism in Afar

The question of whether the option of small-scale farming is taken up by pastoralists depends on factors such as suitability of the area for agriculture, per capita livestock holding of a household, access to wage employment, and external support. Overall, the study indicates that communal land ownership, which forms the basis for pastoralism, is under pressure as a result of state intervention and natural challenges, confirming results of other studies of pastoral areas.

Afar pastoralists are threatened not only by the coercive actions of the state, but also by natural challenges such as recurrent drought. Two major droughts have hit the area since the mid-1990s, and short dry spells are common. This has had two major consequences. First, the prevalence of drought has reduced total livestock assets and productive capacities of the area. Second, it has recalibrated the terms of trade against the pastoralists.

Faced with such natural challenges, pastoral households employ coping strategies which may involve different ways of using the available resources, even looking beyond pastoralism. On the one hand, this natural challenge triggered the intervention of external actors to facilitate cooperation among pastoralists, providing a catalyst for them to take up farming. On the other hand, it increased pastoralists' expectations that they would benefit more by taking advantage of external assistance and participating in collective efforts. These expectations, realized or not, produced cooperative decisions toward engaging in organized activities such as farming.

Implications for Action in Pastoral Areas

Averting state coercion: Current experiences in non-pastoral areas show that undervaluation of land, large variances between what investors pay and what evictees receive, and failure of evictees to start new livelihoods are critical problems associated with the expansion of investments in rural areas of Ethiopia. These problems are attributable to a lack of effective institutions and appropriate governance structures, including lack of clear guidelines on land valuation, marginalization of landholders in the process of land transfers, and a weak organizational setup to administer the transformation process.

Harmonizing policy emphasis with the potentials of pastoral areas: The transformation of property rights due to natural challenges has had important implications for the livelihoods of pastoralists. Poor households (in terms of livestock assets) are more interested in farming compared to better-off ones. Decisions of pastoralists toward farming could reflect their reactions toward recurring natural hazards. Farming is thought to be a post-shock livelihood undertaken by households that cannot call upon their pastoral assets post-drought. Despite this fact, two points can be made about the potential of farming in the study areas in general.

1. Since they are mobile, livestock appear to be somewhat more tolerant of drought conditions than crops. The existence of mobile pastoralism in dry regions of the world also implies the relative viability of livestock production as compared to rain-fed agriculture in these regions. Efforts to produce food crops under rain-fed conditions may not provide any substantial remedy to the decline of food security when drought occurs; during a prolonged spell it presumably will not.

Current Situation in Afar

The coercive expropriation of pastoral land has slowed since 1991, and Afar pastoralists have regained some of their lost rights over their traditional land. However, current national policies are not immune from the anti-pastoral sentiment. The 2005 National Land Use Proclamation declares that communal rural land holdings may be converted to private holdings if the government finds it necessary. There is also a plan to expand irrigated land in the Awash basin. Implementation of such a plan would require evicting pastoralists.

2. Although crops can be produced using irrigation in some ecological niches, an irrigation-based production system is less appealing in many parts of Afar given the scarcity of water. Consequently, livestock production appears to be the best, and in some areas the only option under the existing technologies.

Conclusion

The relatively low participation level of better-off pastoralists in collective action to start farming implies that crop production is not a substitute for, but is rather subsidiary to, livestock production in such dry areas. Therefore, instead of overrating the sustainability and impact of farming on poverty reduction, it would be worthwhile to focus on livestock production. In this regard, improving key services, such as the livestock market information system, veterinary and financial services, investing in infrastructure, and enhancing feed management are key to turning the silent transformation of commons into a viable development path for the Afar. Moreover, other alternative income sources should be promoted in addition to farming as means of improving the capacity of (poor) pastoralists to overcome potential livelihood challenges.

Suggested Readings

Beyene, Fekadu. 2008. Challenges and Options in Governing Common Property: Customary Institutions Among (Agro-)pastoralists in Ethiopia. Institutional Change in Agriculture and Natural Resources Vol. 32. Aachen: Shaker.

Hundie, Bekele. 2008. Pastoralism, Institutions and Social Interaction: Explaining the Coexistence of Conflict and Cooperation in Pastoral Afar, Ethiopia. Institutional Change in Agriculture and Natural Resources Vol. 34. Aachen: Shaker.

Little, P. D.; K. Smith, B.. Cellarius, D. L. Coppock and C. Barrett. 2001. Avoiding Disaster: Diversification and Risk Management among East African Herders. *Development and Change* 32: 401-433.

McPeak, J. 2005. Individual and Collective Rationality in Pastoral Production: Evidence from Northern Kenya. *Human Ecology* 33 (2): 171-197.

Padmanabhan, Martina (ed)(2008) Special Issue I+II, Collective Action and Property Rights in Ethiopia, Part II "Rural Development and Natural Resource Management". Quarterly Journal of International Agriculture. 47 (2+3).

The Role of Collective Action and Property Rights in Climate Change Strategies

Importance of Institutions in Addressing Climate Change

SOURCE:

Meinzen-Dick, R., H. Markelova and K. Moore. *The Role of Collective Action and Property Rights in Climate Change Strategies.* CGIAR CAPRi Policy Brief 7, International Food Policy Research Institute, Washington, D.C.

The well-documented threats posed by climate change are serious and potentially devastating to the global community. The geographic areas that are most susceptible to the effects of climate change episodes such as increased droughts and flooding are also the regions where the majority of the world's poor live. Evidence suggests that these effects may be especially severe for disadvantaged communities in developing countries. The poor have few assets and few income diversification opportunities, which severely limit their ability to cope or adapt to climate changes.

Ensuring that poor people can adapt to climate change and benefit from mitigation measures such as payments for carbon sequestration requires more than technology. Key institutions must also be in place.

The Structure of Mitigation and Adaptation Strategies

Climate change has two manifestations: global warming and an increased number of extreme environmental events. Response strategies are usually divided into mitigation and adaptation (see Figure 1).

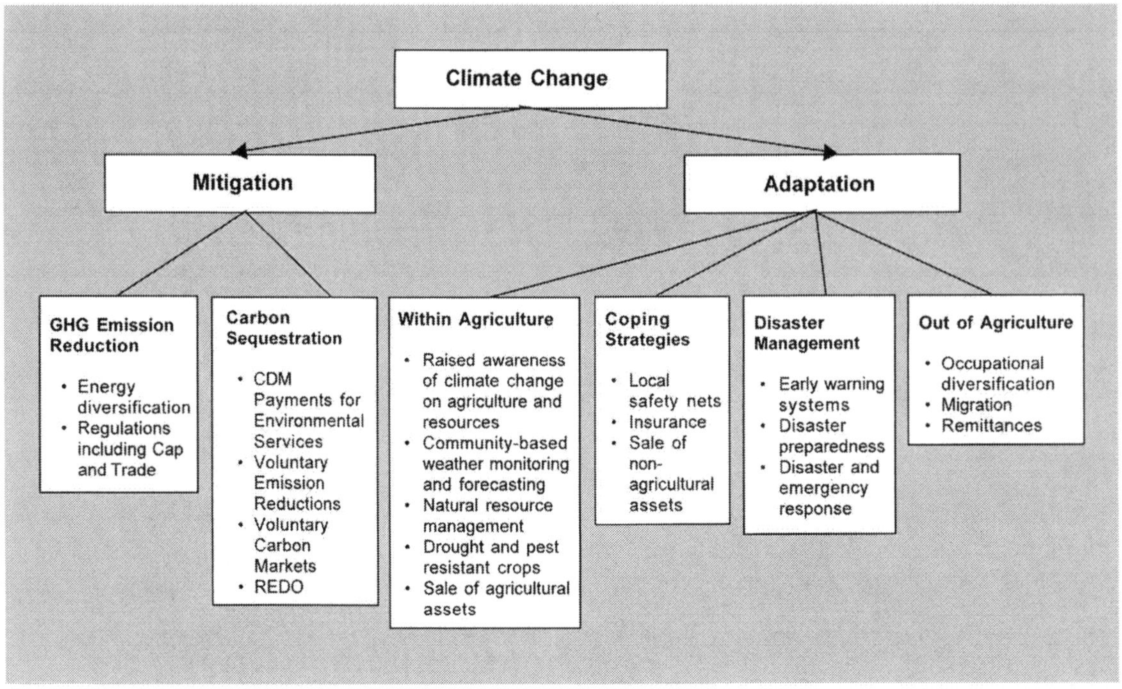

Figure 1. Responses to Climate Change.

Collective Action, Property Rights, and Climate Change Responses

Mitigation refers to strategies utilized to reduce the probability of climate change through sustainable practices that mitigate the increased occurrence, severity, and unpredictability of weather resulting from climate change. The two major forms of climate change mitigation are emissions reduction and carbon sequestration. Emissions can be reduced through a range of technologies, regulations, or economic incentives such as cap and trade systems. Other mechanisms include energy diversification to renewable sources or those that do not emit carbon or other greenhouse gases. Mitigation options for rural smallholders include energy diversification through development of biofuels and alternative energy sources, such as solar-powered stoves. Carbon can be sequestered through afforestation, avoided deforestation and degradation, as well as through sustainable land management practices such as restoring degraded organic soils or using zero- or low-till farming practices.

Payments for environmental services (PES) were introduced to provide incentives for land users to engage in sustainable practices, especially those that sequester carbon above or below ground, and to provide them with some form of compensation for the positive externalities of their actions. Carbon sequestration can receive financial rewards as carbon offsets in carbon markets (such as the Clean Development Mechanism [CDM] set up by the Kyoto protocol), government instituted markets, and voluntary carbon markets. Soil carbon sequestration and avoided deforestation projects, which are important for climate change mitigation in many African countries, were excluded from the CDM but may be covered through new proposals for Reducing Emissions from Deforestation and Forest Degradation in Developing Countries (REDD).

Many compensation payments, however, are available to land owners but not to people with customary tenure, and carbon sequestration plans usually require that land remains unused for other livelihood activities, such as agriculture, livestock raising, or harvesting natural resources such as firewood. As a result, not only do such schemes exclude millions of poor people, but also they also have on occasion, resulted in the displacement of households and communities that do not hold the formal title but depend on that land for their livelihoods. Such communities are pushed out when governments or private interests acquire the land to participate in reward schemes.

Adaptation involves actions that communities and individuals can undertake in response to changing conditions. These approaches include strategies within agriculture such as raising awareness of climate change, community-based climate monitoring and forecasting, changing planting dates, crop varieties, or cropping patterns, and implementing water harvesting or irrigation schemes. Adaptation strategies within agriculture are connected with effective natural resource management (NRM), such as improved land and water management practices. People may also adapt to climate change by moving out of agriculture through occupational diversification of some or all members of the household, or temporary or permanent migration, with increased reliance on remittances. Coping strategies for short-term climate-related shocks such as floods or droughts include reliance on local safety nets or mutual insurance schemes, as well as disaster management, which entails early warning systems, disaster preparedness, and emergency responses. Overall, a community's capacity to adapt requires a number of collective action institutions and property rights arrangements that would enable the smallholders to accumulate various types of assets and knowledge.

To identify the institutional arrangements relevant for climate change response strategies, it is useful to look at the spatial and time scales of each action or program. Figure 2 provides examples of several common response strategies involving natural resource management practices. The spatial scale helps to identify what types of institutions are required, both for policy development to set the enabling conditions, and for actions to carry out the necessary activities. These can vary from the global to the national, local, or even individual level.

Actions at the individual level, such as planting a drought-resistant annual crop or building a farm pond, generally do not require much in the way of institutions for coordination, though coordination at higher levels may be needed to produce the new varieties and develop seed systems that distribute them. Moving up to response options at the group or community level, such as a community pond or small reservoir, some form of coordination becomes necessary. At the local level, collective action institutions are often the most appropriate. Some state institutions may also be relevant, for example, to provide technical advice to a group of farmers constructing or operating the reservoir.

At higher spatial scales, local governments or other state agencies become increasingly important for coordination, although collective action institutions may still be relevant, as in Nepal's National Federation of Forest User Groups. The relative roles of state and collective action are illustrated by the triangles on the right-hand side of Figure 2. In general, if the relevant scale for policies or action is the global level, then international institutions are required for coordination, either through existing international bodies such as UN agencies, or by creating new institutions such as the carbon credit exchanges formed after the Kyoto Protocol in 1997.

The time frame for actions also provides insight into the nature of institutional arrangements needed. While climate change response schemes need to be set in motion very soon, some will show results in the short term (a year or two), others over the medium term (two to ten years), and still others have a much longer time horizon. The longer the time lag between actions and results, the more difficult it will be to gain and maintain support and to monitor progress. Some actions, such as responses to crises like drought or flooding, will only be intermittent. These call for institutional structures for preparedness and ability to respond quickly, but do not need to operate all the time. The time scale may also indicate the relevance of property rights issues when there is a significant lag between an action and its outcomes, especially between investment and returns such as for planting trees.

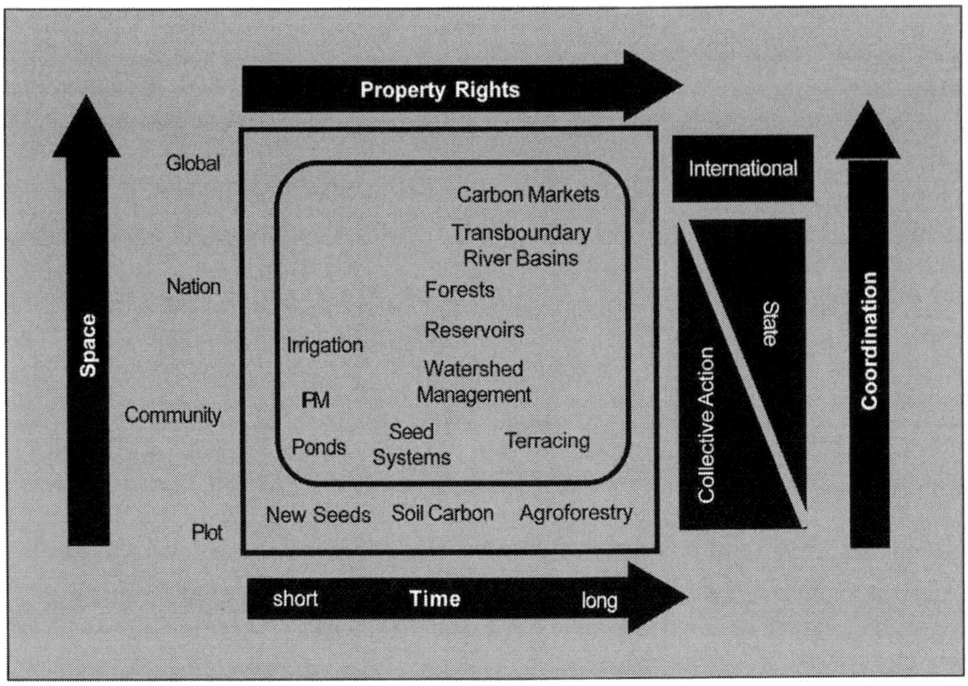

Figure 2: Role of Institutions in Climate Change Responses.

Policy Implications

Recognize the Importance of Collective Action for Successful Mitigation and Adaptation Strategies

Research and practice have shown that collective action institutions are very important for technology transfer in agriculture and natural resource management among smallholders and resource-dependent communities. In the same way, they will also be important for spreading information, technologies and practices for various climate change response strategies, both for mitigation and adaptation.

Smallholder groups can facilitate effective implementation of PES schemes focused on carbon sequestration. Cooperatives or other forms of collective action among smallholders can help to achieve economies of scale in overcoming transaction costs in verification and payment. Groups of smallholders cover more area, and the cooperatives assume the transaction costs of developing and enforcing contracts with individuals. *Fondo Bioclimatico* in Mexico provides an example of a program that restores land, previously deemed useless because of soil degradation, to profitability through use of agroforestry and forestry systems that sequester carbon. Additionally, it is a cost-effective strategy for collective income generation because the contracts are created and brokered by the farmers, allowing them to design, manage, and monitor their programs on individual or communal land. External assistance can help to make the initial contacts between smallholders and CDM programs, and to develop the capacity of local groups to negotiate and meet technical monitoring criteria.

Coping strategies for short-term climate-related shocks also include reliance on collective action in disaster preparedness.

Local institutions are also important for helping farmers adapt to climate change through knowledge and information sharing. Research shows that improved information on climate change increases a farmer's likelihood of adapting. For example, in several Andean communities farmers have developed a knowledge system on climate change and its potential effects on their productivity through community education and sharing observations on gradually changing weather patterns. For areas that are most vulnerable to sudden natural disasters such as hurricanes or typhoons, collective action can help to disseminate information through community meetings, volunteer emergency response teams, and community response plans that include an early warning system.

Enhancing resilience to climate-related shocks is a goal of many adaptation strategies employed by smallholders. Local safety nets built on collective action can help poor people cope with climate-related shocks, for example, by turning to a neighbor for emergency funds or using food reserves and seed banks. Mutual insurance schemes such as funeral societies that have traditionally served as a coping mechanism for illness or death in the family are now being used to cope with climatic shocks such as drought. However, local collective action is less able to deal with shocks that affect many people in a community; for severe and widespread shocks, national or even international assistance is needed.

Ensure that Tenure Insecurity does not Exclude the Poor from Mitigation and Adaptation Strategies

The focus of most mitigation and adaptation programs has been on the global and national level. For climate change policies to be sound development policies, however, the impact of response strategies on the poor needs to be examined. In many cases, customary property rights need to be recognized and made more secure if millions of smallholders are to benefit.

Adopting perennial crops that withstand drought and pests, sequester carbon, or hold moisture, requires land and perhaps also water rights to guarantee a return on these investments. Secure property rights are also important for natural resource management practices like tree planting and water harvesting that involve long-term investment in land and promote sustainable use. Secure tenure can also allow people to migrate or diversify their occupations to pursue alternative income sources. Finally, disaster preparedness requires a certain amount of investment, not only in public infrastructure, but also for protecting livelihoods through practices such as seawall containment, irrigation canals, erosion prevention, and watershed management, all of which require secure property rights.

Knowledge and information sharing increase adaptation.

The rise in demand for land by international fuel developers for biofuel production can weaken local institutions and lead to people with insecure tenure losing rights to land and water resources. There have been reports of land seizures and denial of customary land rights related to biofuel cultivation in parts of Africa (Tanzania, Mozambique), Latin America (Colombia, Brazil), India, and Papua New Guinea. Water use for biofuel plantations is also threatening community resource bases. In other instances, land acquisitions of areas considered underutilized or unused take place, even though these lands may be used for animal grazing or fuel wood collection by the poor. Despite their contributions to climate change mitigation, land acquisitions and land clearings for biofuel production may have detrimental impacts on the livelihoods of the resource-dependent poor.

To allow rural poor to benefit from biofuel production, an array of options for tenure security must be available. Allowing communal systems to participate in the local biofuels market is particularly important. For example, the Kavango Biofuel Project in Namibia is a collaborative effort between local farmers and a Namibian company to grow jatropha on communal land. The company provides capital costs, food, and cash for the farmers to replace annual maize and millet crops with perennial jatropha. Those community members without access to land can participate in other jobs made available through the project, such as working in the processing plants or in product transport.

The design of many carbon payment schemes has excluded small farmers who lack clear land ownership. Whether new REDD schemes will affect smallholders and forest communities positively or negatively will depend on the provisions made for the allocation of benefits from carbon trading. If the land tenure of forest-dependent communities is not secure, and governance around land tenure is not effective, there is a danger that the benefits from REDD projects will be appropriated by governments, the private sector, and even conservation NGOs. Secure tenure rights will give local people more leverage in negotiating the terms of these schemes; insecure rights could lead to dispossession because REDD will increase land values.

As for adaptation mechanisms, property rights are critical in facilitating income diversification because secure tenure will provide a fallback option in case the other sources fail, or can be used as a collateral for other livelihood activities. Without secure property rights, smallholders may not have sufficient capital or a fall-back option to support diversification.

Consider Various Levels of Governance in Designing and Choosing Mitigation and Adaptation Strategies

The need to consider the wide-ranging effects of climate change policies and programs, including their impact on the rural poor, calls for the participation of various levels of governance in designing and choosing response strategies. For example, effective carbon payments will require international market mechanisms to match those who wish to pay to offset their emissions with those who will sequester carbon; national governments that will broker agreements, such as through a Designated National Authority (DNA) as currently employed for CDM agreements; and collective action groups to monitor compliance among local smallholders. While local collective action can provide an effective means of measuring and ensuring compliance, whether a group will continue to fulfill this role on an ongoing basis will depend on whether there is an incentive to do so. Long-term participation is more likely if the group has been involved in the negotiations, has had a say in setting the rules, and receives a substantial benefit, either for the group or its members. Experience with collective action in other types of natural resource management suggests that systems that are developed in a top-down manner and do not engage local people in the design of rules and systems are unlikely to create viable institutions that operate at the local level in the long run. Additionally, local policy responses are necessary to complement national policies that do not specify benefits or support for smallholders. This provides a caution against focusing only on national-level negotiations and systems for climate change mitigation or adaptation, because they are unlikely to create effective institutions to execute the programs, especially among smallholders.

A range of central and local institutions, public and private, is therefore needed. Rather than focusing exclusively on any single type of institution, policies need to develop harmonious, multilevel governance arrangements in which multiple institutions each play a role. Through coordination among different institutions, institutional as well as ecological resilience will be created and the poverty impacts of climate change will be targeted more effectively.

The lack of property rights will discourage people from planting perennials that better withstand climate change, sequester carbon and hold moisture, and require land (and water) rights to guarantee a return on investments.

Suggested Readings

Cotula, L., N. Dyer, S. Vermeulen. 2008. Fuelling Exclusion? The Biofuels Boom and Poor People's Access to Land. IIED and FAO. Rome: FAO.

Knox, A., Meinzen-Dick, R., and P. Hazell. 1998. Property Rights, Collective Action, and Technology for Natural Resource Management. CAPRi Working Paper 1. Washington, D.C.: International Food Policy Research Institute,

Swallow, B. and R. Meinzen-Dick. 2009. Payment for Environmental Services: Interactions with Property Rights and Collective Action. In *Institutions and Sustainability,* ed. V. Beckmann and M. Padmanabhan, eds. Dordrecht, The Netherlands: Springer.

Ruth Meinzen-Dick (r.meinzen-dick@cgiar.org) is a senior research fellow at the International Food Policy Research Institute (IFPRI) and coordinator of CAPRi. Helen Markelova (h.markelova@cgiar.org) is a research analyst with IFPRI/CAPRi. Kelsey Moore (kamoore@uw.edu) was a consultant to the CAPRi program.

Chapter 6

Decentralization

Decentralization and Democratic Governance

Decentralization is often part of a number of related policy reforms, in which central government agencies transfer rights and responsibilities to more localized institutions. Although there are a number of different types of reforms that are sometimes referred to as "decentralization," most call for some kind of greater organized involvement of local people.

SOURCE:

Meinzen-Dick, R., M. Di Gregorio and S. Dohrn. 2008. *Decentralization, Pro-Poor Land Policies, and Democratic Governance*. CAPRi Working Paper No. 80. International Food Policy Research Institute, Washington, D.C.

Types of Decentralization

One useful way of sorting through the various types of reform that are sometimes referred to as "decentralization" is to examine the accountability structures of each. While particular programs may combine these in different combinations, in practice there are several broad patterns:

- **Deconcentration** or **delegation** refers to administrative decentralization in which functions are transferred to lower-level units of a government agency. This represents the least change, because authority remains with the same type of (government) institution, and accountability is ultimately still upward to the central government.

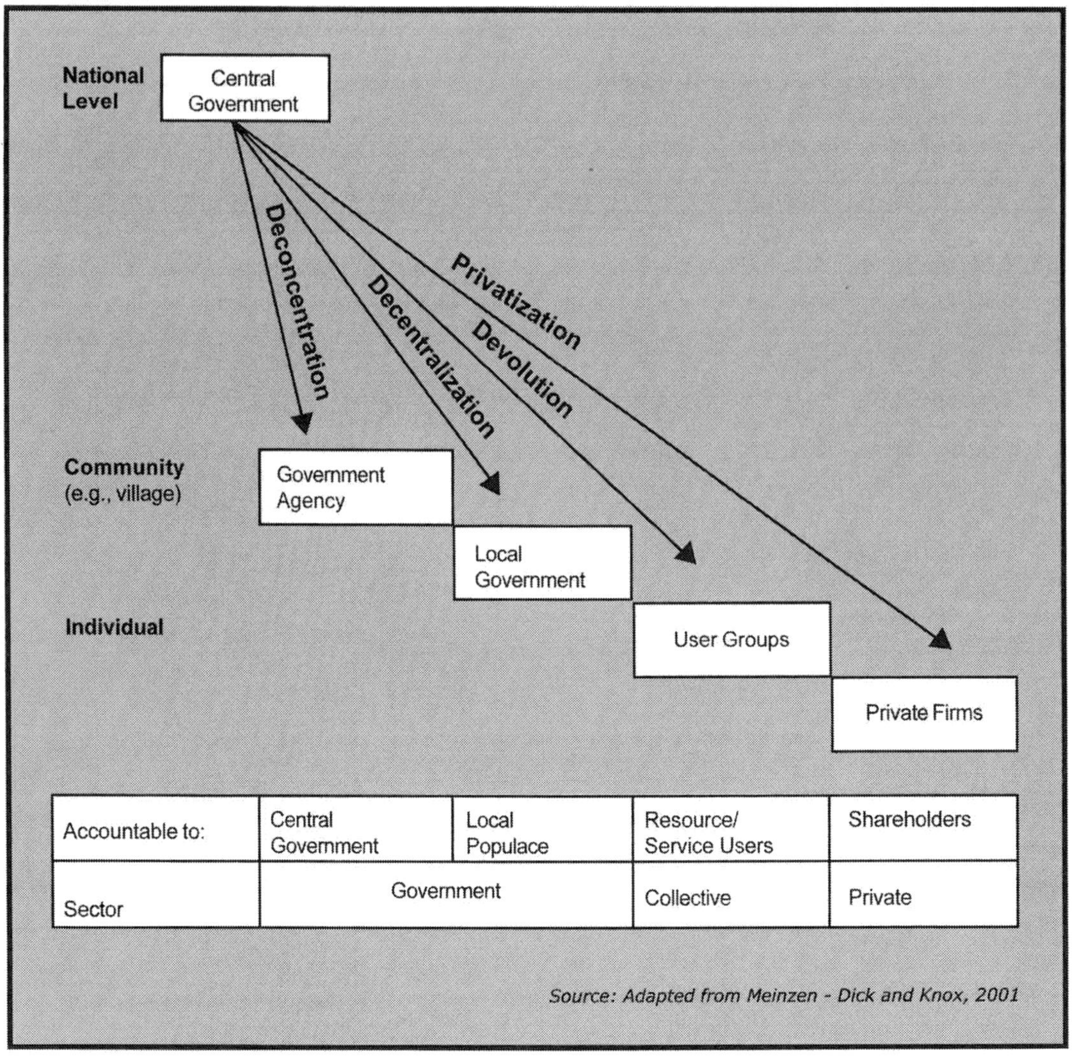

Figure 1: Types of Decentralization Reforms.

- **Political decentralization** transfers authority and functions to local government. Where local government is elected (as in the *panchayts* in India or *municipios* in Mexico), such reforms are referred to as "democratic decentralization", and may be assumed to be responsible to all local citizens. However, for this to hold in practice requires effective local democratic representation and accountability of local authorities to the local populace.

- **Devolution** of natural resources to user groups at the local level creates accountability to their membership, usually those who depend on the resource, but these members do not necessarily represent others in the local community, nor society at large. The extent to which these groups (like local governments) are, in practice, accountable to their members or are dominated by the elites will depend on the degree of checks and balances within these groups, and their extent of democratic decision-making.

- **Privatization** reforms are also seen where state resources are transferred to private groups or individuals rather than to some form of public body. Privatization therefore reduces accountability to the public at large.

Understanding Decentralization Objectives

There has been a wide range of programs related to the forms of decentralization. The objectives are also varied, but include the following:

- delegating administrative functions of the central state to local state agencies, as a means to increase efficiency of government functions including containing central expenditures;
- strengthening participation, rural development, and the maintenance of national unity;
- introduction of direct election at the local level and increased local legislative powers vis-à-vis executive and bureaucratic apparatus as vehicles to strengthen people's participation and empowerment; and
- overcoming the limitations of state capacity to manage natural resources, including reducing the fiscal costs of the state, improving resource management by tapping into users' greater local knowledge of the resource, and empowering local resource users.

One way to strengthen people's participation is to conduct a direct election at the local level.

Decentralization Outcomes

Although decentralization can foster democracy and participation, there are many limits. For example, the limits of financial decentralization in countries affected by regional inequalities, the limits of political decentralization when old political coalitions live on, and the limits of decentralization on policy results when there is a lack of social consensus.

There are many political and economic factors influencing the outcome of decentralization. "Instilling democracy" from the top or from external actors is likely to work only where the preconditions for real democracy are in place, with strong civil society or customary mechanisms for checks and balances. Strong local organizations are needed to take on the additional responsibilities implied in any form of decentralization.

The technical capacity of the body ultimately delivering various services and regulation also plays a key role in shaping the outcomes. The degree of economic and social inequality in each location will also shape whether decentralization will lead to equitable outcomes or a capture of the benefits by local elites.

Decentralization has the potential to empower local people and improve resource management as well as delivery of other poverty reduction programs. However, the outcomes are not always as expected. Attention to the structure and accountability of the local bodies that receive authority, as well as the capacity of the state agencies and local forms of collective action, provides a starting point for more effective local governance.

Suggested Readings

Conyers, D. 1983. *Decentralization and Development: A Review of Literature.* Public Administration and Development 4:187-197.

Meinzen-Dick, R. S. and A. Knox. 2001. *Collective Action, Property Rights, and Devolution of Natural Resource Management: A Conceptual Framework.* In: Meinzen-Dick, R.S., A. Knox and M. Di Gregorio, (eds). 2001. *Collective Action, Property Rights and Devolution of Natural Resource Management: Exchange of Knowledge and Implications for Policy.* Feldafing, Germany: DSE/ZEL.

Ribot, J.C. and A. Larson (eds). 2005. *Decentralization through a Natural Resource Lens: Experience in Africa, Asia and Latin America.* London: Frank Cass.

Land Tenure Reform and Decentralization

There is renewed interest in land tenure reform policies in many countries as resources become more scarce and competition for land increases. Although the term "land reform" is still associated with redistribution of land, there are many types of land tenure reform or land policy.

SOURCE:

Meinzen-Dick, R., M. Di Gregorio and S. Dohrn. 2008. *Decentralization, Pro-Poor Land Policies, and Democratic Governance.* CAPRi Working Paper No. 80. International Food Policy Research Institute, Washington, D.C.

The following are the four major types of reform:

1. ***Land Registration.*** This involves the recording of existing rights. Registration can include marking of plot boundaries, local mapping of holdings, and community land registries, up through full cadastral surveys and titling. In most cases, registration focuses on individual rights, but in some cases collective rights are registered, as in Liberia or Mozambique.

   Codification can strengthen existing rights by making it clear that the state will enforce the rights that are duly registered. However, this may come at a cost to other users of the resource whose rights are not recorded. For example, when rights are registered in the name of the male head of the household only, it can also increase women's insecurity of tenure. In Africa, some find the titling process a source of insecurity because elites would have an advantage in acquiring titles.

2. ***Redistributive Land Reforms.*** These reforms have been variously associated with objectives of increasing equity or productivity, reducing poverty, and responding to political demands and agitation. Redistributive reforms require a strong central government commitment, either to expropriate land from private land owners or to transfer state lands to individuals (a form of privatization).

3. ***Restitution.*** Land restitution can be seen as a variant of redistributive land reform that addresses past injustices, as in South Africa, Zimbabwe, in post-socialist societies such as Eastern Europe and Central Asia, or after a violent conflict. In addition to the challenges of regular land redistribution programs, land restitution is invariably linked to rectifying injustices of the past, and the state has to decide what constitutes legitimate claims to that end.

4. ***Recognition of Land Rights.*** State recognition of land uses that are already being exercised without government approval represents a fourth category of land tenure reform. The recognition of the land rights of customary land users or indigenous peoples provides an important example of such reforms. The rights of people living on land that the state claims as government property for protected areas (such as national parks), forests, or rangelands may also be strengthened or transformed through state recognition.

Informal Land Registration in Madagascar

Madagascar is an example of a highly decentralized informal registration system practiced at the local level, which runs parallel to official land administration. Instead of updating the land titles, which is a very costly process (in terms of both money and time), local people go to the village head to have their land transactions certified in the form of contracts. These have the advantage of tapping in to local knowledge of who is the rightful holder of the land by calling witnesses.

This system of using contracts, generally called "petits papiers," to serve as proof of purchase and ownership is also practiced in other African countries. While it often serves as adequate security of tenure within the community, it may not withstand challenges from outsiders who may use their greater access to formal titling systems to place a claim on the land.

Restitution in South Africa

The Chatha "betterment" claim in South Africa is an example of the importance of the involvement of all stakeholders in negotiation around restitution. Starting in the 1950s, the so-called betterment policies were used to control rangeland degradation by redefining land use in rural villages, and forcibly resettling villagers into new residential areas.

Because returning to the original settlement pattern was seen as undesirable by all parties, negotiations led to the creation of a development package and support to develop and implement a development plan, which again resulted in the creation of a Settlement Support and Development Planning division within the Regional Land Claims Commission to support claimants after settlement.

Restitution claims over nature reserves constitute another complicated situation. The case of Dwesa-Cwebe resulted in a decentralized management scheme, handing over two reserves to a trust and establishing co-management between claimants and national conservation authorities.

Land Tenure and the Role of the State and Communities

The successful implementation of all forms of land tenure reform calls for some substantial role of governments, as well as some forms of organized local involvement. However, this does not imply that all have to be subsumed into one formalized arrangement subject to state law.

Pro-Poor Land Policies

The analysis of different types of decentralization programs and land tenure reforms provides a starting point for identifying appropriate strategies to develop the central/local and state/civil society partnerships that can enhance land tenure security for the poor.

Table 1. Comparison of Different Forms of Land Tenure Reform.

Type of Reform	Registration	Redistribution	Restitution	Recognition
Strengthen existing or transfer rights	Strengthen existing rights	Transfer from large landowners to landless	Transfer land back to original holders	Strengthen existing rights
Context	Customary tenure	Highly unequal landholdings	History of expropriation or conflict	Indigenous people, others using forests, rangelands, etc.
Common bundles of rights	Ownership	Ownership	Ownership	Use, some management rights
Individual/ collective	Usually individual	Usually individual	Usually individual	Usually collective
Potential role of local organizations	Identify rightholder, keep local registry, conflict resolution	Identify recipients (and sellers if market-based), conflict resolution	Identify rightful claimants, conflict resolution	Identify claimants, manage resource on continuing basis
Care needed for pro-poor outcomes	Include recognition of secondary rights important for poor and marginalized groups, including women	Support (e.g. credit, marketing) to enable poor to access land and use it productively	Avoid further exclusion of poorer sections without restitution rights, but who have been investing in land	Safeguard women's rights in patriarchal systems

Finally, millions of farmers, fishers, and foresters have no formal rights to the resources they depend upon. State recognition of such rights can do much to strengthen the tenure security, livelihoods, social cohesion and dignity of these people. Many of the unrecognized users are indigenous groups or other disadvantaged minorities, so strengthening their land rights can contribute to overall human rights.

Suggested Readings

Alden Wily, L. 2006. *Land Rights Reform and Governance in Africa: How to Make it Work in the 21st Century?* New York: UNDP Dryland Development Centre.

Chilundo, A., B. Cau, M. Mubai, D. Malauene and V. Muchanga. 2005. *Land Registration in Mampula and Zambezia Provinces, Mozambique: Securing Land Rights in Africa.* Research Report 6. London: IIED.

World Bank. 2003. *Land Policies for Growth and Poverty Reduction.* World Bank Policy Research Report. Washington, D.C.

Devolution of Natural Resource Management

From fishers in the Philippines to pastoralists in Morocco and rubber tappers in the Amazon, local communities have been actively participating in the management of natural resources.

SOURCE:

Katon, B., A. Knox and R. Meinzen-Dick. 2001. *Collective Action, Property Rights, and Devolution of Natural Resources Management.* CAPRi Policy Brief No. 2. International Food Policy Research Institute, Washington, D.C.

Since the 1990s, there has been a growing recognition of the benefits that can be derived from transferring control over natural resources from central governments to local bodies. At the international level, this trend is seen in agreements such as the Convention to Combat Desertification and the Convention on Biological Diversity that commit signatories to principles of decentralization, subsidiarity, and local participation. At the national level, many countries in Africa, the Americas, Asia, and Europe have devolved management responsibilities over rangelands, forests, fisheries, and irrigation to local government authorities, resource users, or both.

Devolution, defined as the transfer of rights and responsibilities to user groups at the local level, has made its way to national policy agendas for the following reasons:

1. Recognition of the limited effectiveness of the state in managing natural resources, especially at the local level.

Local users often have intimate knowledge of the resource, which is especially important where resources vary greatly over space and time. Users who live and work in the area also may have an advantage over government agents in monitoring use of the resource and compliance with rules. Because their livelihoods depend on the resource, local users often are assumed to have the greatest incentives to maintain the resource base, particularly if they make the decisions, devise the rules, and take part in them.

2. Few developing countries have the financial capacity to adequately monitor the use of large areas of forests, fisheries, range lands, or irrigation schemes. As a result, these resources have not been properly managed, and deforestation, overfishing, overgrazing, and deterioration of irrigation facilities have become major problems.

3. Devolution shifts greater authority and decision-making to rural people, giving them greater control over their assets and livelihood and making it an effective tool for poverty alleviation.

Devolution in Action

- In San Salvador village in Zambales, Philippines, collective action by village fishers, the Haribon Foundation, and local government units (LGUs) at the municipal and village levels led to the establishment of a 127-hectare marine sanctuary and marine reserve. Co-management arrangements have redefined access to resources, encouraged fishers to shift to non-destructive practices, and formally instituted measures to guard the coastal waters from poachers and illegal fishers. Coral reef conditions have improved remarkably, and catch per fishing trip has increased. Fishers, moreover, have perceived positive socio-economic changes over time.

- In Andhra Pradesh, India, more than 10,000 water-user associations have been organized to take a more active role in managing irrigation systems, which cover 4.8 million hectares. Farmers who repair facilities receive part of the irrigation fees. "We were able to finish maintenance work that has not been done for 30 years," reported one farmer. In pilot projects, the irrigated area increased from 30 to 60 percent of the possible command area with simple repairs, such as removing accumulated silt, and by negotiating with farmers at the head end of the canals.

- In Niger, the 1993 legal reforms embodied in the *Principes d'Orientation du Code Rural* recognize traditional resource management systems, particularly of pastoralists, and involve customary rule makers and decision makers in promoting better natural resource management and conservation practices on pastures as well as agricultural land. The *Code Pastorale,* passed in Mauritania in 2000, has gone even further in defending the rights of transhumant pastoralists to rangeland resources.

- Research on community forests in Nepal has shown that many user groups can devise rules that are well matched to their ecological problems. Local institutions have enabled these groups to sustain and, in some cases, improve the condition of their forest.

- In Peten, Guatemala, more than 100,000 ha of tropical rainforest were granted to local people under community forest concessions in the early 1990s. Since then, user groups have earned and maintained "good forest management" certification by the Forest Stewardship Council and acquired logging machinery and timber mills. Community forestry contributes to local employment and development while preserving the rain forest areas more efficiently than the neighboring biosphere reserve.

The result of the above has been a range of co-management arrangements involving government agencies and local users. Although obvious social and economic benefits can be gained from devolution, countries that have done this have experienced mixed outcomes due to issues of power inequality and incomplete devolution policies.

Collective

For resource users to effectively manage natural resources, there is a need for collective action. Studies show that certain prerequisites can sustain such collective action. These are:

- the resource being managed is important to local livelihood;
- the cost of collective action is low and benefits are tangible;
- local leaders endorse social justice and resource management objectives;
- an atmosphere of cohesion and trust exists among users; and
- social structures and values support cooperation.

However, even when such prerequisites are in place, a number of factors can still weaken the legitimacy of local resource management institutions and therefore the potential for collective action. Population pressures, mounting competition for natural resources, incentives created by expanding markets, and policies and laws contradict local rules for resource use and protection that also undermine local authorities.

In Zambales, Philippines, efforts of the people, NGOs and government units led to the establishment of a marine sanctuary.

The Role of External Organizers in Collective Action

Where local cooperation is weak, external organizers can be catalysts for collective action by strengthening awareness of the benefits of cooperative resource management. Staff of non-government organizations (NGOs), or government extension staff trained in community development and organizing, can also facilitate the building of organizational capacity and leadership. These capabilities not only are critical to developing rules for and carrying out resource management activities, but also are necessary for creating legitimate local institutions for resolving disputes. Social processes like this take time, however, and must adapt to their unique socio-economic, political, and physical contexts while developing local legitimacy. Donors and policymakers looking for quick solutions by imposing organization on resource users may even harm existing local forms of organizations.

Property Rights

Devolution programs that transfer responsibilities for resource management to local users often fail to transfer commensurate rights. Nonetheless, property rights that assure users the ability to derive benefits from resources over the long term are necessary to induce them to bear the management costs.

The strength of management incentives depends on how the collection of various rights is distributed. For example, if forest users are allowed to gather non-timber products but are prohibited by the state from cutting trees, and live with the threat of being evicted if forest areas are converted to logging or mining concessions or to restricted areas, sustainable management is unlikely.

The Role of the State in Enforcing Property Rights

Even with the most complete transfer of rights and responsibilities to users, the state retains a critical role in enforcing regulations, punishing violators, and settling disputes between local groups and outsiders.

Devolution as a Means of Achieving Local Control

Legal frameworks and government enforcement mechanisms need to support the rights of local users, respect their management institutions, and provide responsive backup. The actual nature and extent of co-management arrangements are likely to depend on local capacity to undertake certain roles and functions. Devolution can be an evolving process of greater local control as investments are made in building the organizational, administrative, and technical capacity of communities, local and regional organizations, and local and regional governments.

Equity

Aside from resource access rights, equity issues also need to be considered. Protecting the interest of less powerful groups, for example, calls for representative and robust conflict resolution mechanisms that all stakeholders consider legitimate.

Addressing Poverty to Help Conserve Natural Resources

In spite of its potential, devolution will not entirely resolve the problem of degradation of natural resources. There is a strong need to address poverty, particularly in remote areas, where resource users may have few subsistence and income-generating alternatives beyond exploiting their natural resource base.

In Andhra Pradesh, India, more than 10,000 water-user associations have been organized to take a more active role in managing irrigation systems.

This calls for greater attention to policies and investments that will enhance opportunities for livelihood diversification. Such measures include investments in rural infrastructure and enhancing access to markets, credit, and insurance to reduce the high costs of setting up and operating industries, markets, and finance facilities in rural areas. Combining such measures with policies and legislation that enable the poor to have access to and control over natural resources, policymakers will make substantial gains in empowering citizens and reducing poverty.

Suggested Reading

Meinzen-Dick, R. S. and A. Knox. 2001. *Collective Action, Property Rights, and Devolution of Natural Resource Management: A Conceptual Framework*. In: Meinzen-Dick, R. S., A. Knox and M. Di Gregorio (eds). 2001. *Collective Action, Property Rights and Devolution of Natural Resource Management: Exchange of Knowledge and Implications for Policy.* Feldafing, Germany: DSE/ZEL.

By-laws for Natural Resource Management: Insights from Africa

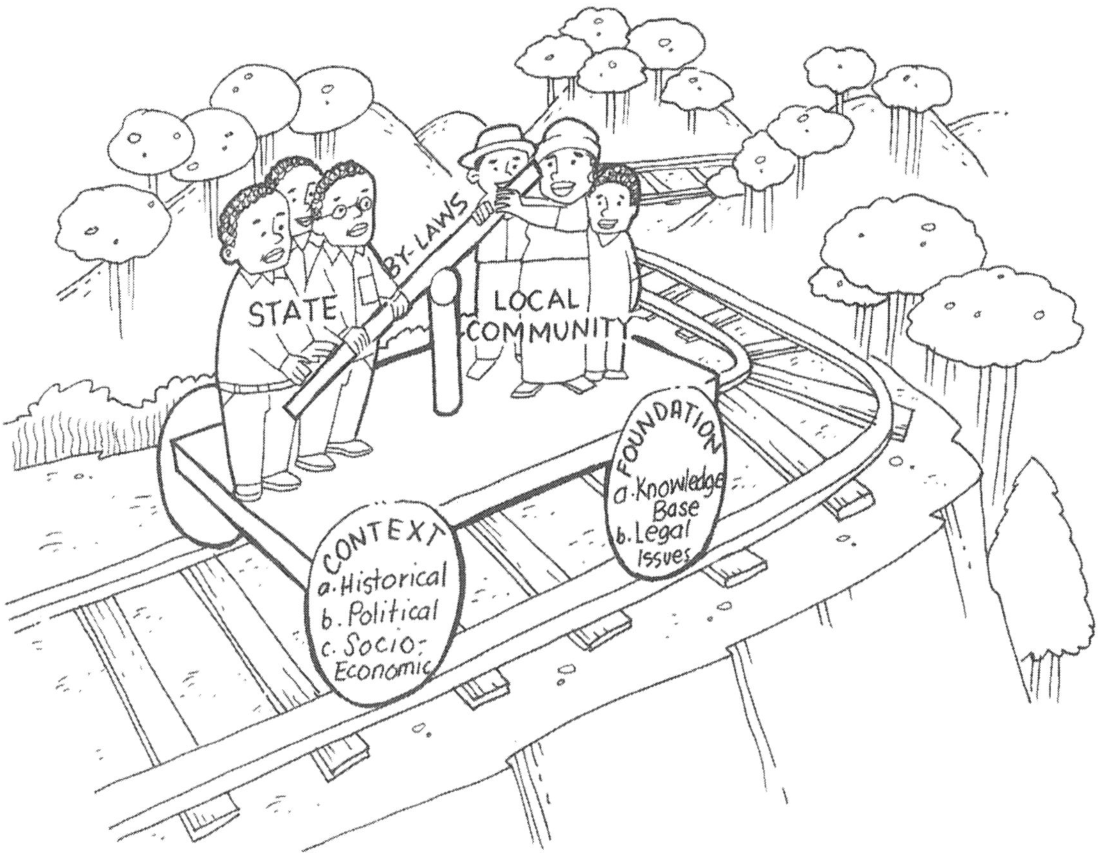

SOURCE:

Markelova, H. and B. Swallow. 2008. *By-laws and their Critical Role in Natural Resource Management: Insights from African Experience.* Paper presented at the 12th Biennial Conference of the International Association for the Study of Commons (IASC) in Cheltenham, England, July 14-18. Available online at http://iasc2008.glos.ac.uk/iasc08.html

Africa's rural populations depend heavily on natural resources, which have been continuously deteriorating due to rapid population growth, increasing market pressures, high rates of poverty, and inappropriate natural resource management (NRM) policies of governments. The failure of top-down approaches to the regulation and administration of natural resources has increased attention on the role of decentralized administrative structures, user groups, and customary governance institutions.

Until recently, local users were seen as unfit to be entrusted with decision-making regarding natural resources. Even though this bias still holds true in many parts of Africa, the waves of decentralization that have been sweeping through the continent since post-colonial independence have led to increased attention to the role of decentralized administrative structures and customary governance institutions.

By-laws Defined

In the realm of natural resource governance, by-laws have emerged with three distinct definitions:

1. **By-laws as local laws** emphasize the role of local communities in the management of resources. Local by-laws can particularly be important to NRM, as they connect the decentralized bodies to their constituents at the local level. They can also result from local processes that fill an institutional vacuum created by the absence or weakness of federal or state laws regarding local resource use. Local laws also emerge either from the resource users themselves (often through elected representatives or selected committees) or from the lowest level of empowered local authority in decentralized governance structures (with fiscal and decision-making powers independent of central government), and can be formal (approved by government authorities or project organizers) or informal.

2. **By-laws as organizational rules** can be important determinants of the success of rural organizations or resource user groups. They provide the actual rules that guide the functioning and operations of organizations.

3. **By-laws as secondary laws** may serve as framework laws that create new authorities, with new mandates that must be implemented. They can be implemented and enforced directly by government agencies at various levels or through local community groups acting on behalf of central government agencies as part of the implementation of specific legislation, or by legally constituted entities that have responsibilities consistent with the national law.

Functions of By-laws

By-laws, whether existing, updated, or newly created, can fulfill several important functions in the communities where they are present.

1. By-laws create space for productive investment, particularly when closely linked with economic profitability.
2. By-laws contribute to the conservation and sustainability of natural resources, as they devolve conservation activities to the local level where these rules are created and implemented.
3. By-laws can help ensure equitable use of resources when there is a balanced representation and active participation of all stakeholders from by-laws formulation to implementation.
4. By-laws play an important function in conflict management and resolution.
5. By-laws may serve as a channel to interact with local and central government officials who may serve as the enforcement agency for locally crafted rules. Such interactions are important as a means of community empowerment.

Factors Influencing By-laws Processes

By-laws can fulfill several important functions for communities and their natural resources. The effectiveness of these rules and regulations depends on their content, applicability, and acceptance in the communities. Processes associated with by-laws include their formulation and implementation. Several factors affect each process.

By-laws Formulation

Historical Context

The varying historical, political, and socio-economic settings across the African continent have affected the conditions and process of by-law formulation. Differences in ethnicity, religion, and other cultural and ecological conditions further complicate the establishment of uniform regulations. Colonial history and differences between the governing styles of colonial powers have influenced the nature of by-laws formulated. Despite these differences, the customary governance structures have been overshadowed by newly established systems.

After independence, many colonial-style institutions persisted, with continued prejudices against customary systems of governance. In recent decades, most nations have embarked on the path of administrative, political, and fiscal decentralization, which has not, however, been a uniform process across Africa. These processes have taken different shapes across the continent, and, due to the legacy of various colonial powers, have had different impacts in Anglophone and Francophone regions of the continent.

Bases of By-laws

The issue of the source, or foundation, of by-laws can be divided into two components: the *knowledge base* and the *legal aspects*. The main question for both areas lies along the lines of customary/traditional versus statutory/modern.

The co-existence of two sets of norms, customary and legal, has influenced the development and refinement of by-laws, some that had existed for centuries and others that have been recently established. In some societies, customary institutions were outright pushed aside, while others have been successful in harmonizing customary and statutory laws. Whatever the case may be, practitioners and policymakers are faced with the challenge of comparing and assigning a value to the two sources of rules, or the norms that prescribe the nature of by-laws, when designing or updating rules and regulations for NRM.

- **Knowledge Base**. When considering theoretical foundations for by-laws, especially for conservation and management purposes, it is important to consider the role of *scientific knowledge*. In fact, when it comes to appropriate technology for conservation or certain agricultural practices (such as seed dissemination), there is a need for informed and tested approaches.

Indigenous Knowledge

For a complex issue such as resource degradation, indigenous knowledge may be limited in its ability to deal with the landscape-wide challenges, especially in the context of climate change. The foundation of by-laws should then be grounded in both local knowledge and scientific facts behind rural development and NRM. A cross-fertilization between scientific and indigenous knowledge could result in higher acceptance and better implementation, since multiple interests are served.

- **Legal Issues.** By-laws can be derived from either *customary* or *statutory law*. If the source comes from both the state and traditional institutions, then the outcome depends on the context and the interaction between the traditional and statutory. At times, donors, NGOs, or mandates based on international agreements (such as the Kyoto Protocol) provide bases for by-laws according to program and project rules. There are both limitations and advantages to both types of laws functioning as the sole basis for by-laws.

National governments and international agencies perceive customary laws as weak and inefficient, which could render them ineffective unless backed by statutory laws. Many customary institutions

and laws have good accountability structures, enjoy legitimacy and respect, promote cooperative decision-making, and carry behind them the richness of local knowledge and cultural heritage.

Customary rules for natural resource use and governance are often linked to customary tenure rights, making them more effective and accepted. Statutory law, on the other hand, carries the backing of the government, which may contribute to the effectiveness of regulations based thereon. Since it is not sensitive to the situation on the ground, by-laws that are based on statutory provisions may lead to elite capture and even worsen natural resource conditions as power is transferred into the "wrong" hands.

Potential contradictions between by-laws and state laws deserve special consideration. Therefore, it appears that a combination of customary and statutory laws may become the best option for the legal basis for by-laws.

Dangers of Elite Capture

It has been shown that customary institutions are not always equitable, especially to the poorest and women, and in some cases become the mechanisms for elite capture, as in the case of Zimbabwe, Uganda, and Ethiopia. In many African nations, traditional norms and institutions have eroded due to demographic change, various government policies, and penetration of the global economy to the local level.

In Tanzania, only the vestiges of traditional institutions remain because of the socialist movement and the subsequent centralization of power that encouraged the breakdown of tribal identity. Even with the introduction of multi-party democracy, decentralization efforts contributed to the breakdown of traditional resource management systems as power was formalized in village governments.

Some evidence of statutory laws leading to elite capture has been found in the case of CAMPFIRE in Zimbabwe, where the Rural District Councils have used the program to generate revenue and use it to their political purposes, disregarding the original conservation and welfare-enhancing objectives of the program.

By-laws formulation and enactment are inherently political processes, since any regulation that deals with natural resources has to account for the multiplicity of interests from different parties with a stake in the resource. Unequal power may arise between the state and the communities and within the communities themselves. Failure to consider power relations may result in elite capture in the formulation and implementation of by-laws, as well as in inequitable distribution of benefits.

Implementation of By-laws

Closely connected to the process of by-laws formulation are the issues of implementation and the monitoring of how they are complied with, observed, and enforced.

- Externally imposed rules that do not take into account local conditions may be perceived as unfair by local resource users, thus lowering any willingness to abide by them.
- People may not comply with internally created rules because of established relationships of hierarchy and norms of mutual support in communities.
- Compliance with by-laws is higher when regulations are relevant to local conditions and are drafted in consultation with local communities.
- By-laws are meaningless unless there is some enforcement. In West Africa, communities tend to bypass formal institutions or disregard by-laws ratified by local governments during the formulation of group rules governing national resources. However, several case studies across India and Nepal have shown that statutory law may contribute to the effectiveness of local regulations by serving as a mechanism for enforcement and compliance. There can be a role for state and local enforcement.
- Because of the norms of reciprocity, internal enforcement may be less effective in monitoring compliance and imposing sanctions.

Conclusion

By-laws are at the core of many governance structures that frame the access, use, and conflict resolution around vital resources across Africa. The necessity for creating and supporting local by-laws becomes vital when considering their linkages to larger trends in the area of sustainable and equitable NRM and poverty reduction in general, and climate change mitigation in particular. To make these rules truly pro-poor, participatory approaches to the formulation and enactment of all three types of by-laws should be explored.

Suggested Readings

Agrawal, A. and C. Gibson. 1999. *Enchantment and Disenchantment: The Role of Community in Natural Resource Conservation.* World Development 27 (4): 629-649.

Alinon, K. and A. Kalinganire. 2008. *Effectiveness of By-laws in the Management of Natural Resources: The West African Experience.* Working Paper No. 92. CGIAR Systemwide Program on Collective Action and Property Rights for Poverty Reduction (CAPRi). International Food Policy Research Institute: Washington, D.C.

German, L., W. Mazengia, W. Tirwomwe, S. Ayele, J. Tanui, S. Nyangas, L. Begashaw, H. Taye, Z. Admassu, M. Tsegaye, F. Alinyo, A. Mekonnen, K. Aberra, A. Chemangeni, W. Cheptegei, T. Tolera, Z. Jotte and K. Bedane. 2008. *Enabling Equitable Collective Action and Policy Change for Poverty Reduction and Improved Natural Resource Management in the Eastern African Highlands.* Working Paper No. 86. CGIAR Systemwide Program on Collective Action and Property Rights for Poverty Reduction (CAPRi). International Food Policy Research Institute: Washington, D.C.

Mandondo, A. 2001. *Allocation of Government Authority and Responsibility of Tiered Governance Regimes: The Case of the Chivi Rural District Counci Landuse Planning and Conservation Bylaws.* African Studies Quarterly 5 (3): [available online].

Mwebaza, R. 1999. *How to Integrate Statutory and Customary Tenure? The Uganda Case.* Paper presented at the DfID Workshop on Land Rights and Sustainable Development in Sub-Saharan Africa, Berkshire, UK, 16th-19th February.

Community-Driven Development:
Treating Poor People as Partners

Community-Driven Development (CDD) is an effective mechanism for poverty reduction, complementing market- and state-run activities by achieving immediate and lasting results at the grassroots level. Experience has shown that CDD can enhance sustainability and make poverty reduction efforts more responsive to demand.

SOURCE:

Dongier, P., J. Van Domelen, E. Ostrom, A. Rizvi, W. Wakeman, A. Bebbington, S. Alkire, T. Esmail and M. Polski. 1995. *Chapter 9: Community-Driven Development*. In *A Sourcebook for Poverty Reduction Strategies. Volume 1: Core Techniques and Cross-Cutting Issues.* The World Bank, Washington, D.C.

Well-designed CDD programs include the poor and vulnerable groups, build positive social capital, and give the poor greater voice both in their community and with government entities. CDD empowers poor people to decide for themselves and take charge of managing their community resources. Building on their institutions and resources, CDD treats poor people, not as targets of development, but as assets and partners in the development process.

In order for CDD to succeed in its goal to help poor people reduce poverty, it has to first prepare communities. Such preparation comes with strengthening and financing inclusive community groups, facilitating community access to information, and promoting an enabling environment through policy and institutional reform.

Partnership as the Key Element of CDD

CDD gives control of decisions and resources to community groups. These groups often work in partnership with demand-responsive support organizations and service providers, including elected local governments, the private sector, NGOs, and central government agencies.

Clear rules, access to information, and appropriate support can effectively facilitate poor men and women to organize and provide goods and services that meet their immediate priorities.

Core Techniques of CDD

At the heart of CDD are core techniques which include: providing social and infrastructure services, organizing economic activity and resource management, empowering poor people, improving local governance, and enhancing security of the poorest.

However, not all goods and services are best managed through collective action at the community level. Public goods that span many communities or that require large, complex systems are often better provided by local or central government.

Similarly, private goods or toll goods are often better provided using a market-based approach, relying more on individual enterprises than on collective action. CDD can, however, fill gaps where markets are missing or imperfect, or where public institutions or local governments fail to fulfill their mandates.

Why Community-Driven Development?

Interviews with 60,000 poor people in 60 countries reveal that poor people demand a development process driven by their communities. When the poor were asked to indicate what might make the greatest difference in their lives, they responded:

- Organizations of their own so they can negotiate with government, traders, and NGOs.
- Direct assistance through community-driven programs so they can shape their own destinities.
- Local ownership of funds, so they can end corruption. They want NGOs and governments to be accountable to them.

Benefits of Community-Driven Development

a. ***Complements Market and Public Sector Activities.*** Policies that promote national economic competitiveness and state-run public investment programs are essential, but insufficient for poverty reduction. CDD offers the opportunity to fill this critical gap by achieving immediate and lasting results at the grassroots level.

b. ***Enhances Sustainability of Services.*** Community-developed facilities such as health centers, schools, and water supply systems tend to have higher utilization rates and are better maintained than when investment decisions are made by actors outside the community.

c. ***Improves Efficiency and Effectiveness.*** Community management of development investments usually results in lower costs and more productively employed assets. In Asia, systems constructed and operated by the farmers themselves generate a higher level of agricultural productivity than more modern systems constructed by government agencies.

CDD can contribute to reduction of poverty and complement market- and state-run activities by achieving immediate and lasting results at the grassroots level. Experience has shown that CDD can enhance sustainability and make poverty reduction efforts more responsive to demand.

Recommendations for Adapting CDD

Scaling Up. The challenge of scaling up is not about bigger projects or bigger organizations, but rather about achieving sustainable results in a large number of communities. Principles for scaling up CDD are, for the most part, the same principles for making CDD more sustainable.

Invest in an Exit Strategy. An exit strategy for external support is a critical component of all CDD interventions. Temporary services, such as initial intensive capacity building support to community-based organizations, may, however, not require sustainable financing. For such temporary services, explicit exit strategies need to be designed and implemented.

In addition to market development, health care for the poor is also an essential service.

Suggested Readings

Adato, M., T. Besley, L. Haddad and J. Hoddinott. 1999. *Participation and Poverty Reduction: Issues, Theory and New Evidence from South Africa.* Discussion Paper No. 98. International Food Policy Research Institute: Washington, D.C.

Lam, W. F. 1998. *Governing Irrigation Systems in Nepal: Institutions, Infrastructure and Collective Action.* Oakland, Cal.: ICS Press.

Narayan, D. 1995. *Designing Community-Based Development.* Environment Department Working Paper 7. World Bank, Washington, D.C.

Narayan D., R. Chambers, M.K. Shah and P. Petesch. 2000. *Voices of the Poor Crying for Change.* Oxford University Press. New York.

Sara, J. and T. Katz. 1997. *Making Rural Water Sustainable: Report on the Impact of Project Rules.* United Nations Development Programme (UNDP) and World Bank Water and Sanitation Program, Washington, D.C.

Chapter 7

Gender, Collective Action and Property Rights

Gender and Collective Action:
A Conceptual Framework

This paper presents a framework for investigating the intersection of collective action and gender to illustrate how gender-oriented analysis can foster more effective collective action in the context of agriculture and natural resource management, and how collective action can be used as a vehicle for gender equity.

SOURCE:

Pandolfelli, L., R. Meinzen-Dick and S. Dohrn. 2007. *Gender and Collective Action: A Conceptual Framework for Analysis.* CAPRi Working Paper No. 64. International Food Policy Research Institute, Washington, D.C.

The Analytical Framework

The Context or Initial Conditions

Particular attention is given to the cultural context where gender roles are constructed by society and influence the extent to which women and men can use their assets and institutional infrastructure at their disposition. For example, physical assets such as roads will enhance access to markets, yet a gender norm which confines women to their homes, e.g. *purdah* in India, can hinder women from meeting their livelihood objectives.

The context includes the assets, vulnerabilities, and legal governance (norms, legal structures, power relations) systems that influence a range of outcomes.

1. ***Assets.*** These refer to a pool of resources or assets available to an actor. These can be categorized as physical (e.g. roads, markets), natural (e.g. water, soils), financial (e.g. bank account), social (e.g. group membership), political (e.g. government representation), and human capital assets (e.g. education), as well as property rights vis-à-vis these assets. Property rights can only be effective if they are recognized as legitimate, as when they are sanctioned by governance structures to enforce such rights.

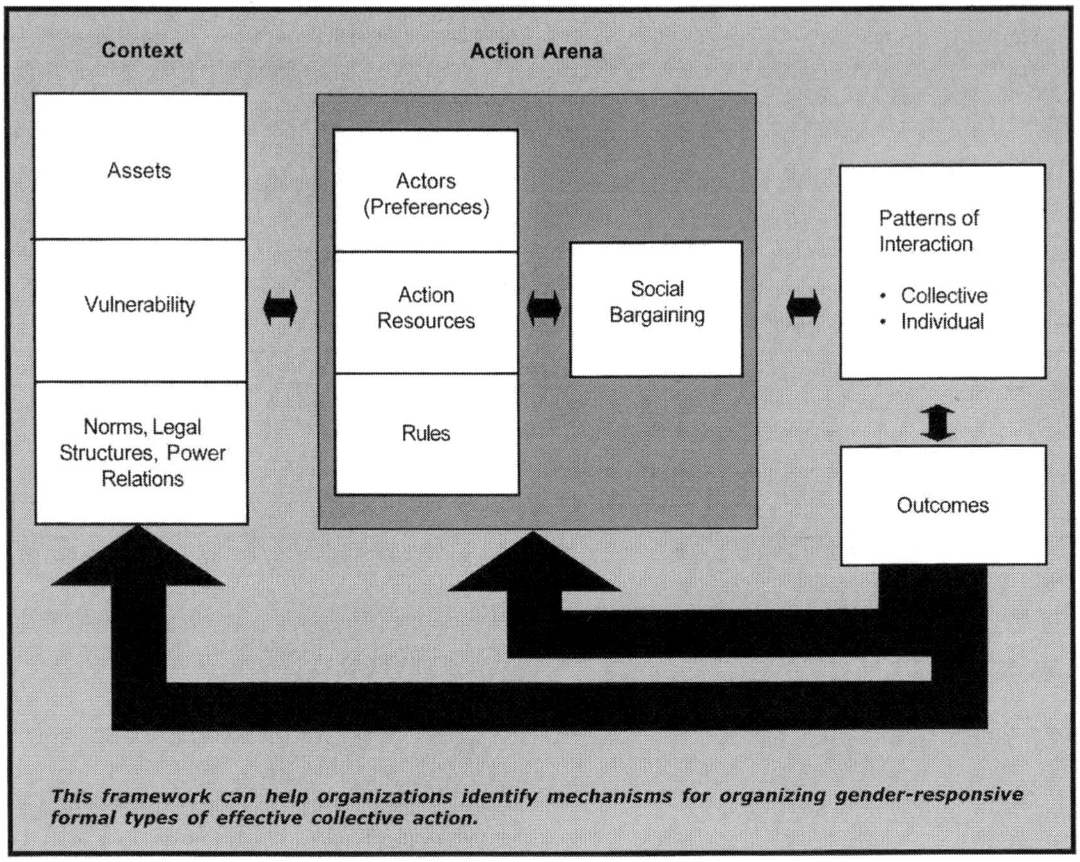

Figure 1. Analytical Framework to Analyze Gender and Collective Action.

For example, a woman may have access to a piece of land for firewood collection but have no rights to plant trees on that land, as this activity is often reserved for those who own the land. There is evidence that shows that property rights raise women's status in the household as well as in the community, which translates into greater bargaining power.

2. ***Vulnerabilities.*** Aside from lack of available assets, women are vulnerable to lack of government services, crises in agricultural production such as drought, declines in landholding, seasonal unemployment, and gender-based harassment and violence. Women are more strongly affected by these factors because they have less access than men to credit and employment in alternative labor markets.

   Women are often limited by accepted cultural gender roles, which in turn may affect their ability or willingness to engage in collective action. Such vulnerabilities include dependence on, or subordination by, male household members and in-laws, which may result in a husband's refusal to allow his wife to engage in, or control the benefits accrued from, collective action.

3. ***Legal Governance.*** Gender biases towards women as reflected in the norms embedded in cultural, political, and economic institutions do not change overnight, and in fact, attempts to directly challenge gendered norms and upset power imbalances may result in backlash and further disempowerment of women.

   To stimulate gender equality, changes in statutory law (e.g. in laws pertaining to inheritance, divorce, and property rights) will provide a basis for women's appeals for more substantial rights, i.e. changes in gendered norms. Decentralization can also help to change existing power structures by enhancing women's participation in the public arena.

Action Arena

This is the heart of the framework and is shaped by a host of initial conditions. Here, *actors* and their preferences, *action resources* (such as information and the ability to process it, social status, time), and *rules* determine which actions are carried out, and how they are implemented.

- ***Actors and their preferences.*** To understand the motivation of the actors, it is important to understand their preferences. Usually men and women differ in their preferences: for example, women prefer crop varieties that have good taste and cooking properties, while men first consider the market price.

- ***Action resources.*** These are the assets and internal capabilities that are relevant to the specific situation and increase the bargaining power of the actors. For example, having the confidence to stand up and speak in front of the community can be an important action resource. However, if women are forbidden from speaking in public, this particular asset cannot be translated into an action resource.

- ***Rules.*** Rules clarify expectations about the costs and benefits of participation. They shape the bargaining process and/or may be shaped in the process of bargaining. They can be written or unwritten. For example, a woman may remain silent in the presence of her husband during a public meeting, even though she is more informed about the subject matter. Both groups and assets strengthen women's bargaining power.

Gender roles (women taking care of children) may affect women's willingness to engage in collective action.

Women often prefer crop varieties that have good taste and cooking properties.

In northern Nigeria, women must observe seclusion under *Shari'ah* law; thus, they cannot organize. However, they can capitalize on the resurgence of Islam to form women-only associations that teach Islamic education. Through this informal rule that permits these schools, women are able to develop additional support networks to help with childcare and ceremonial expenses.

- ***Bargaining power.*** This is the ability of an actor to engage in social bargaining, based on their action resources and the rules. Both groups and assets strengthen women's bargaining power.

Outcomes: Impact on Gender Relations

Whereas effectiveness of collective action refers to the ability of groups to meet their immediate purposes (e.g., the management of a natural resource), the impact of collective action refers to changes (in this case, changes in gender relations) that go beyond that. For example, a microcredit scheme designed to raise the income of its members would measure its effectiveness in terms of income earned while measurements of impact on gender relations would include the ability of women to control that income within the household.

The framework described here undertakes a "gendered poverty lens" to consider collective action outcomes in terms of all the critical aspects of poverty, as well as how these aspects are experienced differently by women and men. Impacts on gender equity can thus be evaluated by several indicators, including: the level and distribution of income, as well as the recognition that women may make trade-offs, or tactical choices, between different material, psychological, and symbolic aspects of poverty; the ability to secure basic needs; the degree of social and political inclusion; security against violence (including violence against women); vulnerability to shocks; and, more broadly, the opportunity set for livelihood improvement.

Four levels of impact on gender relations can be distinguished: relations within the household, relations within the collective action group itself, relations of the group vis-à-vis the community, and relations of the community vis-à-vis the outside. Analysis of the impact of collective action on gender equity cannot be divorced from analysis of the household because activities undertaken as a collective feedback into women's and men's social bargaining within the household. For example, income-generating collective action schemes may increase a woman's fallback or exit options within the household if she is able to strengthen her asset endowments (e.g., financial capital) and draw upon them as action resources to increase her bargaining power within the household.

At the community level, collective action groups, particularly mixed-sex groups, may alter perceptions of women's socioeconomic contributions, thereby increasing their status within the community. Collective action groups may also mobilize enough social and political capital to contest the state. For example, the Green Belt Movement in Kenya grew into a significant political force. Collective lobbying efforts have also been influential in strengthening women's legal rights and share of state expenditure at the national level in countries such as Uganda, Tanzania, and South Africa. Even at the international level, the global women's movement may be seen as a form of collective action that has had an impact on development discourse and policy, such as through the *Convention on the Elimination of All Forms of Discrimination Against Women (CEDAW)* and the Beijing Platform for Action. Changes in gender relations may feed back into the action arena, the initial conditions, or both.

Conclusions

For researchers, this framework can help identify key aspects of the environment that influence collective action outcomes and how these may differ for men and women.

It can also help to look at the various resources that different actors have to draw upon, and how the rules affect the bargaining power of different actors, especially men and women. This information can be used to redress power imbalances by building up the critical resources needed for both men and women to participate effectively.

This framework can also help government and development organizations to learn from and strengthen informal forms of collective action that women may engage in, and identify mechanisms for organizing gender-responsive formal types of effective collective action.

Suggested Reading

Pandolfelli, L., Meinzen-Dick, R., and S. Dohrn, eds. 2008. *Gender and Collective Action: Motivations, Effectiveness and Impact.* Special Issue of Journal of International Development 20 (1): 1-116.

Involving Men and Women for Effective Groups

SOURCE:

Pandolfelli, L., S. Dohrn and R. Meinzen-Dick. 2007. *Gender and Collective Action: Policy Implications from Recent Research.* CAPRi Policy Brief No. 5. International Food Policy Research Institute, Washington, D.C.

Collective action plays a vital role in many people's lives, particularly for income generation, risk reduction, public service provision, and the management of natural resources. While women are important users of natural resources (land, water, forests, fisheries), they are often excluded from management of those resources, and men's and women's voices are often not equally represented or valued when people act together. Understanding how men and women interact, what motivates them, and what capacities they have (or do not have) for effectively working together can result in natural resources being managed more effectively and equitably.

Collective Action with Both Men and Women in the Group

In many instances, the gender composition of groups is an important determinant of effective collective action, especially for natural resources management in two key dimensions:

1. **The ability of groups to meet their immediate purposes,** whether that purpose is the management of a natural resource or the disbursement of funds to members of a burial group.

2. **The process by which the group works to meet that purpose.** Specific measures of effectiveness might include tangible indicators such as economic returns to group members' compliance with rules, transparency, and accountability in managing funds or the incidence and severity of conflicts, as well as less tangible indicators, such as members' satisfaction with the group.

Strong common identity and interests among members make it easier for groups to establish management rules that are easy to understand and enforce. It is often easier to get all-female or all-male groups established, especially where women and men do not mingle freely. However, involving both men and women may lead to more effective groups in the long run, because they draw on their gender-based strengths. For example, in Bangladesh, women ensure community compliance with sanctuaries and fishing rules because they are the ones who decide whether to catch or not to catch fish.

Success Stories of Both Men and Women Participating in Collective Action

What are the gains when both men and women participate in collective action that aims to protect natural resources? The success stories below feature how men and women can best work together:

- ***Madhya Pradesh, India.*** Control of illicit grazing of livestock has increased by 24 percent, control of illicit felling of trees by 28 percent, and regeneration of allotted forest by 28 percent when women participate in forest protection committees.

- ***Bangladesh.*** Compliance with rules limiting fishing in protected areas is higher when both men and women collectively manage floodplain and fishery resources. Women's participation in fishery management is widely accepted by the community because much of the pressure to ensure community compliance with sanctuaries and fishing rules comes from women, who control what is cooked, discuss fish catches in group meetings, and decide to catch or not to catch fish. However, men's participation is also vital for ensuring compliance with the rules because they are better able to guard the fish sanctuaries at night when it is unsafe for women to do so.

- ***Kenya.*** Better governance practices can be seen in mixed-sex groups in the highlands of central Kenya, where women are regarded as more trustworthy with money than men. Men express more satisfaction with the way group finances are managed when women manage the money. In these groups, women frequently act as treasurer, while in all-male groups, men who act as treasurers are perceived to be more vulnerable to corruption.

However, simply adding women to a group does not automatically lead to greater group effectiveness. To actively participate, women need to be able to make management decisions and take on leadership responsibilities.

In mixed-sex groups, women frequently act as treasurers because people regard them as more trustworthy.

Recommendations

Planners need to consider how to overcome the barriers to active participation of both men and women working together in groups.

At a practical level, this means:

1. ***Assessing women's and men's motivations for joining groups.*** Since development policies and programs prefer to work with groups rather than individuals, a better understanding of women's and men's reasons for joining groups can help policymakers and practitioners assess whether their programs are hitting or missing their targets. Men and women have different capacities and motivations for joining groups. For example, men often have more land and financial resources. If financial resources are critical to the success of the joint activity, microfinance targeted at women may be a critical intervention.

2. ***Assessing the level of gender segregation in the community.*** In communities where high levels of gender segregation exist, a more effective initial intervention may be to promote women's groups and build their capacity, while sensitizing men about the benefits of women's participation.

3. ***Promoting approaches and rules of engagement that foster women's inclusion in collective action, whether through mixed or single-sex groups.*** Formal or informal rules of participation often exclude women, for example, when only the land owner or head of household can be a member. Planners need to consider the opportunity cost of women's time for engaging in collective action and approaches enabling women to actively participate. Timing of meetings, for example, can be critical if women are to attend. Furthermore, women often do not speak up in public for various reasons, so strategies to overcome this may be needed (e.g. parallel discussions).

4. ***Working with women to strengthen their technical and organizational capacities.*** Where gender segregation hinders women from participating in the public sphere, capacity building initiatives aimed at enabling them to assume leadership roles may be helpful.

In drafting measures to empower women, planners need to ensure that all women's interests within a group are represented, including the voices of poorer and less-educated women, as well as those from marginalized communities.

Women may need to be trained to enable them to assume leadership roles.

Suggested Readings

Agrawal, A., G. Yadama, R. Andrade and A. Bhattacharya. 2006. *Decentralization and Environmental Conservation: Gender Effects from Participation in Joint Forest Management.* CAPRi Working Paper No. 53. International Food Policy Research Institute: Washington, D.C.

Kariuki, G. and F. Place. 2005. *Initiatives for Rural Development Through Collective Action: The Case of Household Participation in Group Activities in the Highlands of Central Kenya.* CAPRi Working Paper No. 43. International Food Policy Research Institute: Washington, D.C.

Pandolfelli, L., R. Meinzen-Dick and S. Dohrn. 2007. *Gender and Collective Action: A Conceptual Framework for Analysis.* CAPRi Working Paper No. 64. International Food Policy Research Institute: Washington, D.C.

Sultana, P. and P. Thompson. 2006. *Gender and Local Floodplain Management Institutions: A Case Study from Bangladesh.* CAPRi Working Paper No. 57. International Food Policy Research Institute: Washington, D.C.

Community Forestry in Nepal: Women and Collective Action

Community forestry has remained Nepal's forest management strategy since its introduction in 1978. Local communities make decisions regarding the use, distribution and management of forest resources, and are organized into Community Forest User Groups (CFUGs) where each CFUG elects a set of officers composed of a chairperson, a vice-chairperson, a secretary, and a treasurer.

SOURCE:

Acharya, K. P. 2005. *Improving the Effectiveness of Collective Action: Sharing Experiences from Community Forestry in Nepal.* CAPRi Working Paper No. 54. International Food Policy Research Institute, Washington, D.C.

There are currently 14,000 CFUGs controlling approximately 1.2 million hectares, or 25 percent, of Nepal's forest area. Forest conditions have improved upon the implementation of this strategy but concerns are being raised regarding equity and the role of women.

Women's Participation in Nepal Through User Groups

There are 143,000 CFUG members, but only 24 percent of them are women. Wealthier upper-caste men tend to dominate major decisions. The interests of women and other marginalized sectors, who earn their livelihood through common resources, are seldom addressed. It is essential for women to be an active part of the CFUG, not only in the interest of equality, but also to ensure that the initiatives of the CFUGs are sustained and women are able to fulfill their roles in the community.

Several factors explain in part why women have very little participation in CFUG activities which impact decision-making. Traditionally, women are in charge of gathering produce from the forest, silviculture, forest management and other such tasks. These tasks consume most of their time and energy and limit the amount of time and effort that can be spent on active participation in CFUG activities.

Some initiatives were launched to encourage women to participate in the decision-making of CFUGs, although these initiatives had limited success. When community forestry was first introduced, the Ministry of Forest and Soil Conservation (MFSC) created a policy that women should make up 33 percent of the executive committees of CFUGs.

CFUGs composed entirely of women were also organized. Although this meant that women would monopolize the decision-making in this case, it was established that the household size

SAMARPAN Case Story: Creating Opportunities for Women

CARE Nepal, through the funding of the United States Agency for International Development (USAID), ran the Strengthening the Role of Women and Civil Society in Democracy and Governance (SAMARPAN) Program in order to create opportunities for women. SAMARPAN aimed to improve the skills of women through advocacy and to get women elected into influential positions within the CFUGs. The program provided skills training that would enable facilitators to discuss policies and procedures, champion causes and thus have significant influence on decisions made by the CFUG. These facilitators, on the other hand, would pass on the knowledge they gained to the members of their community.

SAMARPAN drove women's participation in making decisions that affect the distribution of forest resources. Moreover, the program increased interaction between civil society groups and federations. As a result, there are more public hearings and audits being held regarding finances and more funds are being allocated for marginalized communities and women's needs.

To observe the benefits of the program at a micro level, a case study was conducted of six CFUGs implementing SAMARPAN methodologies. The six groups that were chosen shared several characteristics. Inasmuch that they had at least one woman in a key position, showed interest in tracking progress, had been founded two years or more ago, were stable in terms of migration, and were composed of members from different castes and of different lifestyles.

The information obtained from committee meeting minutes, along with financial and administrative records was used to substantiate information from other sources. Dissenting and similar comments were noted down. Focused group discussions and one-on-one interviews with both members and officers were also performed.

in these CFUGs was 1.5 times smaller than the household size in any mixed-sex CFUG. In addition, the average forest area per household in these CFUGs is only 50 percent of the average forest area per household for mixed-sex CFUGs. Furthermore, decisions were made according to the interest of women from land-rich, high-caste households.

Despite these initiatives, women's roles in decision-making in mixed CFUGs are not fulfilled because very few women are elected to key positions and gain tenure in those positions.

Conclusions and Recommendations

Several observations/conclusions were arrived at, based on the experience of the CFUGs in Nepal (see SAMARPAN case study in the box above).

Women should be involved in decision-making processes. It is more beneficial to enable women to fill key positions in mixed-sex CFUGs, rather than creating a CFUG that has only women members.

An inclusive decision-making process is vital. All sectors of the community should be allowed to have a say in the decisions that are made about the appropriation and use of forest resources.

The critical mass theory versus the critical act. It is said that once the number of people considered as a minority in a population reaches 30 percent, change can take place. While there is safety in numbers, it is also important to consider the impact of the existing culture of the community and the existing hemogeny. This means that rather than just have the minority gain critical mass and instigate changes, the existing majority should also work towards improving the situation of the minority.

More women in the decision-making process means better governance. The women leaders of all six CFUGs took an active role in reviewing the appropriation of funds. In most instances, misappropriated funds were recovered and channeled towards the benefits of CFUG members.

The election of women into key positions in a CFUG remains a challenge. In two instances, women leaders resigned from their post after being elected in a key position. Reasons given were lack of experience, lack of confidence, lack of support from family, lack of time in which to perform duties, and other risks and threats inherent to the job. There was also resistance from men and the reigning majority.

Opportunities should be tied to continuous training and empowerment. It is not enough to merely put women in the position to make the decisions. It is also vital that the community works towards equity and understanding, and recognizes the role of women in the CFUG. The minority does need to be listened to, but the majority also needs to be considered.

Suggested Readings

Acharya, K. P. 2002. *Twenty Four Years of Community Forestry in Nepal.* International Forestry Review 4 (2):149-56.

Acharya, K. P. 2003. *Changing the Strategy for Community Forestry in Nepal: The Case for Active Management.* The Journal of Forest Policy 10(1): 43-50.

Acharya, K. P. 2004. *Sustainability of Supports for Community Forestry in Nepal.* Forest, Trees and Livelihoods (Formerly called International Tree Crop Journal) 13(3): 247-260.

O' Brien, P. and A. Jones. 2002. *Human Rights and Rights-Based Programming: Basic Training Manual.* Atlanta, USA: CARE.

Gender Roles in Collective Management of Aquatic Resources in Bangladesh

Floodplain wetlands are the major common natural resource in Bangladesh. Their rivers, *beels* (lakes), *baors* (oxbow lakes), *haors* (large deeply flooded depressions), and floodplains support some 260 fish species.

SOURCE:

Sultana, P. and P. Thompson. 2005. *Gender and Local Floodplain Management Institutions: A Case Study from Bangladesh.* CAPRi Working Paper No. 57. International Food Policy Research Institute, Washington, D.C.

Bangladesh wetlands also have over 2,900 local rice varieties, at least 13 species of edible wetland plants, many other plants that are used for fodder, medicine, mat making and fuel wood, shrimps and crabs used as human food, and molluscs that are used as feed for domestic ducks and in prawn culture. Wetland plants also provide natural protection against wave erosion.

About 80 percent of rural households catch fish for food or to sell. About 60 percent of animal protein consumption comes from fish, and of this, 80 percent is from freshwater fish. However, fish consumption declined between 1995-96 and 2000 by 14 percent to 11.1 kg/person/year.

This decline has been attributed to increasing the area cultivated to rice, expansion in irrigation, construction of flood control embankments, and natural siltation. Nevertheless, fisheries remain key floodplain resources, and the restoration of floodplain fisheries through community-based management promises to be a major strategy to improve and make more sustainable the livelihoods and quality of food consumed by poor people.

Gender Roles in Aquatic Resources Management

Poverty and opportunity have changed practices in fishing, the second most important occupation in the non-farm sector in Bangladesh. In the past, only the men were engaged in fishing, but extreme poverty and growth in shrimp farming have increasingly involved women in the livelihood.

Women in Bangladesh

Rural women in Bangladesh are caught between two very different domains, one determined by culture and tradition that confines their activities inside their homes and the other shaped by increased landlessness and poverty that forces them into wage employment.

The role of women in society is subsidiary to that of men. Women are primarily concerned with the household, reproduction, childcare, and family management.

Today, about 80 percent of the workforce collecting "shrimp fry" is composed of women and children. Shrimp fry refers to shrimp post-larvae captured for use in aquaculture. In inland areas, some Hindu women catch fish in the bodies of water near their houses. Women also catch fish by hand in shallow water and paddy fields, particularly in coastal areas. Much of the work in shrimp processing and fish post-harvest and storage are the women's domain. Women also make fishing gear such as nets and traps, while both women and men take care of the cleaning and mending of nets. In shrimp processing, men confine themselves to the breaking of ice slabs used in preservation, and most work in processing factories is done by women.

The rapid expansion of shrimp and prawn farming has given rise to the snail trade, a very popular business in the southwest of Bangladesh. The snail trade has provided another income source for women who sell snails to duck and prawn farmers or work as laborers paid to break the snails.

Women make fishing gear such as nets and traps.

Comparison of Different Beel Management Cases

Since the 1980s, non-government organizations (NGOs) have concerned themselves with and made impressive strides to economically empower and emancipate women. One such NGO, Banchte Shekha, working mainly with women, organized community-based fishery management in some beels in Southwest Bangladesh.

Beels are natural depressions covering large areas of land (from hundreds to thousands of hectares) that are flooded by rainwater and the tides (in coastal areas) during the five to six months of the monsoon each year.

In three such beels, the Community-Based Fisheries Management (CBFM) model was implemented to improve overall floodplain productivity. The three beels showcase management approaches that were dictated by circumstances such as social norms, culture and religion. For comparisons, these three cases are referred to as BMC-A, BMC-B and BMC-C.

For additional income, women sell snail to duck and prawn farmers or work as laborers paid to break the snails.

1. **Beel Management Committee (BMC) "A" was composed of representatives from a mixture of professions in the community, some of whom were members of primary all-female groups organized by Banchte Shekha.** Its group members are representatives of beel stakeholders concerned with adopting fish conservation measures. They save regularly, arrange income generating activities, and have access to credit. The BMC is responsible for coordination with other stakeholder groups and organizations. It makes decisions through participatory discussion.

   BMC "A" has succeeded in implementing rules and enforcing penalties to protect beels' resources. Women and men guard the beel with the support of local leaders. BMC "A" has successfully appealed to the local council chairman to get the lease to a canal without any fees imposed for making it into a fish sanctuary. BMC "A" has a small community center located next to the beel, the land on which it stands having been donated by one of its members.

   In 2002, representatives from BMC "A" and stakeholders organized an integrated floodplain management committee that works as an apex body to coordinate the activities of all local institutions. The 15-member committee includes six women from the BMC and the farmer field school.

2. **BMC "B" is similar to BMC "A" but only women are members, and they have taken the lead in fishery conservation and management in the beel.** The women first discussed with the men the need to improve fishery management by forming an institution. However, the men were not interested in this proposition. The women then sought the help of respected men from the community to constitute an advisory committee, since they saw that in a male-dominated society, they could more easily persuade men to follow BMC rules with the help of an advisory committee.

   The women also enlisted the advisory committee's help to talk to violators of rules in using the beel's resources, including those who just wanted to test the authority of the all-women group. Moreover, the committee also negotiated with local government to support water retention and fish sanctuaries, and helped them establish linkages with local experts and officials.

   BMC "B" has a legal identity, group savings, access to credit for income generation activities for women, and a fund for the BMC. Its chairperson has been chosen to head a women's group that fights against repression of women and to act as secretary of a cluster committee of five connected beels including their own beel and Beel "A."

3. **BMC "C" is all-male, and was established in an area that previously had no local institutions for resource management or experience in any development work.** The community is comprised mostly of Muslims, and women's voices are not heard. NGOs are not allowed to work freely with the women in the area. When they started the CBFM project, Banchte Shekha faced problems forming women's groups. The men did not allow women to take part in the BMC and no women were included in any committee, nor were they allowed to take part in any discussions.

   BMC "C" has always had all-male decision-making committees. When Banchte Shekha refused to lend money to BMC "C" to fund its project, it finally allowed women to form a few groups. Women are now receiving credit, something the men have gotten used to. Except for a brief time, women never became part of the committee and did not have a role in decision-making.

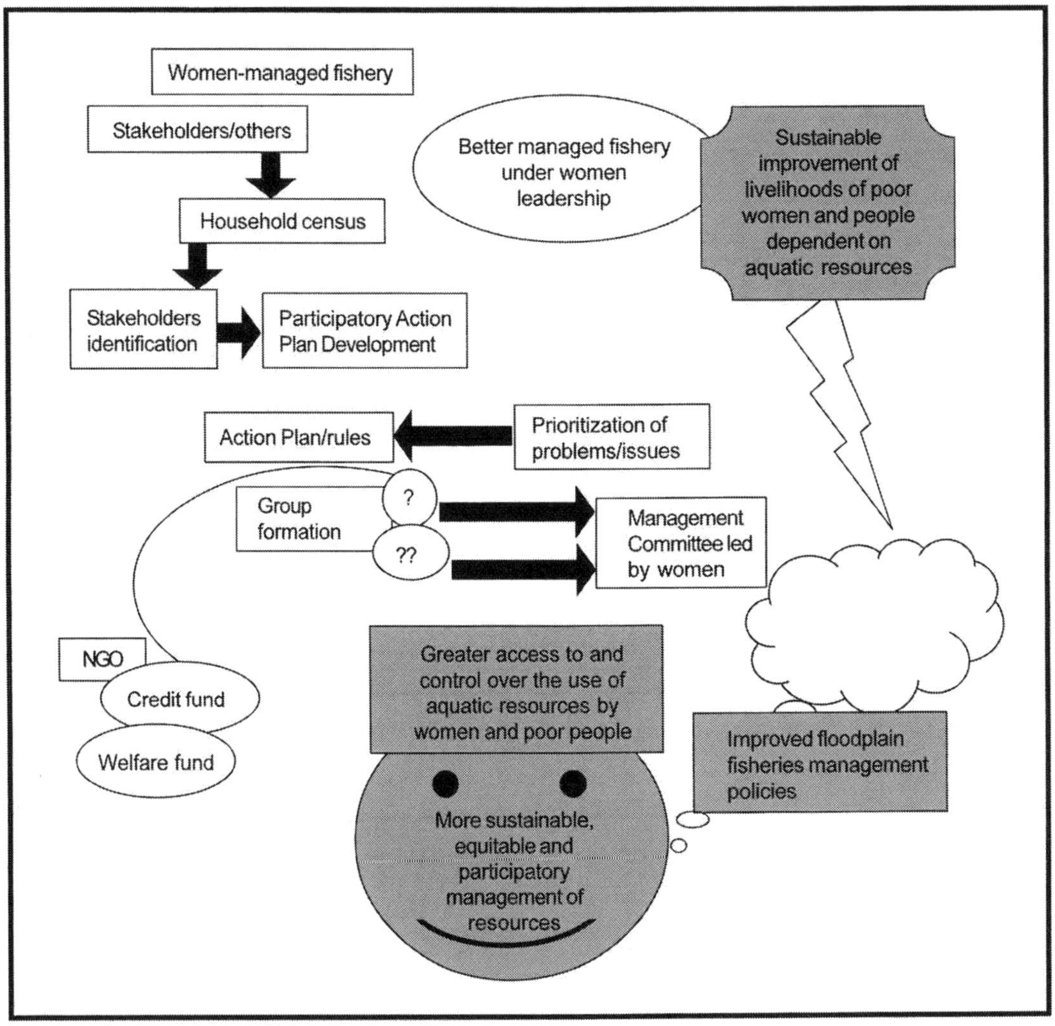

Figure 1. CBFM Approach Adopted in Maliate Beel.

Impacts of CBFM on Fisheries and Livelihoods

In all three communities, both men and women saw gains and improvements in the health of the fisheries resource, even where women did not have a role in decision-making. The BMCs reported high acceptance and compliance with the limits they set on resource use, although compliance was higher in sites where women had a role in decision-making and men also were active decision-makers (BMC "A"), or where men advised and endorsed decisions (BMC "B"), than in the site where women played no role (BMC "C"). In each case, the number of conflicts decreased over time and the BMCs have been recognized, with their plans accepted by the communities which now follow rules set by the BMCs.

Collective action in beel management in Bangladesh has given women the ability to judiciously manage resources such as choosing the right size of fish to harvest.

BMC "B" has been more adaptable, slowly introducing and adjusting rules through the years. For example, if the members see small-sized fish or new species in the closed season, they prolong the closed period through motivational work with the community. They tell the community that the fish price will be higher after a month when fish size increases.

Involving women in decision-making is an important policy direction that has great impact in natural resource management.

The ability to establish community-based organizations where women play an active or leading role is influenced by local community norms and culture and the acceptance of women's involvement in economic activities outside the home. In the study area, this is greater among Hindu communities than in Muslim-dominated areas, where women do not normally have much, if any, say in public affairs. This is also affected by education levels — in beel "C," few women have attended school whereas the average education level of women and men in the other two beels is almost equal. There appears to be a compounding effect of education, social norms, economic activity, and mobility which constrain or permit women to have equal roles with men for natural resource management.

The status and recognition given to women by the local community and leaders reflected this experience and was highlighted by the women themselves. In BMC "A" and "B," women reported increasing recognition of their voices and willingness to listen to their opinions, which in turn led to increased willingness of the women to join local institutions and greater acceptance by men of their decision to do so.

By comparison, in BMC "C," women have not been given any place in the BMC by the men, who do not recognize the fact that some women do actually depend on using non-fish aquatic resources. Consequently, women have no power or role in decision-making in BMC "C," and although they now recognize the value to the community of fishery-related rules, the BMC has not addressed many of their concerns.

Conclusion

It is evident that facilitation by an NGO that focuses solely on women's development is not sufficient to ensure their participation in decision-making and community institutions, because their participation is also affected by cultural norms and the extent to which women and men directly use the resources. Hence, it is important for those planning to support and facilitate community-based management of natural resources to follow processes that include women and help both sexes to recognize the uses, opinions, and relevance of those resources.

Where local social norms and culture limit the public voice of women, they cannot be expected to take a lead in resource management and will therefore need a long-term plan for developing their capacity and changing men's opinions. However, it is clear that at least in the context of Bangladesh floodplains, women-led community organizations can improve fishery management. Involvement in fishery management appears to be associated with greater community-wide acceptance of management rules and reduced conflict. Policy should aim for community-wide participation, including an active role for women.

Suggested Readings

Ali, M.Y. 1997. *Fish, Water and People*. Dhaka: University Press Ltd.

Sultana, P., P. Thompson, H. Ahmed and A. Hossain. 2005. *Better Options for Integrated Floodplain Management in Bangladesh: Uptake Promotion Piloting of IFM Options: Narail Site.* Dhaka, Bangladesh: Centre for Natural Resource Studies and WorldFish Center.

Thompson, P., P. Sultana and N. Islam. 2003. *Lessons from Community-Based Management of Floodplain Fisheries in Bangladesh.* Journal of Environmental Management 69(3): 307-321.

Sourcebook on **Resources, Rights, and Cooperation**, produced by the CGIAR Program on Collective Action and Property Rights (CAPRi)

Empowering Women Through Land Rights

Command over property is arguably the most severe form of inequality between men and women today. Despite their prevalence, gender differences in rights to land are some of the most poorly documented dimensions of gender inequality and figure in few statistical systems.

SOURCE:

Crowley, E. 2001. *Empowering Women to Achieve Food Security.* 2020 Focus Brief 11, International Food Policy Research Institute, Washington, D.C.

Land rights increase women's power in social, economic, and political relationships. Rural women claim that secure land rights increase their social and political status, and improve their sense of self-esteem, confidence, security, and dignity. These rights can also increase women's bargaining power in their families and participation in public dialogue and local political institutions.

Customary vs. Formal Systems

In considering land rights, one must determine which system can provide women with greater and more secure access to land: customary tenure systems or formal statutory systems. The former are locally enforceable and have adapted over time, while the latter are legally or morally bound by universal conventions.

Customary systems are based on membership in lineage, community or household. These systems are most effective when land is relatively abundant and most land users know one another and have regular and direct contact. Formal systems are most effective where land values are high and land transactions among strangers are frequent. These transactions require transparency and public records to reduce informational asymmetries.

In formal tenure systems, unwritten rights often coexist with the limited number of rights that are actually recorded in registries or titles. On the other hand, the codification of customary rights has often strengthened and concentrated land rights of individual, senior, male household heads over other interests, resulting in only a small percentage of the population, and strikingly few women, holding land certificates or titles in developing countries.

Securing Rights for Women

There are essentially two ways to enhance women's land rights. One is to protect or increase the security of existing rights. The other is to create new rights or increase the range of rights over which women have control. The customary tenure systems support or secure existing land rights, while formal systems create new rights.

A woman's rights are secure when she can use or manage land in a predictable fashion for a defined length of time. Customary of tenure consists of three dimensions: definition, independent control, and enforcement.

In defining security of tenure, policy can be developed towards the clarification and registration of women's customary use rights. Tenure security for women can be improved by establishing contracts protecting widows and children from eviction or by developing leasehold contracts documenting the duration and scope of women's land rights to permit planning and managing of land and income use.

For most women, land rights are defined by their relationships to men: fathers, husbands, or brothers. The difficulty in distinguishing rights of different household members also contributes to the (sometimes false) assumption that women in landed households share these rights and that women's specific land rights need only be defined when they head households. However, in most cases, unlike men, women cannot liquidate, trade, or retain derived land rights when the male link is lost.

Enforcement of tenure security depends upon women's capacity to lobby for and promote their interests. It also relies upon whether the formal and customary authorities vested with the power to protect women's land rights share these interests and have a strong imperative to uphold them.

For improvements in tenure security to become operational, they need to be socially acceptable to formal and informal governing bodies with different norms and values. Policymakers need to identify partners capable of influencing the attitudes, priorities, and incentives that govern political and group decisions. Proposals for improved tenure security also need to be administratively viable.

The challenge then for government planners is to build a land administration capacity capable of more efficient land transfers than customary inheritance systems. Another challenge is to develop a robust, affordable and accessible dispute resolution procedure.

Creating Rights for Women

Formal tenure systems can be better suited than customary ones to rapidly create new land rights for women. However, two major formal mechanisms — land reform and land markets — have not resulted in positive change. Land reforms associated with new political regimes and government- or project-based land redistribution have induced significant changes in landholding patterns, poverty, and inequality while adversely affecting women almost universally. To improve women's property rights, land reform policy must focus on favoring women in redistribution through stable and capable institutions.

Changing the policies that regulate land markets is a second formal mechanism for creating new rights. However, in practice, only wealthier women and women's groups have the income to buy land through formal markets. Nepotism, preferential treatment, and complex, expensive procedural requirements restrict entry to land markets. Policy should focus on reducing the administrative transaction costs and barriers faced by poorer buyers and women.

To create the convergence of values that support changes in tenure systems, a shift in public attitudes is needed. Coalition building and negotiated reform can help to induce positive change. Cross-sectoral alliances, unions and lobby groups can build a shared awareness of common positions among women, encouraging joint action.

Integrated Action for Enhancing Women's Land Rights

Enhancing women's land rights requires that they become a political priority and a legal possibility; it also requires administrative viability, social acceptability, and moral legitimacy. Complementary policies must address women's limitations in exercising and enjoying their land rights.

Even with assured land rights, investments in property require access to financial markets and information, extension, and other services. Policymakers should be aware of the complexity of tenure systems and how legal principles associated with land rights can be subverted when put into practice.

To bring about substantial progress, integrated joint action is required to meet the following objectives:

- Women must know what rights to land they can claim and how to claim those rights.
- Formal and customary land administration officials and services must develop the administrative capacity and discipline to process records and claims in support of women.

- The general public must recognize and accept that women's rights to land are ultimately in the interests of a broader populace, and create the popular support needed for political change.

Leveraging Power of Influence

Women and like-minded citizens who have formed viable civil society groups or cooperatives have, on a small scale, not only succeeded in purchasing land, but have also increased their capacity to leverage relationships of power and manipulate public opinion and legal contexts.

Suggested Readings

Agarwal, B. 1994. *A Field of One's Own: Gender and Land Rights in South Asia.* Cambridge University Press.

Gray, L. and M. Kevane. 1999. *Diminished Access, Diverted Exclusion: Women and Land Tenure in Sub-Saharan Africa.* African Studies Review 42(2): 15-39.

Chapter 8

Strengthening Property Rights and Collective Action

Strengthening Property Rights for the Poor

Although many of the poor in the developing world are landless, most of the rural poor have some access to land.

The landed poor are a heterogeneous group who hold rights to their landed assets in diverse and complicated ways.

SOURCE:

Bruce, J.W. 2004. *Strengthening Property Rights for the Poor.* 2020 Vision for Food, Agriculture and the Environment. Focus Brief 11 Collective Action and Property Rights for Sustainable Development. International Food Policy Research Institute, Washington, D.C.

- They may hold the land in tenancy passed from father to son, in which landlordism is a class, caste, or ethnic phenomenon.
- They may be farmers under a system of leaseholds from the state or a collective and may be deprived of any long-term interest in their improvements on the land, even the homes they have built.
- They may be land reform beneficiaries whose landholdings, because of neglect, paternalism, or political change, have never been legally regularized.

- They may be users of forest lands that their families have occupied and cultivated for generations but who are barred from acquiring secure property rights because of its classification as a forest.
- They may hold land under customary tenure systems unrecognized by the state, with no legal basis for resisting the claim of the person with a title document granted by the national government.
- They may be women in societies where land passes from generation to generation in the male line and only have access to land as daughters and wives.

Strengthening the Property Rights of the Poor

The "landed poor" remain poor not simply because their holdings are small, but also because their land rights are weak and insecure. Strengthening the property rights of the poor is a complex project but the following guidelines can help direct efforts to strengthen these rights.

Trust land users with stronger property rights. Owners, responding to the incentives implicit in ownership, produce better land management than top-down schemes, which soon sour and often become corrupt.

Legislate for stronger property rights. The state must provide a robust legal framework of rights for land users. An adequate legal framework is a first and essential step.

Improved property rights means different things in different contexts. It may mean co-ownership of land for husbands and wives; empowerment of tenants to buy out their landlords; provision of unconditional, inheritable land rights to settlers; or state recognition that customary, community-based rights are equal with land rights created by national statute.

Adopt local definitions of tenure security when appropriate. Adequate tenure security does not necessarily mean ownership in the Western sense. Many customary or community-based tenure systems can provide adequate tenure security.

Always ask, "security of tenure for whom?" Consider which beneficiary is most likely to use the land effectively. Titles are commonly awarded to male household heads, but others may be more likely to undertake investments in the land.

Protect common property rights. The poor often depend disproportionately on common property resources. Tenure security is not only about individual property rights, but also about legitimate common property and state rights in some categories of land.

Provide for adequate proof of property rights. In urban and peri-urban contexts, and where rural land is highly valued, adequate proof may entail formal surveys, titling, and registration of holdings. Elsewhere, where land rights are of lower value and transferred largely within the community, adequate proof may involve demarcating community boundaries and empowering local communities to maintain simple but reliable records of individual and family landholdings and transactions.

- ***Educate people about their rights in land.*** Rights not understood will not be defended, and rights must be defended every day or they will be lost to the powerful.

- ***Establish adequate dispute settlement mechanisms.*** Rights that cannot be defended against challenges provide no incentives and no security.

Institutionalizing Property Rights Reforms

Be politically astute. Each group of stakeholders has its own interests and objectives. You may have to facilitate compromises among divergent interests and objectives to achieve reform.

Embody new property rights in law. Ensure that new rights have a legal basis. When the political economies of nations change, legal reform can be forgotten and reforms processed administratively, without firm legal basis.

Exploit all possibilities for legal change. All avenues, from national legislation to judicial reform through court decision to community-based reform of customs, can be effective on the ground.

Ensure capacity and finance for sustained implementation. Strengthened property rights systems are costly — they often require substantial state or community investment in systems for survey, adjudication, and titling, for registration of transactions and inheritances, and for dispute resolution. Many property rights reforms have stalled for lack of financial support.

Involve non-government organizations in the reform process. Non-state organizations of the marginalized can voice the demands of the poor and press for reforms. Such organizations have skills in areas like rights education and dispute settlement that are vital to implementing reforms.

Exercise caution in replacing inadequate property rights systems. If an existing system of property rights is culturally embedded but is judged inadequate, be careful in replacing it. Attempts at reform of customary systems that do not succeed in changing behavior can create confusion and conflict between claims based on custom and others based on national law.

Aim for equitable strengthening of property rights. The rights of all stakeholders should be considered together. Reforms to strengthen the property rights of one individual or group, especially those under customary tenure, should not inadvertently weaken the property rights of others.

Look out for unintended consequences. Even well-conceived reforms can be hijacked by the powerful. A classic case is the appropriation of common areas by the powerful through land titles, depriving the poor of a resource upon which they rely.

Recognize that new property rights alone are insufficient. Property rights reforms, particularly those seeking to strengthen the marketability of land rights, may be unable to achieve their goal when credit markets are badly distorted and the credit supply system is in its infancy.

Increasing the land rights of the poor is a complex project, and it must recognize the diversity and complexity of land ownership, especially in customary systems. Any moves to enhance security of tenure for the poor must be sensitive to specific circumstances that characterize each case, the existing legal conditions, the strength or weakness of available financial and property registration systems, the needs of each group of stakeholders, and the possibilities of unintended consequences. Common property rights must also be protected.

Representation of Vulnerable Groups

Vulnerable groups are often unrepresented in local implementation authorities, and mechanisms must be built into the implementation process to ensure their participation in reform processes and benefits.

Suggested Readings

Ghimire, K.B. (ed). 2003. *Whose Land? Civil Society Perspectives on Land Reform and Rural Poverty Reduction.* Rome: Popular Coalition to Reduce Hunger and Poverty, International Fund for Agricultural Development, and United Nations Research Institute for Social Development.

Toulmin, C. and J. Quan (eds). 2000. *Evolving Land Rights, Policy, and Tenure in Africa.* London: Department for International Development, Natural Resources Institute, and International Institute for Environment and Development.

World Bank. 2003. *Land Policies for Growth and Poverty Reduction*: *Policy Research Report.* Washington, D.C.: World Bank.

Commons, Customary Law and Formalization of Land Tenure

SOURCE:

Alden Wily, L. 2005. *The Commons and Customary Law in Modern Times: Rethinking the Orthodoxies. In: Land Rights for African Development: From Knowledge to Action.* CAPRi Policy Briefs. International Food Policy Research Institute, Washington, D.C. and UNDP, and International Land Coalition.

Common properties refers to those lands which by tradition rural communities own collectively. They usually embrace lands like forests, woodlands, pastures and rangelands, which are not logically owned on an individual or family basis. And yet it is because these lands are collectively owned which has made them so vulnerable to losses. Expansion of towns and cultivation, including by community members, have been sources of the reduced area of commons now available to communities. However, the greatest losses have incurred by the hand of governments. Because they tend to follow imported European systems of land ownership which are individual-centric, it has been easy for governments to regard communal lands as unowned lands, or 'public lands', and even to be made the private property of the state. The high value of communal lands has been the main incentive. Many commons have accordingly been designated as forest and wildlife reserves or sold or leased by governments to private sector interests for mining, logging, ranching, or agribusiness exports. This represents mass dispossession. However, more than land rights have been lost; communities have also lost their rightful share in the revenues which mining, logging, ranching or farming by government or investors earn from their traditional lands. Generally, the loss of commons is most serious for poorer families. Often their share in the commons is their only real potential capital asset. This is quite aside from the many ways in which commons support the daily livelihood of up to three billion rural families around the world.

It is fair to say that governments, not communities have so far reaped the enormous benefits of the commons in rural economies this last century.

More worrying for reformers and communities, this often remains the case today, even after two decades of land reforms in Latin America and Sub-Saharan Africa especially. Even where wars have been fought over the massive loss of commons (such as in Sudan between 1984 and 2002) governments often find it convenient to persist in treating the commons as unowned, and to use or allocate these at will. Many such areas in Africa are today vulnerable to leasing to Middle Eastern governments and enterprises seeking land to grow food or agrifuels for their own home economies.

Recording of Common Property

Clarifying and entrenching the rightful tenure of commons is needed to enable customary owners to hold on to and reap benefits from these estates, for immediate or future gain. This requires adjudication and recording. Until today, individually held properties have been the focus of registration. These are the wrong target. The properties that are by far and away most at risk of involuntary loss are not family farms or house plots, but the commons. This is not to say insecurity of tenure does not affect individual estates in the customary sector, but that the risk of wrongful appropriation and failure to pay compensation when acquired for public purpose is much higher for the commons. Generally, when a farm or house is taken, the owner at least gets some small recompense.

A second and rising pool of insecurity that also needs prioritization is at the rural-urban interface where farms and commons are often forcibly converted into building plots, often to the manipulated benefit of parties other than the customary owners.

State Recognition of Customary Rights in Africa

Statutory recognition of all customary land interests as private property rights needs purposive acceleration. Only a handful of African states have achieved this.

The purpose of titling itself is long overdue for review. The conventional justification has been that titling is necessary to enable land owners to get bank loans on this basis. While collateralization can be important for better-off farmers, the outstanding reason for certification of holdings today must be simply to enhance tenure security. This is especially so where national constitutions or land laws do not guarantee customary land holding, even when it is unregistered. In Africa, Tanzania and Uganda, both give such guarantees, which have the effect of making all customary properties including those owned collectively less vulnerable. It also makes case-by-case certification and registration of those properties less urgent.

However, in most cases it is important to double-lock customary properties against wrongful dispossession, through certification procedures.

What Is Required

In pursuit of registration, clearer understanding is needed in order to establish the relationship between statutory and customary law (not an either/or). Statutory support, i.e. parliamentary enacted laws, is essential to recognize, sustain, and uphold customary rights, irrespective of whether or not these are held by individuals, families, clans, groups, or whole communities.

Nor should it be assumed that the codification of customary law is prerequisite to formal recognition or registration of customary land interests: it is not the rules themselves that need modern law support, as these do and should continue to alter with changing circumstances such as those already widely experienced over the last century. Rather, it is the exercise of customary land administration which needs support, the founding principle that a customary system is logically exercised by and at the community level. This nature of indigenous or customary regimes is in tune with modern demands for devolved and democratic land governance and upon which living customary owners can slowly build more modern 'customary practice'.

An equally important requirement is to make real the message that formalization procedures must be simple and cheap to enable mass uptake and sustained use. Reversion into expensive and remote systems too often still occurs in new administration programs. While desirable in principle, registration based upon a cadastral title system may never be applicable or sustainable at scale. It is also unnecessary for the vast majority of small estates like rural farms and houses. Legal recognition of detailed boundary description, lodged in community land registers, is usually sufficient.

Ten Steps to Implementation

In a growing number of countries it has become important to assist rural communities to define their overall community land areas or 'domains' as the first step to securing common properties found within. The steps listed below are derived from practical experiences in community-based land securitisation carried out by the author in Tanzania, Afghanistan and Sudan. Similar work is being undertaken by others in some West African states, building upon rural land plans. The following ten-step model may serve as an example:

> **Empowering Community Members**
>
> Community members determine beforehand how they want the land council constituted, with what proportion of elected and traditional leadership and the procedures through which land councilors will be accountable to itself and how decisions will be implemented.

1. A technical facilitator calls representatives of rural communities to a meeting to decide the basis upon which they will identify and operate their customary domains, with a village basis generally preferred.

2. A representative boundary committee from each community is formed. Each works with neighboring committees to agree the exact location of their shared boundary. This is done by walking every step of the boundary and recording the description agreed by the two committees. Expert facilitation should be available to promote compromises. A detailed boundary description should be prepared and approved before full community meetings.

3. Where the customary domain has been routinely used by outsiders (e.g. pastoralists) who now hold acknowledged customary access rights to products or areas these users need to be consulted. It is generally the case that their rights are clarified as access rights, to distinguish these from the local ownership rights held by residential communities. Alternatively other co-owning agreements can be reached.

4. Each community is assisted to form a community land council (with seasonal user representation as appropriate) to serve both as trustee owner of the land itself within the defined domain, and to serve as the local land authority over the domain, responsible for zoning, regulation of access and land use, procedures for transfer and the establishment in due course of simple registers of ownership and transaction of properties within the domain.

5. Policy and legal support is secured, ideally founded upon at least a reasonable degree of trial implementation in the field, to ensure that legal constructs and procedures will be workable and easily replicated and sustained. New legislation may outline how customary land authorities operate and provide for registration of community domains and registers of common properties within them, and, in due course, individual properties on a demand basis.

6. Communal domain registers are established at local government level and simple procedures for this disseminated. Final registration of communal domains takes place only after boundaries have been finally agreed and the community land council is up and running. Registration of the council as the lawful local land authority is part of the process.

7. Councils use simple land-use planning to divide domains into zones — for example, current farming zones, potential investment zones, community pastures, and protected areas — and they devise and put into effect any needed regulations for each zone.

8. Community lands councils have to be assisted to identify and claim wrongly appropriated customary land with the help of law provided in the constitution. Where such lands are in the possession of outsiders, rigorous financial accountability has to be insisted upon.

9. Identification and registration of common properties must be encouraged. This ensures protection from wrongful occupation or appropriation by government agencies, local elites, and corrupt leaders.

10. Reworked and modernized community-based regimes are put in place for resolving disputes between and within communities, with appeal to higher levels.

A process that includes these ten steps may restore and develop the right and practice of communities to create and control their own tenure norms. It begins by inducing the critical mass of popular ownership that mobilizes the effort and sustains implementation. Conflicting land interests are unpacked by the parties themselves, making it more likely that compromises and agreements will be upheld. The process clarifies customary rights and access rights. It also uses existing community organization upon which to build modern, community-based land administration while providing relevant local institutions for their modern administration.

Suggested Readings

Fitzpatrick, D. 2005. *Best Practice Options for the Legal Recognition of Customary Tenure.* Development and Change 36(3):449-475.

Alden Wily, L. 2003. Governance and Land Relations: A Review of Decentralisation of Land Administration and Management in Africa. IIED, London.

Alden Wily, L. 2006. Land Rights Reform and Governance in Africa. How to Make it Work in the 21st Century. UNDP, New York.

Alden Wily, L. 2005. Guidelines for Customary Land Securitization in Central Sudan, USAID/ USDA, Khartoum.

Innovations in Land Tenure Reform and Administration in Africa

Land and the institutions that govern its ownership and use greatly affect economic growth and poverty reduction. Lack of access to land and inefficient or corrupt systems of land administration have a negative impact on a country's investment climate. Well-functioning land institutions and markets improve it, reducing the cost of accessing credit for entrepreneurs and contributing to the development of financial systems.

SOURCE:

Augustinus, C. and K. Deininger. 2006. *Innovations in Land Tenure, Reform and Administration in Africa.* In: *Land Rights for African Development: From Knowledge to Action.* CAPRi Policy Brief. International Food Policy Research Institute, UNDP, and International Land Coalition.

Access to even small plots of land to grow crops can also greatly improve food security and quality. Broad-based land access can provide a basic social safety net at a cost far below alternative government programs, allowing governments to spend scarce resources on productive infrastructure. Policies that foster lease markets for land can also contribute to the emergence of a vibrant nonfarm economy.

Increased demand for land may lead to public investment in infrastructure and roads and increased land values. When well-functioning mechanisms to tax land are added, this can contribute significantly to local government revenues and provide resources needed to match decentralization of responsibilities for service

> Insufficient innovative tools exist to deliver affordable security of tenure and property rights at scale for most of Africa's populations.

delivery. Improving land administration may also contribute to broader public service reform and provide a basis for wider reforms.

Innovations and Options Needed

Conventional land administration systems in sub-Saharan Africa do not fit customary structures of group and family rights, do not function adequately or solve land conflicts, and are not useful to most people. Registering a title can take between six months and 10 years, records are poorly kept, most people do not have title deeds, and millions of titles await registration. Furthermore, most systems are centralized, inaccessible, too expensive, not transparent, and do not protect women's land rights sufficiently. Transforming such systems is a time-consuming and complex task which normally entails the reform of a number of separate agencies, alterations in power and patronage, and extensive civil society debate at national and local levels.

Innovations in land reform and land administration that are adapted to current conditions are being attempted in some countries in sub-Saharan Africa. However, insufficient innovative tools exist to deliver affordable security of tenure and property rights at scale for most of Africa's populations. New tools need to be developed, but these are not simple, easy to produce, or easily adapted to the diverse needs of various countries.

No single tenure option can solve all problems. Policy on land tenure and property rights can best reconcile social and economic needs by encouraging a diverse range of options, adapting and expanding existing systems when possible, and introducing new ones selectively.

Another approach seeks to eliminate gender-based discrimination regarding land, housing, and property rights. This is particularly needed because individualization of land tenure, land-market pressure, and other factors have eroded customary laws and practices that used to protect women. The HIV/AIDS crisis has worsened the situation, and land-grabbing and discriminatory practices have increased evictions of women by their in-laws or husbands. Secure tenure would be a mitigating factor for these women, and would assist those widowed by conflict who meet legal or customary discrimination against widows inheriting land.

Though some African countries have passed land legislation that is advanced in many respects, they are struggling to modernize and equip their land institutions to deal with the demands of implementation. In doing so, they often try to copy unaffordable and sometimes inappropriate approaches (such as high-precision surveying) from other parts of the world that cannot be scaled up quickly.

To reach the Millennium Development Goals (MDG) whose achievement is mediated by security of tenure, more focus is needed on implementation of policy at scale, along with cost-effective, easy-to-use and pro-poor land tools.

> **Millennium Development Goals**
>
> MDGs are a set of eight goals that the global community pledged to achieve by 2015. The targets were established at the world summits of the 1990s. Poor countries have pledged to govern better, and invest in their people through health care and education. Rich countries have pledged to support them, through aid, debt relief, and fairer trade.
>
> - Goal 1: Eradicate extreme poverty and hunger
> - Goal 2: Achieve universal primary education
> - Goal 3: Promote gender equality and empower women
> - Goal 4: Reduce child mortality
> - Goal 5: Improve maternal health
> - Goal 6: Combat HIV/AIDS, malaria and other diseases
> - Goal 7: Ensure environmental sustainability
> - Goal 8: Develop a global partnership for development

One example is computerization of land records in some states in India, which the evidence suggests, can significantly reduce the scope of the extracting of bribes by officials and increase their accountability. The computerization also linked formerly disparate institutions, effected improvements in tenure security, and increased the government's revenue collection.

Affordable Pro-Poor Tools for Advancing Security of Tenure and Property Rights

Affordable pro-poor tools that are needed include the following:

- NGO enumeration information that becomes first adjudication evidence for land rights for slum upgrading and post-disaster housing delivery;
- gender-friendly approaches to adjudication;
- land administration appropriate for post-conflict societies;
- just-deceased estates administration, especially for HIV/AIDS areas and to protect women's land rights;
- expropriation and compensation for the management of urban growth and improved agricultural production;
- a regulatory framework for the private sector that takes into account poverty issues;
- capacity building programs for in-country sustainability of land administration systems, particularly for the poor;
- an affordable geophysical database and indicators for Africa, possibly using NASA's information;
- Land/Geographic Information System (LIS/GIS) spatial units as framework data;
- high accuracy, off-the-shelf global positioning system units for non-professionals;
- robust indicators or benchmarks to measure tenure security for the delivery of Millennium Development Goals; and
- non-titled land rights that can be upgraded over time.

Conclusion

What is needed is a global assessment to establish which tools exist, the options for scaling them up and widely disseminating them, and estimates of their cost-effectiveness. New tools also need to be developed. This agenda will take many years, significant funding, and a comprehensive global framework.

Suggested Readings

Augustinus, C. 2005. *Innovations in Africa: Pro-Poor Land Approaches.* Paper presented at the African Ministers Conference on Housing and Urban Development (AMCHUD), 31 January - 3 February, 2005, Durban, South Africa (unpublished).

Food and Agriculture Organisation of the United Nations. 2005. *Access to Rural Land and Land Administration after Violent Conflict.* FAO Land Tenure Studies, Rome.

Fourie, C. 2001. *Land and Property Registration at the Cross Roads: A Time for More Relevant Approaches.* Habitat Debate 7(3):16. Additional information can be found at: http://www.gltn.net/.

Sourcebook on **Resources, Rights, and Cooperation**, produced by the CGIAR Program on Collective Action and Property Rights (CAPRi)

Securing Dryland Resources for Multiple Users

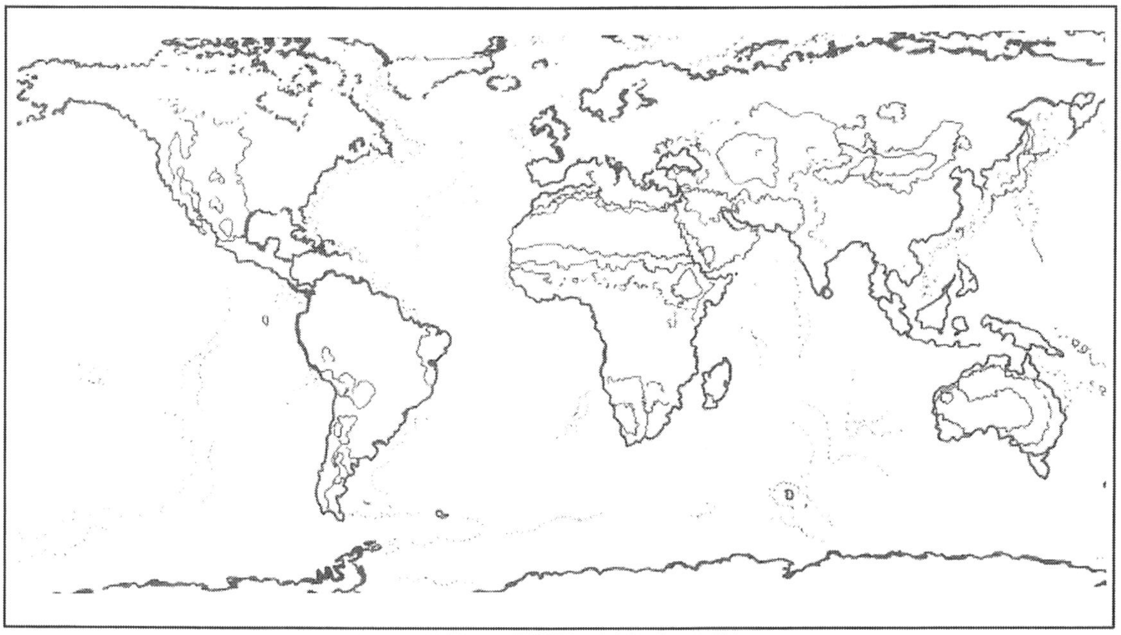

SOURCE:

Mwangi, E. and S. Dohrn. 2006. *Biting the Bullet: How to Secure Access to Drylands Resources for Multiple Users,* CAPRi Working Paper No. 47, International Food Policy Research Institute, Washington, D.C.

Close to one billion people worldwide depend directly on drylands for their livelihoods. Because of their variable and erratic climate and political and economic marginalization, drylands have some of the highest rates of poverty, including the world's poorest women and men. Users of dryland resources — including pastoralists, sedentary farmers, hunter-gatherers, and refugees — need to be assured of appropriate and effective access to sustain their diverse livelihood strategies in their risky shared environments.

Pastoral and sedentary production systems that coexist in drylands very often use common property arrangements to manage their access to and use of natural resources. However, despite their history of complementary interactions, pastoralists and sedentary farmers increasingly face conflicting claims over land and other natural resources. Past policy interventions and existing regulatory frameworks have not offered lasting solutions to problems relating to land tenure and resource access for multiple and differentiated drylands resource users. These users require flexibility of access; they adopt opportunistic strategies to cope with the uncertain conditions in which they operate.

> Instead of the allocation of rights, tenure regulation needs to center on rules and mechanisms for regulating access and use among multiple interests.

It now seems to be recognized that drylands resources need to be secured for their users against some form of threat, often external. So too is the idea that some legal solution premised on local customary rules may be appropriate and effective in protecting group rights. These realizations are informed by earlier top-down, state-led approaches of individualization or nationalization that privileged some customary users over others, undermined authority systems regulating resource access, and opened up opportunities for non-customary users and immigrants to appropriate resources.

However, in seeking legal solutions for recognition and strengthening of group rights, there is increasing empirical evidence that threats to tenure security may also originate from within the groups themselves, with women's rights being particularly vulnerable. The question thus remains of how resources are to be allocated, accessed, used, and managed within groups. Another concern is not only how tenure security can be enhanced for multiple resource users, but also how it can be strengthened for multiple uses of drylands resources.

A Focus on Process

Among a range of innovations tackling these problems are legal reforms that seek to adapt customary and local systems to wider statutory obligations. However, key concerns are the oversimplifying of complexities and the exclusion of secondary and temporary users in rural areas. In such multi-use environments, process—rather than content—should be the focus of policymakers. Instead of the allocation of rights, tenure regulation needs to center on rules and mechanisms for regulating access and use among multiple interests.

Attempts to secure access for multiple users in variable drylands environments should identify frameworks for negotiated conflict resolution. This requires crafting rules from the ground up, in addition to a more generalized or generic identification of rights. Elite capture and exclusion of women and young people continue to pose significant challenges in decentralized processes.

Local actors are the competent authorities to determine the forms of insecurities that exist and levels of appropriate action that might alleviate them. To secure access options to drylands resources and opportunities for differentiated local actors, negotiated processes must have meaning in local settings, and elite influence must be strategically confronted. Efforts to reform rights systems may yield little benefit if pushed too soon, too quickly, or without appropriate synchronization between different components of institutional change. These efforts will be more effective if timing matches local priorities and schedules, allowing continuous learning and integration between changes in policy, regulation, and practice.

Negotiating Access Rights

Attempts to support tenure policies must try to reconcile legitimacy, legality, and practice of tenure rights. To create legitimacy on the ground requires promotion and support for dialogue and negotiation among resource users. This works best within a legal framework that centers on process, leaving details to local people and enabling them to adapt their local systems to specific external and internal threats to tenure security. Law thus sets the principles and procedures of accountable, transparent, and inclusive negotiation and dialogue. Even then, the state would need to function as a capable mediator and enforcer.

Multiple Users and Uses of Resources

Many resources, including private property and the commons, are used by different people for a wide variety of purposes. For example:

- The same piece of land may be used for growing different crops, grazing, and gathering.
- The same water source can be used for irrigating, washing, taking care of the farm animals, or income-generating activities.
- The same area of forest can be used to produce timber, fruits, leaves, firewood, shade, or other commodities.

Most analyses of the efficiency of natural resource management have failed to recognize that resources often have multiple uses, and that sub-groups of users often can be characterized by their use patterns. As resources become increasingly scarce, strategies need to be devised that will minimize conflicts for resources among different categories of users and put forth enduring solutions that respond to the interests of multiple users, particularly those whose livelihoods depend on the utilization of natural resources.

The process may also benefit from an explicit description of what constitutes security of access for different categories of users or different resources, at different times and scales. Seeking answers to the fundamental question of what security means, for whom, and against what threats may well open up a range of useful policy options for securing land access rights. Unpacking tenure insecurity may also provide some clues on how powerful interests may be countered for the benefit of a wider segment of society. For rights to be meaningfully secured, there is need to identify the nature and sources of threats that create insecurities.

Addressing accountable, inclusive, and transparent procedures for negotiating and arbitrating disputes at local levels provides an avenue out of the need to record and legalize all manner of rights and negotiations. These should be based on local, salient values of what is fair and equitable. Recent attempts at decentralizing authority and functions to local and district levels have remained incomplete, thus strengthening local elites and increasing the vulnerability of those already marginalized. A system of incentives is required to ensure that central and local institutions are more responsive and accountable to local populations as a whole.

There are, however, limitations: negotiation may not be practicable, either due to prior injustices or unequal capacities of parties, and the elite may capture the process. Though the state's theoretical role as the ultimate guarantor of property rights and mediator of conflicts is fairly clear, the complement of institutions and actors that comprise the state have proved incapable (and perhaps unwilling) to perform this role effectively. A state's institutional weakness is bound to lead to the failure of mediation, without which there can be no consensus and no general framework of dynamic relations between actors in rural development.

Conclusions

Instead of allocation of rights, tenure recognition needs to center on the rules and mechanisms for regulating access and use among the multiple interests. While enhancing security of tenure is the question on one hand, it is also important to see to it that there are mechanisms for strengthening the access of multiple users to the dryland resources in question.

It is critical to involve local people to come up with appropriate actions to negotiate access rights. Legal solutions based on customary rules are appropriate to protect rights of various groups dependent on the same resources. Legal reforms need to take customary and local systems into account.

The process of negotiation needs to take into account the capacity of differentiated local actors to facilitate continuous learning for integrating policy, regulation and practice. The state should limit its function to mediation to bring and build consensus.

Suggested Readings

Juul, K., and C. Lund (eds). 2002. *Negotiating Property in Africa*. Portsmouth, NH: Heinemann.

Payne, G. (ed). 2002. *Land, Rights and Innovation: Improving Tenure Security for the Urban Poor.* London: ITDG.

Facilitating Collective Action

Through collective action, forest users, fishers, irrigators, herders, and other rural producers improve and sustain resources vital for their lives. In cases where it has weakened or seems absent, citizens, non-government organizations (NGOs), and government agencies can work to stimulate, strengthen, or sustain collective action.

SOURCE:

Bruns, B. and P. C. Bruns. 2004. *Strengthening Collective Action.* Collective Action and Property Rights for Sustainable Development, 2020 Vision For Food, Agriculture, and the Environment. Focus Brief 11, International Food Policy Research Institute, Washington, D.C.

Facilitating Collective Action

Extension agents, community organizers, and similar change agents have catalyzed communities to organize bottom-up identification of priorities, planning, and action. They have helped farmers organize themselves to transform a situation of conflicts into one of effective cooperation.

Facilitators have included recent university graduates, retrained agency field staff, local community members, and "farmer consultants." Facilitation approaches have built on earlier methods in community development and community organizing, combined with reforms, to enhance the capacity of technical agencies to work with communities.

Changes in policies and regulations, and in everyday attitudes and practices of agency staff can make it much easier for communities and agencies to work together in managing resources. Where additional stimulus is helpful, facilitators can reduce the initial barriers and costs of organizing.

Care is needed, however, to avoid dependence on facilitators and instead build sustainable local capacity. Facilitators can reach out to include poorer and more marginalized people in collective action.

Participatory application of planning methods such as logical framework analysis empowers local stakeholders to make decisions. Integrated pest management, which relies on coordinated action among neighboring farmers, has shown the value of integrating local and scientific knowledge. Technical tools, such as geographic information systems and computer models, can support better-informed decision-making by local stakeholders. Sustaining changes beyond the stages of initial enthusiasm requires good follow-through from planning to action and a supportive institutional environment.

Participatory Learning and Action

Joint walkthroughs, transect walks, sketch maps, scale models, cropping calendars, matrix ranking, buzz groups, and other techniques not only quickly generate valid information and support analysis by stakeholders, but also are fun for those involved.

"Icebreaker" activities and listening skills exercises help bring groups together and build trust and mutual understanding. Including a diverse mix of participants — women, poor people, ethnic minorities, elders, youths, and others — encourages a full range of concerns to be voiced.

Where conflicts among stakeholders are severe, alternative dispute resolution methods of negotiation, mediation, and arbitration may be useful.

Redesigning Institutions and Incentives

Research has identified key design principles that promote collective action. Resource management institutions must adapt to local conditions, offering local organizations the autonomy to devise and revise their own rules. Participants will address problems they identify as important, so it is essential that the actions taken will benefit those involved.

Groups need the power to set boundaries and control access to the resource, to monitor rule violations, and to enforce sanctions. Rules need to be workable in terms of local ideas and resources. For example, fishers find it simpler to control locations and kinds of fishing gear rather

Participatory techniques such as transect walks encourage joint learning between farmers and researchers.

than to regulate the amount that can be caught. Crafting and applying such rules depends on both local agreements and adequate legal backing from government. Small face-to-face groups with strong, shared interests can combine into larger federations.

Where resource boundaries do not fit administrative units, resource user groups need support to organize themselves in suitably specialized organizations, backed by necessary legal authority, that still accommodate village and other administrative bodies.

Incentives matter not just for ordinary resource users, but also for leaders and for those who spend long hours, often at night or in bad weather, patrolling forests, canals, or other remote areas. Local organizations need authority and autonomy to establish a structure that fits their conditions, with adequate incentives for members and leaders, enforceable sanctions against those who violate rules, and feedback mechanisms to learn from experience.

Policy Reforms

In programs such as irrigation and forest management, national governments are partially or fully devolving authority to user groups or local governments. States are not only withdrawing from some activities, but are also building capacity to provide new services such as technical advice, dispute resolution through courts and other forums, and regulatory arrangements to protect broader societal concerns. Strengthening the resource tenure of existing local institutions, i.e. formalizing community rights to regulate land use, reinforces incentives for collective action.

Harnessing Social Energy

Successful change often depends heavily on intangibles: political will, trust, reputation, and legitimacy. When these are lacking, communications strategies — such as political advocacy, public relations campaigns, training programs, study tours, and dissemination of success stories — may be ineffective. They may even backfire, breeding cynicism and disappointment, and discrediting future efforts. Where suitable conditions exist or have been created, good communications are key to bringing about change.

Assurance that fellow resource users share a willingness to try new approaches, reinforced by visible support from leaders in government, can be crucial in changing expectations and transforming decisions about joining in and supporting collective action.

One of the most powerful tools available for promoting collective action lies in changing how governments provide financial assistance. Subsidies can be offered to stimulate, rather than displace, sustainable collective action. Social funds have pioneered creative approaches to financing for community infrastructure development. New approaches to agricultural extension allow users to choose from a variety of service providers. Grants, loans, vouchers, and demand-driven "menus" for training and other services can all be designed to increase incentives for collective action and local resource mobilization.

Potential Problems

Communities are not homogenous, and attention needs to be paid to the implications of economic and social differences. Innovative efforts to initiate collective action should be based on a pragmatic assessment of the strengths and weaknesses of communities, markets and governments, and the opportunities for appropriately combining different institutions. Whereas local resource users possess valuable knowledge and social links that help create and enforce rules, governments often retain advantages in providing technical information, resolving disputes, and strategically promoting wider societal interests such as equity and environmental sustainability.

Incentives for members and leaders help facilitate collective action, while social appreciation makes it a non-monetary recognition.

Governments have an important role in counterbalancing the potential for local corruption and other abuses. They can limit local elites' efforts to grab the lion's share of benefits from collective action. Government's role includes promoting democratic processes for choosing leaders and making decisions, establishing accountability mechanisms for reporting the use of funds, and taking proactive initiatives to help the poor, excluded, or disadvantaged, to organize themselves and protect their interests.

Pilot projects often pioneer ideas about strengthening collective action. Success stories have, however, often benefited from extra attention, special resources, strong charismatic leaders, and other exceptional factors. Expanding innovations successfully will require developing approaches suited to actual conditions and sustainable on a routine basis with ordinary levels of resources.

Conclusion

There is no one best way, no magic bullet or uniform recipe, to strengthen collective action, in general or within a single sector. Research and experience show that reforms to strengthen collective action need to employ multiple approaches and be customized by local resource users to fit their local conditions in ways that allow for continuing learning and adaptation. A variety of techniques are available that have been proven to be effective in different circumstances and contexts.

Suggested Readings

Participatory Learning and Action (PLA) Series, International Institute for Environment and Development (IIED), http://www.planotes.org/

Uphoff, N. 1991. *Learning from Gal Oya: Possibilities for Participatory Development and Post-Newtonian Social Science.* Ithaca, NY: Cornell University Press.

Sourcebook on **Resources, Rights, and Cooperation**, produced by the CGIAR Program on Collective Action and Property Rights (CAPRi)

Catalyzing Collective Action in Natural Resources Management

Working with communities or groups within communities and helping them to reach their goals is a challenge. This paper provides guidelines in catalyzing collective action, especially in natural resources management, based on: the global literature on community-based management of forests and other natural resources; experience in catalyzing collective action within communities in more than 30 communities in 11 countries, using the approach called Adaptive Collaborative Management (ACM); and through experience trying to catalyze collective action in two communities in Sumatra, Indonesia.

SOURCE:

Colfer, C.J. P. 2007. *Simple Rules for Catalyzing Collective Action in Natural Resources Management Contexts*. Indonesia: Center for International Forestry Research.

Understanding the Socio-Cultural Conditions

It is important to be aware of local socio-cultural conditions in order to learn to expect and accept the unpleasant and unexpected events that may emerge during interactions.

- ***Learn about the people and their conditions before bringing about any kind of change.*** Do not assume that local people have the same motivations as you do and that they behave in the same way. Understand their personal motivations and values, how they think people ought to treat each other, and what differentiations they make within their own group and in relation to outsiders.

- ***Things are interconnected.*** External changes, over which no one in the community may have any control, can also result in changes in the local system. The use of holistic, anthropological methods can help anticipate *some* of the effects of change — whether initiated by you, by the local people, or coming from outside — but it will not be possible to anticipate all of the effects of such changes.

- ***"Emergence" exists.*** Effects of actions cannot be predicted. Things happen (emergence), from the interactions among parts of systems, and it is not always understandable how they have come about. However, accept that surprise exists and be prepared to deal with the results when things come together unpredictably to produce an unexpected result.

Facilitating Collective Action

Once the local situation is understood, it is time to start the action. Observe the following in bringing about collective action:

- ***Respect and work with existing local institutions.*** Every society has existing institutions based on kinship, common interests, occupation, or any number of other organizing principles. These groups can serve as a basis from which to build collective action. Work with an existing group and there is no need for new communication patterns (at least initially). People attend fewer meetings and the value of their existing way of life is acknowledged. Such acknowledgement can be very important for developing or strengthening people's self-confidence and is also important for bringing about effective collective action.

- ***Respect and build on local knowledge.*** Local knowledge is not always obvious but it exists everywhere. Usually a marriage of local and outsider, knowledge is needed, bringing in local people's key knowledge about their environment, its uses, their hopes for the future, and their patterns of human behavior that can contribute to or detract from future uses of the environment.

- ***Identify and work toward shared goals.*** Once the groups have been identified, facilitate a process whereby the group members themselves determine what their goals are. Only if the goals are truly theirs will they be willing to go to the significant trouble of acting collectively to achieve them.

- ***Start with easy goals.*** "Start simple" to allow the group to gain experience and build confidence. Approaching a comparatively short-term goal with a high probability of success first will give them skills and confidence to pursue something more difficult.

- ***Build in mechanisms for assessing progress.*** For any goal, develop indicators of progress that can be monitored to make sure progress is being made. The absence of such monitoring is often a prime constraint in efforts to improve conditions. Routine monitoring can enhance sustainability. If a mechanism has been learned for ongoing assessment, communities have a better chance of continuing to work toward their goals after the project and facilitator are gone.

- ***Focus on opportunities.*** Instead of identifying problems, begin by looking for opportunities. Such opportunities can relate to the small goals suggested as first steps, or they can be part of any step in the process of working with communities and other groups. Problems cannot be ignored forever, but the search for opportunities can be the key to some quick and meaningful successes.

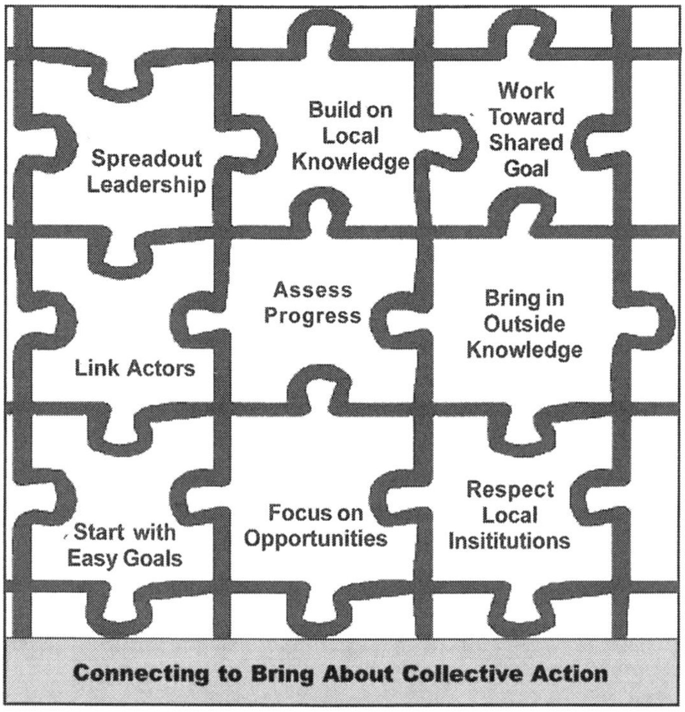

- ***Bring together local and outsider knowledge.*** Local knowledge is important in any attempt to catalyze collective action, but it is also usually important to link this knowledge to the kinds of knowledge that outsiders have. Such linkage works best when there is explicit recognition of the value of local knowledge. When local people's knowledge is recognized as a valuable and useful contribution, this strengthens their self-confidence — again, leading to more effective collective action.

- ***Make links among actors.*** Almost all communities are linked to the outside world, from where resources can be valuable to local people. The facilitator should at least identify relevant links to the outside world (government agencies, NGOs, academics, other communities, networks, etc.), help local people develop the self-confidence and negotiation skills they will need to deal with such outsiders, and serve as a facilitator in the early stages of their interactions. It may also involve helping local people learn to write letters, proposals, complaints, newsletters, and other documents in language that is understandable and acceptable to the outsiders.

- ***Leadership can emerge anywhere.*** Look beyond formal leadership roles particularly when dealing with marginalized groups. Discuss leadership ideas with people, since different groups can have different ideas about who can be a leader, what behavior is acceptable in a leader, what constrains people from becoming leaders, etc. Sometimes an outsider (like a facilitator) who exposes people to different ideas about leadership can open doors for those who have not had such roles in the past — thereby liberating a whole range of skills and knowledge that have not been used adequately.

However, the facilitator should be analytical of his/her own role. Friendships and attention may affect how the community members feel about many different things, including their assessment of the leadership potential of individuals.

- ***Seek justice, via understanding.*** If people are treated fairly, they are more likely to act responsibly and cooperatively. Facilitators must be alert to injustice in the conduct of work. The better the understanding of the context in which the work is done, the more likely that the facilitator will note the inequities and do something about them. Obviously, not all issues can be addressed, but exacerbating existing inequities can be avoided and the facilitator may be able to make progress in correcting some long-standing wrongs (through improved collective action).

- ***Balance power.*** Balancing power is not entirely within the hands of the facilitator. On the one hand, the facilitator's role is to serve as a relatively neutral outsider, facilitating a process. On the other hand, facilitators need to act to strengthen the voice of those in need. It is a delicate balancing act. If too much effort trying to protect those in need is expended, the power as a neutral actor to bring about better communication and cooperation among the parties is lost.

- ***Facilitation is an invaluable skill.*** Make sure that everyone has a genuine opportunity to provide input. Use facilitation skills so that the ideas of the poor, women, and lower castes, can also be heard throughout the process. However, do not disenfranchise the wealthy and the powerful. Avoid what some call "*facipulation*" – facilitation in such a way that it manipulates people to serve one's own ends.

- ***Build coalitions.*** Building coalitions can be extremely useful in the process of balancing power as it may be helpful in achieving goals and it bumps the stakes up a notch, catalyzing collective action on a broader scale.

- ***Diversity leads to more creative solutions.*** When working in communities involving marginalized groups, a problem solving process will strengthen collective ability to come up with innovative ideas and answers. This same principle applies in collaborative efforts between communities and other groups such as government, NGOs, academics, and project personnel.

- ***Dealing with diversity involves significant transaction costs.*** As groups become more diverse, communication among participants becomes harder and social capital is lower (initially); there are likely to be fewer collective actions that "come naturally" to the participants. Be prepared for miscommunications, suspicions, and slow-downs deriving from these inherent difficulties.

Working with Communities on Collective Action Issues

Finally, note these specific guidelines in working with communities on collective action issues:

- ***Practice what you preach.*** Actions speak louder than words. Do not underestimate the power of example.

- ***Listening can be more important than talking.*** Encourage people to take action. If we are constantly telling them what to do, they will not develop the skills they need to continue the process after we are gone.

- ***Be patient.*** Any attempt at collective action involves various barriers and constraints that must be overcome. The processes of collective action all take time — even when things go smoothly.

- ***Give up the love of control.*** Try to adjust and respond to an uncertain world in creative and persistent ways, moving iteratively and slowly toward the set goals. Encourage community members, government officials, project personnel, NGO workers, and others to do the same.

- ***Try to find long-term funding.*** Catalyzing collective action is a long-term commitment and takes an uncertain amount of time. If you truly respond to the needs and wishes of community members, then you cannot pre-determine even what the project will entail, let alone the amount of time it will take. This kind of uncertainty is very uncomfortable for donors (and others), making securing funding a difficult task. Your task must be to educate donors to the need for both flexibility and long-term commitments and carry on until they are convinced!

Collective Approaches for Facilitating Farmer Innovation

SOURCE:

Knox, A. and N. Lilja. 2004. *Collective Action and Property Rights for Sustainable Development: Farmer Research and Extension.* Collective Action and Property Rights for Sustainable Development, 2020 Focus Brief 11 International Food Policy Research Institute: Washington, D.C.

Participatory application of planning methods such as logical framework analysis empowers local stakeholders to make decisions. Integrated pest management, which relies on coordinated action among neighboring farmers, has shown the value of integrating local and scientific knowledge. Technical tools, such as geographic information systems and computer models, can support better-informed decision-making by local stakeholders. Sustaining changes beyond the stages of initial enthusiasm requires good follow-through from planning to action and a supportive institutional environment.

Local innovation is the key to sustainable improvement in agricultural production, natural resource management, and rural livelihood systems. One of the main lessons of participatory research is that involving stakeholders in the early stages of research and development leads to better targeting of technologies, a greater sense of local ownership, and often more economically secure livelihoods. Participatory research approaches have been shown to reduce the time between the initiation of research and the adoption of new technologies and to increase both the rate and speed of adoption. The process of participating in research can also have a significant impact on farmers' human and social capital.

Combining technical innovations with collective action initiatives has been shown to lead to substantial farmer benefits. A number of farmer-led research and extension (FRE) approaches incorporate collective action for different purposes and at different stages in the innovation process. Collective action can be useful in sharing knowledge, setting priorities, and experimenting with, evaluating, and disseminating technologies.

Participatory research and collective action tend to reinforce one another. Where strong norms of collective action and social capital exist, they create a climate conducive to joint experimentation and sharing of innovation. Collective action can be instrumental in motivating participation, coordinating the actions of multiple resource users, spreading risks, managing environmental spillovers, and scaling up the benefits of participatory research. When seeded by external facilitation and scientific partnership, a carefully nurtured process of participation also has the potential to strengthen social networking, cooperation, and organization.

Collective Action Research Programs

Farmers and communities have used a range of FRE approaches based on collective action. This section describes some of the most widely applied participatory research approaches.

Farmer field schools (FFSs) emerged in Indonesia in 1986. By 1998, more than 1 million farmers had participated in FFSs in Indonesia alone, and the method had spread to 12 Asian countries. It also appeared in many African and Latin American countries, and the approach continues to spread globally.

The method typically brings together 20–25 farmers from a community for intensive, field-based learning by doing. It has been used mainly to train farmers in the principles of integrated pest management (IPM). Collective action in IPM is critical because reducing pest infestation depends on widespread adoption of the practices. FFS training, tools, and dynamics aim to build solidarity among participants, thereby promoting knowledge sharing, experimentation, adoption, and diffusion. In one Indonesian case, farmers broadened the scope of the project from targeting a single pest to adopting a more integrated crop management program for cassava production.

Local agriculture research committees (known by their Spanish acronym, *CIALs)* provide farmer-led research on crop technologies to communities. Communities interested in forming a CIAL elect a small team of community members to undertake the research. Through partnerships between farmers, extension workers, and scientists, researchers learn about the farmers' priorities and filter those up to research organizations to shape technology development. At the same time, farmers learn skills in research design and experimentation and gain access to information on new technologies from the scientists. Unlike the farmer field schools, CIALs are permanent and provide ongoing services. The two approaches are increasingly used to complement each other.

Because CIALs work to bring communities together to identify research priorities and learn from their results, their viability depends on large-scale cooperation and support. Joint experimentation is also fundamental. Collective action helps to spread both the experimentation risks and the labor burden, while also enabling more extensive and verifiable experiments. In Colombia and Honduras, CIALs have formed second-order organizations to provide credit, organize exchange visits, and train experienced members to become facilitators who can organize new CIALs.

Farmer research groups (FRGs) also carry out joint scientific experiments.They differ from the CIALs in size (FRGs have between 10 and 45 members) and because their members participate for themselves as individuals, rather than on behalf of the community. Often they build on existing local organizations.

A study of 21 FRGs in Kabale, Uganda, revealed that participation in these groups follows a U-shaped pattern. Participation is initially high when groups are formed, then declines as members drop out and motivation wanes. Once groups show successful results, more farmers join.The poorest farmers appear to participate in equal numbers with less poor farmers, and women tend to dominate FRG membership, although men tend to occupy leadership roles in mixed groups.

Experiments are undertaken on a shared plot that is either rented by or donated to the group. All phases of experimentation, from land preparation to harvesting, are implemented collectively. Members develop common rules for the group's operation and membership. Including a sociologist among the external researchers collaborating with the group is instrumental in building the group's organizational capacity.

Farmer innovation approaches (FIAs) in Africa identify farmer innovators to promote indigenous knowledge.Their focus is mainly on soil and water conservation technologies.

How Do FRE Approaches Compare with Conventional Research?

Much participatory research focuses on farm- and plot-level technologies. FRE approaches that address landscape-level resources and technologies, particularly those held in common, are still the exception. Even participatory watershed research, which starts with a landscape perspective, is mostly oriented toward on-farm soil and water conservation measures. Addressing landscape-level resource management using FRE will undoubtedly require even greater attention to collective action than is already employed in crop and farm technology research. The challenges of fostering successful collective action around natural resource management technologies currently lead programs to focus on less complex systems.

The collective action needs for participatory research can be seen as a continuum (Figure 1). On one end of the continuum are resources that are managed by individuals or households at a plot level and which generate few spillovers for their neighbors. Midway on the continuum are resources that encompass significant environmental flows, such as water or soils in a watershed or hillside context, involve many more stakeholders in resource management, and generate more innovations for their management. On the other end of the continuum are common property resources, for which both the costs and the benefits of management are shared by multiple users

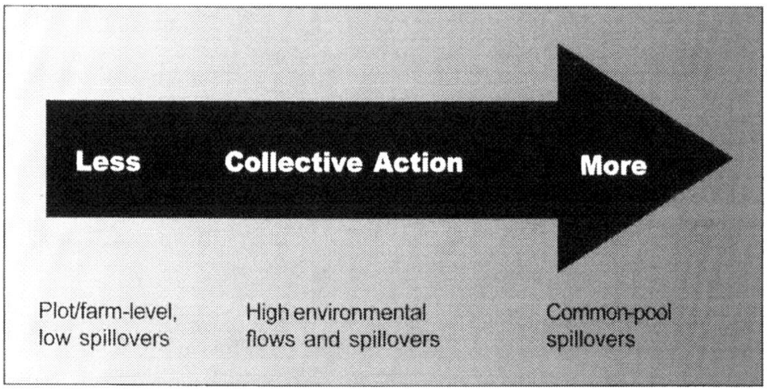

Figure 1. Collective Action Needs of FRE.

who may prioritize the ultimate use of those resources differently. In this case, research cannot be effective unless all users are involved and there is agreement on which technologies are to be tested and the criteria to evaluate them.

Although this framework may be helpful for identifying important collective action constraints for landscape-level farmer research and extension, collective action for organizing farmer participation and knowledge sharing is likely to add considerable value to on-farm research. Collective action may also be necessary for effective scaling up of technologies. Empirical studies show that farmer participatory research, even if conducted at the farm or plot level, leads to rapid scaling up of results to landscape levels if the research is sufficiently linked to local social networks and is designed to enhance local human and social capacity.

Further stakeholder dialogue and research are needed to identify which approaches are most effective at strengthening collective action for FRE so that it:

- better addresses landscape resource issues;
- fosters greater and more widespread human and social capital; and
- accelerates, improves, and scales up the outcomes of the innovation process.

Ultimately, the goal of refining farmer-led research and extension in these ways is to improve the livelihoods of the poor.

Suggested Reading

For further reading see the publications available on the Program on Participatory Research and Gender Analysis (website at http://www.prgaprogram.org/).

Sourcebook on **Resources, Rights, and Cooperation**, produced by the CGIAR Program on Collective Action and Property Rights (CAPRi)

Using Games to Support Collective Action in the Real World

The use of economic games in the field to explore how people's decisions affect individual and collective well-being has increased over the last few years as a tool to study economic behavior (Table 1). There are a number of applications of these games to issues of development and the environment, with quite a number of these addressing particular aspects of collective action such as cooperation, voluntary contributions to public goods, trust, reciprocity, altruism, and social norms.

SOURCE:

Cardenas, J.C. 2009. *Experiments in Environment and Development: Annual Review of Resource Economics.* Vol. 1: 157-183 (Volume publication date, October 2009) (doi:10.1146/annurev.resource.050708.144056).

These games (also called economic experiments) have been replicated in very different cultural settings, and participant pools. Some robust patterns have emerged from these studies; however, variation across experiences has also enriched the understanding of human behavior. While most games are used as research tools, some researchers have observed that the use of games in research-for-development interventions can increase awareness and understanding of collective action in communities and, ultimately, in some cases, increase cooperation.

Economic Games

Economic games are the equivalent of experiments for social scientists. A game consists of players, rules, and reward structures. Games are designed to mirror real life situations, and are especially useful for looking at intangible issues like trust, fairness, and cooperation. Changing the rules of the

Table 1. Questions, Behavioral Aspects, and Experimental Strategies.

Issues in development and the environment	Trade-offs and interesting questions	Experimental designs from the field and the lab
• Risk exposure, risk aversion, and poverty	• Risk versus higher returns • Technology adoption	• Lotteries, varying variance, and expected returns
• Time discounting, saving rates, pensions	• Consumption today versus consumption tomorrow	• Payments spaced in time
• Prosociality toward others today (fairness, inequality) • Prosociality toward kin in the future • Prosociality toward non-kin in the future	• My consumption today versus sharing with kin today • My consumption today versus sharing with others today • My consumption today versus saving for kin tomorrow	Social preferences: • Altruism (dictator, ultimatum) • Reciprocity and trust (ultimatum, trust, gift exchange) • Cooperation (prisoners dilemma, common-pool resources CPR, voluntary contributions game VCM) • Third-party punishment
• Protection of the environment	• Consumption today versus resource exhaustion tomorrow • Consumption today versus extinction tomorrow • Protecting today versus consumption of others (next generations) tomorrow	• WTA/WTP (hypothetical, experimental) offers • Donations to environmental protection programs and charities • Ecological or environmental intrinsic values • CPR and VCM games
• Environmental institutions and mechanisms	• Market versus state versus community-based management of the local and global commons	• Market-based institutions (ITQs, fees, quotas, command and control) • CPR and VCM games
• Market-based growth through competition, specialization and access to credit and microfinance	• Cooperation versus competition (complementary? conflicting?) • Innovation versus risk for the uninsured • Adaptive (resilient) multitasking versus specialization	• Market behavior (double auction, posted offers, etc.)
• Provision of public goods, regulation, and corruption (education, health, security, recreation, etc.)	• Market- versus state- versus community-based provision of local public goods • Rule of law, compliance, rent-seeking	• CPR and VCM games • Endogenous versus external regulations • Corruption
• Self-government and social networks	• Private versus state versus communal insurance over risks	• (Lotteries) risk and risk-pooling games • Existing and controlled social networks experiments in combination with social preferences experiments

game allows researchers to test how regulations or other institutional innovations affect individual behavior and collective outcomes. A key element of the games is that the rewards or payoffs that people earn are real, usually money but possibly also in-kind. Because the playoffs are real, the games are not considered hypothetical.

In a commonly used forestry game, five players exploit a forest with an initial stock of 100 trees. During each round, the forest can grow at a rate of 10 percent, i.e. for each 10 standing trees, one more tree might grow; altogether, the forest can grow up to 100 trees. During each round of the first stage, each player can cut up to five trees and receive a cash payment of say, USD 0.50 for each tree. By the end of the game, each player receives in cash his/her earnings from the total accumulated during the game.

If the stock falls below 25 trees, the maximum trees allowed to each player decreases such that the group maximum does not exceed the total number of trees available. Decisions are made in private and are kept confidential, and during each round only the total group extraction is announced. The first stage consists of a maximum of 10 rounds with no communication allowed among the five players.

During the first stage, a "rational" strategy for an individual player would be to extract the maximum number of trees allowed for each round. If all players adopt this strategy, then in every round 25 trees would be cut and the forest wiped out by the sixth round. Under this individualistic strategy (usually called Nash strategy), the group would amass a total of 119 trees.

In contrast, a socially efficient sustainable path of extraction would be to postpone exhaustion of the forest until the tenth round. This strategy would yield 166 trees. The challenge to achieving this outcome is that players will not voluntarily refrain from extracting unless they have some assurance that the others will also refrain, and the basic game structure does not provide this. Under either the Nash or the socially-optimal solution in this game, the final forest stock will be zero trees, given that at the end of the tenth round, any remaining trees have no value to the players.

In a set of sessions in a village or project, one could try variations of this game to compare the results and discuss them with the participants. For instance, one can compare the case when the game is played among five people who know each other well as opposed to five strangers. One could also introduce changes in the rules and test different institutional arrangements, e.g. allowing the group to have an open conversation before each round of the game, test the effect of public disclosure of individual decisions among players after each round, or test the effect of a system of monitoring and sanctions funded by the players.

Games in Development Research

Games have been shown to create a more interactive environment for researchers, field practitioners and communities. The data collected from the games are used to generate discussion with the participants about the similarities between what happened in the games and their reality.

For instance, in a study recently conducted with this game in six rural villages of Thailand and Colombia, it was found that the participants avoided the tragedy of commons and, in fact, at the end of the 10 rounds trees were left standing despite the fact that within the game, any standing tree had no monetary value for the players. A follow-up conversation with the participants after the games revealed that the participants had assigned an intrinsic value to the standing trees and felt some trees had to remain for symbolic purposes.

There are some advantages to using the games to create an environment for a conversation among actors. These have to do with the two-way interactions between three components of the framework shown in Figure 1: a *theoretical model* that gives us benchmarks to compare the results obtained in the field; a design of the *games or experiments* that allow for testing of different treatments controlling for the rest of the variables; and the *reality* and its stakeholders.

These two-way interactions complement each other in various ways. For instance, a policy discussion (F,C) between a particular theory about conservation of natural resources and the stakeholders could benefit by testing first with these games (A,D) different configurations of such policies and then be brought to the reality (B,E) with adjustments from what was learned in the field lab setting.

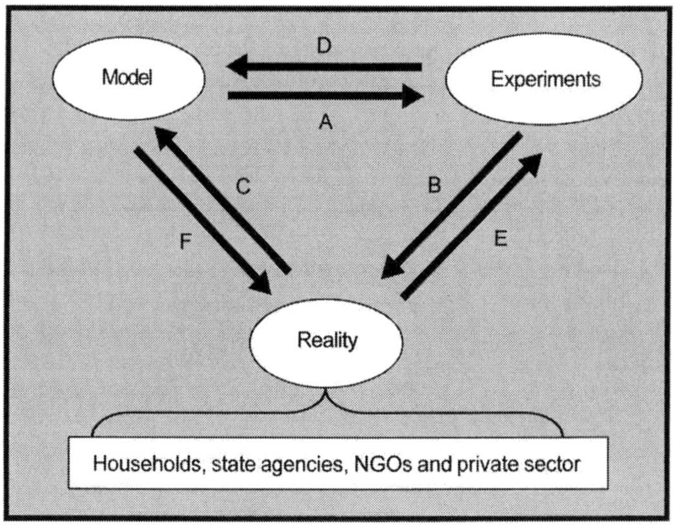

Figure 1. Relationship Between Theoretical Models, Experiments, and Reality.

The possibility of a trial-and-error iteration using games and the feedback obtained from the active participation of community members, NGOs, and local public officers could create a more fertile terrain for the final design and implementation of a policy or program that better reflects the interests and views of the stakeholders.

This is particularly true for problems of collective action and property rights where individual and group interests may be in conflict and where legitimacy and enforcement capacity of regulatory agencies are limited.

Games in Development Interventions

While economic games are used by practitioners to create a space for dialogue with communities, they may also play a role as pedagogical tools for self-reflection and social change.

In a study conducted in three villages in rural Colombia, the researchers conducted a number of these games based on a common-pool resource situation in which each player had to decide how much effort to put into extracting the resource. After the games were completed, there was a community workshop in each of the villages to discuss with the participants and other members of the village the main results from the games and the implications of the different treatments (changes in rules of the game) on behavior and outcomes. About one year later, the researchers were able to return to these same villages with the intention to repeat the exact same games under the same sets of incentives. They recruited not only people who had participated in the previous games a year earlier, but also new participants. Or so it seemed!

The researchers were astounded to see that from the start of the games this time, and without any apparent communication during the games themselves, the rates of cooperation were substantially higher than a year earlier. A new follow-up workshop and interviews revealed that the "experienced" players remembered quite well the functioning of the games. During the recruitment stage, they were able to spread the word among both the ones that participated before and the new ones, that a cooperative strategy by the groups would maximize the amount of cash for the groups, creating an *ex-ante* agreement, or as they said, "we learned from the games at that time that cooperation pays."

Conclusions

The use of economic games or experiments for the study of issues of development and the environment has increased substantially over the last few decades. Behavioral sciences have made large contributions to the understanding of collective action and how rules and norms play a crucial role in problems of managing common-pool resources and solving the dilemmas of group-based property rights.

In addition to helping to understand the foundations of behavior, these games can create a space for an interactive dialogue with communities facing these dilemmas. The games offer some potential for self-reflection in a dialogue among stakeholders, and even for social learning processes that create actual changes in behavior beyond the domain of the controlled game.

Suggested Readings

Cardenas, J.C. and J. Carpenter. 2008. *Behavioural Development Economics: Lessons from Field Labs in the Developing World.* Journal of Development Studies. Vol. 44, No. 3 (March 2008): 337-364.

Holt, C. A. 2006. *Markets, Games, and Strategic Behavior.* Addison-Wesley.

Ostrom E. 2006. *The Value-Added of Laboratory Experiments for the Study of Institutions and Common-Pool Resources.* J. Econ. Behav. Organ. 61(2):149–63.

Planning Together for Sustainable Water Resources Management

Achieving participation in planning and collective action among various stakeholders, even those with different or conflicting interests, is not impossible.

SOURCE:

Sultana, P. and P. Thompson. 2003. *Methods of Consensus Building for Community Based Fisheries Management in Bangladesh and the Mekong Delta.* CAPRi Working Paper No. 30, International Food Policy Research Institute, Washington, D.C.

Participatory Action Plan Development

Case studies in Bangladesh and the Mekong Delta have shown that a method called Participatory Action Plan Development (PAPD) is effective in consensus building, especially in the management of shared aquatic resources. The method, initially tested in Bangladesh, is a three-phased process comprising 13 stages leading to continuous and long-term resource management practice.

Previous efforts to manage inland fisheries in Bangladesh have shown the need for facilitated local institutions and establishment of common property regimes. In the case of floodplain wetlands, these are areas of seasonal flooding that provide fishing and irrigation, transportation, and a supply of wild plants used for food, animal feed, medicines, and construction. Depending on the stakeholders' resources and opportunities, they adopt different means of livelihood resulting in different ways of using the wetlands' resources. These ways may be complementary or competitive.

These variations create a need for management of the floodplains' resources. The PAPD process allows the stakeholders to achieve consensus on the actions necessary. PAPD is a planning process that recognizes diversity among stakeholders and their livelihoods while focusing on common interests.

> **PAPD Applied in Bangladesh and Vietnam**
>
> In its application in Bangladesh and Vietnam, PAPD has proven that consensus among different stakeholders in the community is essential to collective action and the development of co-management institutions. Consensus thus appears to be a good starting point for community-led development; even some social capital indicators among the case study communities have shown a significant change. The PAPD process has also been shown to be transferable to other social settings, as it was first applied in Bangladesh before it was adapted in the Mekong Delta.

The process works to avoid domination by a few powerful voices while trying to come up with a desirable consensus. Stakeholders are grouped into their respective categories. Each group is then asked to enumerate their problems and rank them according to importance. After this, they meet in plenary with the other sub-groups to compile and rank all the problems. Solutions are then discussed separately again before meeting in plenary to agree on collective actions that would lead them to their goals as well as determine how these actions would affect their fellow stakeholders. The process also aims to increase social capital — that is, broadly, those things that help a community develop.

PAPD Application to Resource Management

Community-based management strategies for improving natural resource management and empowering local communities have become common in the past 20 years. These strategies are based on co-management concepts and on the use of local knowledge and common property regimes.

Application of PAPD in both Bangladesh and Vietnam has been in the context of complex floodplain wetland commons. Here there are policies for transferring formally-recognized rights over state-owned water bodies to user groups, and informal community rights over common pool fisheries on seasonally flooded private land. In both cases, it was understood that more participation and consensus are keys to its success.

PAPD is a method originally developed by a Bangladesh non-government organization (NGO), the Center for Natural Resource Studies, and researchers from Newcastle and Durham Universities and

The participation and consensus of user groups develop community rights over common pool fisheries and seasonally flooded private land.

the WorldFish Center. It is based on principles such as the desirability of consensus, the need for inclusivity, neutrality, and information sharing. Its key features include for each stakeholder category:

- identifying and ranking their problems (regarding natural resources management), and for all groups to set priority problems together; and
- considering solutions and their impacts, and then jointly forming a consensus on win-win solutions.

The PAPD method aims to provide a more holistic approach to resource management that is based on the principles of *heterogeneity* and *inclusivity.* This means that the method recognizes that users pursue different livelihood strategies that may or may not interfere with the others' activities. Further, the method recognizes the concerns of all users in the community.

PAPD also recognizes that some groups, due to certain advantages (education, social status, etc.), are likely to be heard, and thus it is designed so that the disadvantaged have equal chances to be recognized. The method even takes into account secondary users (government agencies, etc.) who may also have vested interests in the community's resources. As a process, PAPD tries to raise collective awareness of and action on the problems of the community.

The heart of the whole process is encapsulated in the second phase (stages 4-9). It is in this stage that participatory workshops with separate stakeholder groups and combined plenaries are held. It is here that most consensus building is achieved, thus making this phase the PAPD proper. The aim of the participatory process is to arrive at an agreement between the different stakeholders for sustainable collective actions. If this is to happen, the stakeholders must understand know each other well. Mutual understanding is expected to happen in the second phase and facilitators must

Stages of PAPD Process

The PAPD process was originally conceived as a two-phase process but has since evolved into three stages during its application in Bangladesh. Within this process the actual PAPD workshop forms phase II. The different stages of the PAPD process are as follows:

I. Scoping Phase

1. Situational analysis (through summarizing local knowledge)
2. Stakeholder analysis (through key informants)
3. Household census (invitations sent to households selected by stratified random sampling)

II. Participatory Planning Phase

4. Problem census (within each stakeholder category group)
5. Compiling of ranked problems (separating natural resources problems and combining group rankings)
6. Stakeholders plenary (group representatives and local leaders will review problems, vote on top priorities for solution analysis)
7. Solution and impact analysis (within each stakeholder category group)
8. Stakeholders plenary (primary and secondary users will present whole process, identify feasible solutions, discuss institutional arrangements proposed by groups)

III. Implementation Phase

9. Develop community institutions for community resources management
10. Community organization develops detailed implementation plan for the agreed upon solutions
11. Wider community should review plans for adjustments especially to avoid adverse impacts
12. Implementation of action plan (actual physical work, implementation of rules, etc.)
13. Institutionalization of management arrangements including local policy support

understand this without allowing the participatory process, which encourages the necessary understanding between diverse people, to get lost in the tools that they use. After this, the process moves on to solution analysis. The stakeholders are again separated into their respective groups to find solutions before the second plenary where solutions are discussed altogether and ranked. In the process, part of the solution analysis is an understanding of how the stakeholders' actions, and proposed solutions will affect others in the area, as well as the feasibility of these solutions. These considerations are part of the ranking mechanism. After this, the process moves into the final phase.

Field Experience in Bangladesh and Vietnam: Avoiding Facilitator Influence

In Bangladesh and Vietnam, care was taken to avoid undue facilitator influence on the participants who spent a whole day listing and ranking their problems. In both countries, the problems appear to be simple but with complex backgrounds.

The common problems are a decline in fish catch, polluted waters, and malfunctioning infrastructure, among others. Extra care was taken to make sure everyone was able to air their concerns and have equal control of the proceedings. The problems identified by the separate groups were ranked separately and then validated and revised in plenary.

Meanwhile, action research to address the community's problems happens in the last stage; institutional arrangements and management actions are developed in this stage through the help of various agencies, including NGOs.

Complementary or competitive uses create a need for the management of the floodplain's resources.

Assessing PAPD

Integral to the process is the evaluation of success. In PAPD, possible outcomes include: that stakeholders better understand each other's livelihood and use of shared resources; increased awareness of the resource management issues; greater social equity; and, most of all, that the different actions will be adopted. Eventually, impacts on more measurable indicators such as biodiversity, fish populations, production, and people's overall status can be measured. Possible indicators for assessing the impact of the consensus building process include the extent to which it:

- raises cognitive social capital levels;
- increases trust and reciprocity;
- empowers;

- it is inclusive and representative;
- focuses on common issues/goals;
- it is open for all to speak (civil discourse);
- scientifically informed and adaptive;
- encourages critical thinking;
- maintains stakeholder interests;
- results in decline of reported conflict;
- ensures that consensus is sought only after thorough exploration of issues; and
- applies Alternative Dispute Resolution (ADR) methods.

Conclusion

The core of PAPD is an empowering process that will eventually lead stakeholders to create local institutions. Its success is determined and measured in terms of social capital that allows communities to better manage their resources.

In Vietnam, building on earlier work gave the PAPD process a more comprehensive view of the problems and possible solutions. This allowed the process to come up with an implementation plan, although that one still needed a few modifications. Nevertheless, the stakeholders were able to agree on rules and sanctions with regards to the use of the wetlands.

All in all, the process was proven to be an effective way of allowing people to come together and find ways of working together in their own way. Subsequent assessments in Bangladesh have quantified the advantages of adopting the PAPD process.

Suggested Readings

Barr, J.J.F, P-J. Dixon, M.M. Rahman, M.A. Islam, M.I. Zuberi, A.A. McGlynn, and G.P. Ghosh. 2000. *A Participatory, Systems-Based, Process for Identification of Improved Natural Resources Management for Better Floodplain Livelihoods.* Project Report of R6756. Newcastle, England: University of Newcastle, Centre for Land Use and Water Resources Research.

Edmunds, D. and E. Wollenberg. 2001. *A Strategic Approach to Multistakeholder Negotiations.* Development and Change 32(2): 231-53.

Krishna, A. and N. Uphoff. 1999. *Mapping and Measuring Social Capital: A Conceptual and Empirical Study of Collective Action for Conserving Watersheds in Rajasthan, India.* Social Capital Initiative Working Paper No. 13. Washington, D.C.: Environmentally and Socially Sustainable Development Network, World Bank.

Sultana, P. and S. Abeyasekera. 2008. *Effectiveness of Participatory Planning for Community Management of Fisheries in Bangladesh.* Journal of Environmental Management 86(1): 201-213.

Empowering Communities to Co-Manage Watersheds:
Forum for Citizen Action

Community participation is recognized as an essential part of equitable and sustainable watershed management. Stakeholders play a vital role in ensuring that land use in the upstream does not affect the quality and quantity of water that flows to downstream communities. Regulatory measures could potentially address this concern. However, they entail high monitoring costs and compliance is not certain. In theory, stakeholder participation in watershed management can be a solution to these challenges.

SOURCE:

Candelo, C., L. Cantillo, J. Gonzalez, A.M. Roldan and N. Johnson. 2008. *Empowering Communities to Co-manage Natural Resources: Impacts of the Conversatorio de Acción Ciudadana.* Paper presented at the Second International Forum on Water and Food, CGIAR Challenge Program on Water and Food (CPWF), Addis Ababa, Ethiopia, 10-14 November 2008.

In practice, meaningful participation is difficult to achieve when communities are unorganized, unaware of their legal rights and responsibilities, and lack the information, education, and confidence necessary to interact with other more powerful stakeholders. The Forum for Citizen Action (known by its Spanish acronym CAC) is an innovative methodology developed in Colombia to empower communities to participate actively and effectively in the governance and management of natural resources.

The *Conservatorio De Accion Ciudadana* (Forum for Citizen Action)

The CAC is a political and legal mechanism founded on the idea of civil society and authorities conversing in familiar terms about issues of importance to both, and then arriving at agreements for action. It is designed to address the disparities in power, rights, and information between communities and government institutions that often prevent communities from exercising their constitutional rights to participate and to hold their representatives accountable. The CAC's point of entry is the Colombian constitution and the rights and responsibilities that citizens are entitled to but often do not know how to use.

CACs were conducted in three Colombian watersheds between 2004 and 2007. Together, the three CACs led to 76 concrete commitments on the part of institutions to invest a total of more than USD 15 million to improve the welfare of watershed residents and the management of watershed resources.

An assessment in late 2007 showed that compliance rates were relatively high, especially in the communities that had stronger follow up processes to hold institutions accountable for their commitments. The CAC methodology also had significant human and social capital impacts on community members who participated, and led to changes in the ways that communities and institutions perceive each other, in some cases, moving from antagonism to respectful collaboration.

The CAC Methodology

The methodology consists of three phases: ***preparation***, ***negotiation***, and ***follow up***. A crucial component is the three-pronged environmental, social, and legal capacity building of ordinary individuals and public servants. Topics for the former include concrete legal instruments available to citizens to access information or compel government agencies to act in a timely manner. The latter received training on their roles and responsibilities under the constitution, especially in relation to citizen participation. The CAC also focuses on building social capital and improving people's knowledge of their natural resources.

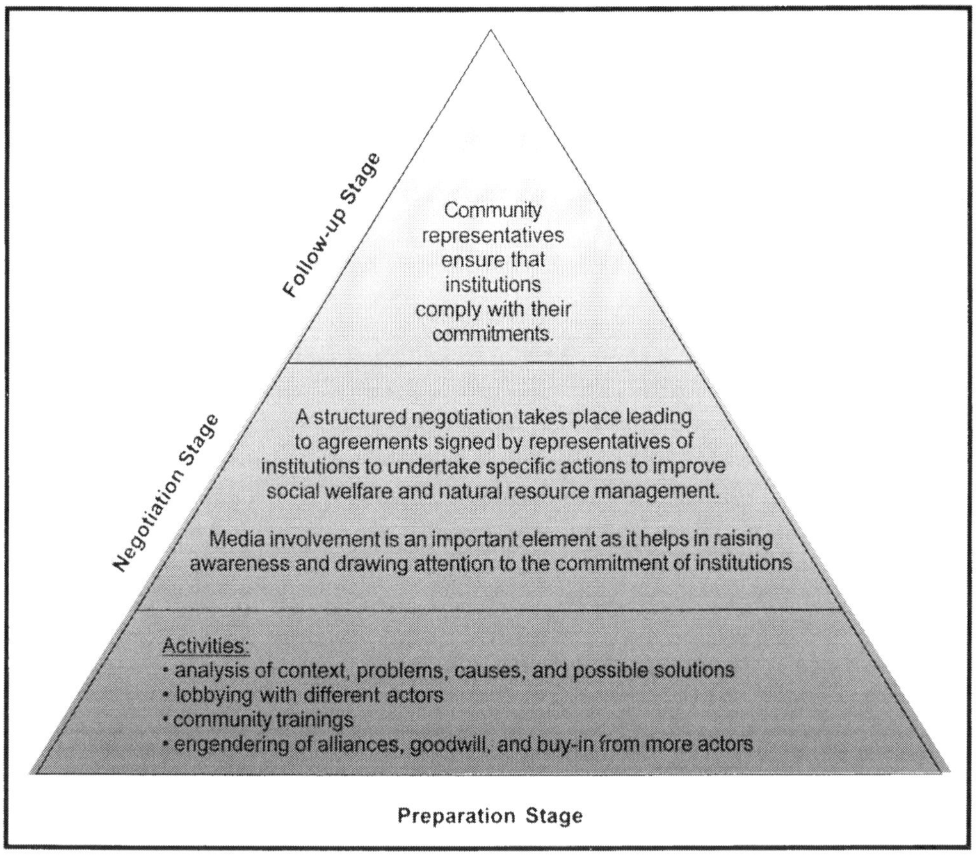

Figure 1. The CAC Methodology

Conclusions

While the same general methodology was followed in the three sites, each *CAC* was implemented in a slightly different way due to differences in the lead organizations, the social, political and biophysical contexts, the available resources, and the level of support from external organizations. The major lessons from these three experiences are:

1. The CAC process cannot be done hastily; it takes time, usually one to two years.
2. Local organizations with experience in community organization as well as research and advocacy are best placed to support a CAC.
3. Links with public institutions need to be established early on to ensure buy-in. Innovative ways of engaging the private sector should also be explored.
4. A core team will always lead the process; however, pressure should be applied to ensure they share and seek feedback from their communities.

Suggested Readings

Beardon, H. 2008. *Building Hope from Chaos: Culture, Politics and the Protection of the Colombian Pacific Mangroves*. WWF-UK, http://www.wwf.org.uk.

Johnson, N., J. García, J.E. Rubiano, M. Quintero, R.D. Estrada, E. Mwangi, A. Peralta and S. Granados. 2007. *Watershed Management and Poverty Alleviation in the Colombian Andes.* Water Alternatives. 2(1): 34-52.

Annex

Glossary

ACCESS
The ability to use land or another resource.

ACCOUNTABILITY
Answerability; having a duty to explain one's conduct and being subject to monitoring and evaluation by a higher authority. (Heywood, 1997).

ADVERSE SELECTION
Adverse selection, anti-selection, or negative selection are terms used in economics, insurance, statistics, and risk management. It refers to a market process in which "bad" results occur when buyers and sellers have asymmetric information (i.e. access to different information): the "bad" products or customers are more likely to be selected. A bank that sets one price for all its checking account customers runs the risk of being adversely selected against by its low-balance, high-activity (and hence least profitable) customers.

AGENCY
- Bureaucratic arm of the government, such as an Irrigation Department, Forestry Service, etc.
- *New Institutional Economics* - Agency relationship: when a principal delegates some rights — for example, user rights over a resource — to an agent who is bound by a (formal or informal) contract to represent the principal's interests in return for payment of some kind (Eggertsson, 1990).
- *Sociology* - Purposeful action. This term implies that actors have the freedom to create, change and influence events (Bilton et al. 1996: 654).

AGRARIAN REFORM
Our broadcast term for the attempt to change agrarian structure, which may include land reform, land tenure reform, and other supportive reforms as well as reform of the credit system.

AGRARIAN STRUCTURE
The pattern of land distribution among landowners.

BIMODAL AGRARIAN STRUCTURE
A distribution pattern for land in which most land is owned by the largest landholders and the smallest landholders.

ALTRUISM
The principle of acting without selfish concern, in the interests of others (Bilton et al. 1996: 654).

ASSOCIATION
A group formed by voluntary action, reflecting recognition of shared interests or common concerns. (Heywood, 1997).

AUTHORITY
The right to influence the behavior of others on the basis of an acknowledged duty to obey; authority may be traditional, charismatic or legal-rational. (Heywood, 1997).

BUNDLE OF RIGHTS
The several rights that constitute tenure; alternatively, all the rights belonging to various persons or groups in a piece of property.

CADASTRAL SURVEY
A survey that determines the ownership, boundaries, and location of a parcel of land.

CADASTRE (or cadastral map)
A map showing the results of a cadastral survey.

CAPITAL
Social Capital
The trust, norms and networks facilitating cooperation and collective action (Putnam, 1993).

Glossary

The shared knowledge, understandings, norms, rules, and expectations about patterns of interactions that groups of individuals bring to a recurrent activity (Ostrom, 1999).

Social capital is the arrangement of human resources to improve flows of future income (Ostrom, 1994: 527-8).

Social capital is created by individuals spending time and energy working with other individuals to find better ways of making possible the achievement of certain ends that, in its absence, would not be possible (Coleman et al. 1966).

Features of social organization — such as networks and values, including tolerance, inclusion, reciprocity, participation and trust — that facilitate coordination and cooperation for mutual benefit. Social capital inheres in the relations between and among actors (UNDP, 1997).

The social resources (networks, membership of groups, relationship of trust, access to wider institutions of society) upon which people draw in pursuit of livelihoods (Carney, 1998:7).

Bonding social capital. Horizontal ties among homogenous groups (Woolcock and Sweetser, 2002).

Bridging social capital. Horizontal ties among heterogeneous groups (Woolcock and Sweetser, 2002).

Linking social capital. Vertical ties with people in power, whether they are in politically or financially influential positions (Woolcock and Sweetser, 2002).

Human capital. The knowledge and skills that individuals bring to the solution of a problem (Ostrom, 1994: 528).

The knowledge, skills, and experience of people that make them economically productive. Human capital can be increased by investing in education, health care, and job training (Soubbotina and Sheram, 2000).

The skills, knowledge, ability to labor, and good health important to the ability to pursue different livelihood strategies (Carney, 1998).

Physical capital. Produced asset: Buildings, machines, and technical equipment used in production plus inventories of raw materials, half-finished goods, and finished goods (Soubbotina and Sheram, 2000).

Physical capital is the arrangement of material resources to improve flows of future incomes (Lachmann, 1978).

The basic infrastructure (transport, shelter, water, energy and communications) and the production equipment and means which enable people to pursue their livelihoods (Carney, 1998).

Natural capital. A stock of natural resources — such as land, water, and minerals — used for production. Can be either renewable or non-renewable (Soubbotina and Sheram, 2000).

The natural resource stocks from which resource flows useful to livelihoods are derived (e.g., land, water, wildlife, biodiversity, environmental resources) (Carney, 1998).

Glossary

Financial capital. The financial resources available to people (whether savings, supplies of credit or regular remittances or pensions) and which provide them with different livelihood options (Carney, 1998).

Cultural capital. Refers to the extent to which individuals have absorbed the dominant culture. Associated with Pierre Bourdieu, who claimed that the greater degree of cultural capital individuals possessed (the more absorbed they were in the dominant culture), the more successful they would be in the educational system (Bilton, 1996:656).

CBNRM

Community-based natural resource management, in which the government plays a relatively minor role.

CENTRALIZATION

The concentration of political power or government authority at the national level (Heywood, 1997).

CIVIL SOCIETY

The realm of autonomous groups and associations; a private sphere independent from public authority. (Heywood, 1997).

COLLECTIVE ACTION

"Action taken by a group (either directly or on its behalf through an organization) in pursuit of members' perceived shared interests" (Marshall, 1998).

"Collective action is the coordinated behavior of groups toward a common interest or purpose" (Vermillion, 2001).

Collective action arises when the efforts of two or more individuals are needed to accomplish an outcome (Sandler, 1992:1).

Collective action arises when individuals join together to work for a collective good (Ensminger, 1992:30).

Action undertaken in a relatively spontaneous way by a large number of people assembled together in a particular place or area. One of the most important forms of collective action is crowd behavior. In crowds, individuals can seek to achieve objectives which in ordinary circumstances are denied to them (Giddens, 1997).

The study of collective action examines the factors that motivate individuals to coordinate their activities to better their collective well-being (Sandler, 1992:19).

COLLECTIVE ACTION DILEMMA

The paralysis that can result when members of a group fail to produce a collective good due to free rider problems (McCay et al., 1999).

CO-MANAGEMENT

"Partnership arrangements in which government, the community of local resource users, external agents (non-governmental organizations, academic and research institutions), and other resource stakeholders share the responsibility and authority for decision-making over the management of a natural resource; it covers various partnership arrangements and degrees of power sharing and integration of local (informal, traditional, customary) and centralized government management systems" (Pomeroy, 2001).

Refers to programs that seek to increase users' direct involvement in resource management in conjunction with a continuing role for the state at some level (Vedeld, 1996; Hesseling, 1996).

Glossary

COMMON PROPERTY
Commons from which a community can exclude non-members and over which the community controls use.

Common property institution - An organization that manages common property tenure arrangement itself.

Common property management - Management of a resource as a common property.

Common property resource - A resource managed under a common property regime.

COMMONS
Land or another natural resource used simultaneously or serially by the members of a community.

COMMUNITY
(1) A group of people living in the same locality and sharing some common characteristics; (2) a group of people having ethnic, cultural, or religious characteristics in common; (3) groups of people who share a common interest and communicate with each other about that interest (including via the internet), and (4) a group of nations having common interests (e.g., Southern African Development Community SADC) (adapted from www.hyperdictionary.com, accessed 01/06/05).

COMPLIANCE
Fulfilling an agreement, formal or informal, based on accepted standards, norms or rules.

CONFLICT
Competition between opposing forces, reflecting a diversity of opinions, preferences, needs, or interests that has a rising probability of violence compared to, say, market competition (Heywood, 1997).

CONSTITUTION
A formal and authoritative set of rules that establish the duties, powers, and functions of the institutions of government. Often these contain basic rights and bases for judicial actions that, among others, define the relationship between the state, corporate persons, and real individuals (Heywood, 1997).

CO-OWNERSHIP
Joint ownership by more than one legal person.

CREDITWORTHY
Term used to characterize a borrower who is a good risk for a lender.

CULTURE
A people's attitude, beliefs, symbols, and values; broadly, that which is acquired through learning, rather than inheritance (Heywood, 1997).

Meaning and social behavior transmitted by non-biological means (i.e., communication and imitation) (McCay et al., 1999).

The total lifestyle of a people from a particular social grouping, including all the ideas, symbols, preferences, and material objects they share (University of Richmond accessed 2002).

DECENTRALIZATION
Transfer of both decision-making authority and payment responsibility to lower levels of government.

"Systematic and rational dispersal of power, authority and responsibility from the central government to lower or local level institutions" (Pomeroy, 2001).

Glossary

Movement of management roles from higher or central levels to lower or local units within the same agency or ministry (Vermillion, 2001).

DE-CONCENTRATION
"The shifting of workload from central government ministry headquarters to staff located in offices outside of the national capital" (Rondinelli et al., 1989).

Transfer of authority and responsibility from national government departments and agencies to regional, district, and field offices of national government offices. Also referred to as administrative decentralization.

DEED REGISTRATION
Registration of title deeds.

DELEGATION
"Passing of some authority and decision-making powers to local officials. The central government retains the right to overturn local decisions and can, at any time, take these powers back" (Pomeroy, 2001).

"Transfers of authority to public corporations or special authorities outside the regular bureaucratic structure" (Ostrom et al., 1993).

DEMOCRATIZATION
The advance of liberal-democratic reform, implying in particular, the granting of basic freedoms and the widening of popular participation and electoral choice (Heywood, 1997).

DENATIONALIZATION
Refers to the selling to the public or to workers of government-owned assets or enterprises meant for the production of goods or services (Dahal, 1996).

DEREGULATION
Involves the dismantling of price controls, quotas, and barriers to entry so that market forces determine savings, investment, and consumption decisions of economic actors (Dahal, 1996).

DEVOLUTION
Transfer of responsibility and authority over natural resources from the state to non-governmental bodies, particularly user groups.

"Increased empowerment of local organizations with no direct government affiliation" (Maniates, 1990).

"Strategy of governance prompted by external or domestic pressures to facilitate transfers of power closer to those who are most affected by the exercise of power" (Agrawal and Ostrom, 2001).

Shift of responsibility and authority for resource management from the state to non-governmental bodies, which includes traditional institutions, the private sector and other organizations of civil society, such as herders' associations or village committees (Meinzen-Dick and Knox, 2001).

Transfer of power and responsibility for the performance of specified functions from national to local governments without reference back to central government. The nature of transfer is political (by legislation), in contrast to de-concentration's administrative, and the approach is territorial or geographical, in contrast to sectoral.

EMPOWERMENT
Multidimensional social process that helps people gain control over their own lives; a process that fosters power (that is, the capacity to implement) in people,

Glossary

for use in their own lives, their communities, and in their society, by acting on issues that they define as important (Page and Czuba, 1999).

EQUITY
The state or ideal of being just, impartial, and fair. The term is often used synonymous with equality.

ETHNIC GROUP
A social group that has a common cultural tradition, common history, and common sense of identity and exists as a subgroup in a larger society. The members of an ethnic group differ with regard to certain cultural characteristics from the other members of their society (Source: www.socialpolicy.ca/e.htm, accessed 01/06/05).

EXTERNALITY
An external economy (diseconomy) is an event which confers an appreciable benefit (inflicts appreciable damage) on some person or persons who were not fully consenting parties in reaching the decision or decisions which led directly or indirectly to the event in question (Meade, 1973).

Effects of a person's or firm's activities on others which are not compensated. Externalities can either hurt or benefit others–they can be negative or positive. One negative externality arises when a company pollutes the local environment to produce its goods and does not compensate the negatively affected local residents. Positive externalities can be produced through primary education–which benefits not only primary students but also society at large (Soubbotina and Sheram, 2000).

FEE SIMPLE or FEE SIMPLE ABSOLUTE
Archaic terms for freehold, from English feudal tenure terminology.

FIXED BOUNDARIES
Boundaries fixed by reference to points in a geodetic network.

FIXED RENT
A rent fixed in cash or a quantity of goods.

Fixed rent tenancy - A tenancy for which the rent is fixed.

FORMAL TENURE SYSTEM
A tenure system created by statute.

FRAGMENTATION
The state of a holding , consisting of several separate parcels.

FRAMES, FRAMING, FRAME ANALYSIS
The concept of frames or framing is used in the contexts of some social movement analysis to mean patterns of perception and/or schemata of interpretation employed by social movement participants or social movement organizations viewed collectively. A frame might be imagined as a kind of template or filter that organizes how one processes new information encountered in the world. Frames organize that information based on previously held beliefs or previously shaped patterns of perception and interpretation.

FREEHOLD
Full private ownership, i.e., free of any obligations to the state other than payment of taxes and obser-

Glossary

vance of land use controls imposed in the public interest.

GENERAL BOUNDARIES

Boundaries established by reference to physical features, such as a river or hedgerow.

GLOBAL POSITIONING SYSTEM (GPS)

A system of survey which establishes and can re-establish points on the earth's surface by reference to orbiting satellites.

GOVERNANCE

"The exercise of legitimate authority in transacting affairs, broadly understood to refer to the maintenance of social order through endogenously evolved sets of rules or authority structures, or some combination of locally evolved and externally imposed rules sets" (Mearns, 1996).

"The exercise of economic, political, and administrative authority to manage a country's affairs at all levels. It comprises mechanisms, processes, and institutions through which citizens and groups articulate their interests, exercise their legal rights, meet their obligations, and mediate their differences" (UNDP, 1997).

"The traditions and institutions by which authority in a country is exercised for the common good. This includes the process by which those in authority are selected, monitored, and replaced, the capacity of the government to effectively manage its resources and implement sound policies, and the respect of citizens and the state for the institutions that govern economic and social interactions among them" (World Bank, www.worldbank.org, accessed 01/06/05).

GOVERNMENT

The mechanism through which ordered rule is maintained; the machinery for making and enforcing collective decisions in society and elsewhere. The core functions of government are to make law (legislation), implement law (execution), and interpret law (adjudication). However, the term "government" is also used to refer to the political executive alone, making it equivalent to the use of the term "the Administration" in presidential systems (Heywood, 1997).

" Exercise of influence and control, through lae and coercion, over a political community, constituted into a state within a defined territory" (Mearns, 1996).

HOLDING

(Verb) Having control of land or another resource; (noun) All the land held by a household or person in whatever tenure.

(Noun) All the land held by a household or person in whatever tenure.

HUMAN RIGHTS

Rights to which people are entitled by virtue of being human; universal and fundamental rights defined in Universal Declaration adopted by UN in 1948, supplemented by 1960s Covenants on social, economic, political, and civil rights. Variously interpreted by states, hence, the subject of global debate.

IMMOVABLE PROPERTY

Property in land and attachments (European Civil Law).

IMPORTED TENURE SYSTEM

Tenure system occupied from another country.

Glossary

INDIGENOUS TENURE SYSTEM
Tenure system of local origin.

INDIVIDUAL PROPERTY
Property held by a natural person.

INFORMAL TENURE SYSTEM
Unwritten customary tenure system.

INHERITANCE
The legal process by which land or other property passes from a deceased owner to his or her heirs.

INSTITUTIONS
"The rules of the game in a society or, more formally, the humanly devised constraints that shape human interaction" (North, 1990).

Institutions are not organizations — although they embrace them — but are best understood as a set of formal and informal rules administered by organizations (North, 1990).

[Institutions are] like the 'rules of the game' in competitive sport. They are created by the participants and they set the social and physical parameters in which the game is played (Evans, 1993).

Encompass both rules and organizations that shape and enforce these rules (Kirk, 1999).

Sociology: A reciprocal typification of habitualized action by types of actors (Berger, 1967).

A partial order for community life which serves specific purposes and has the capacity to undergo further evolution independently. It offers a firm basis for shaping social actions over long periods of time (Schmoller von, 1990:61).

INTEREST GROUP
Groups characterized by the will to influence political decision-making, in order to successfully implement certain political goals or values. They tend to be integrated into the political process, although groups may at times employ destructive methods in order to accomplish their goals.

INTESTATE SUCCESSION
An inheritance under a scheme of intestacy, applicable by law.

JOINT MANAGMENT
See co-management.

LAND REFORM
The attempt to change and thereby improve the distribution of land among landholders.

LAND REGISTRATION
Recording in a register the ownership and other property rights in land (a broad, generic term).

LAND SURVEY
Determining the boundaries and fixing the location of a parcel of land.

LAND TENURE
Right(s) in land.

LEASE
(verb) To make a contract for temporary use; (noun) an agreement for temporary use of a lessee, who pays rent to the lessor (owner).

LEASEHOLD
Tenure for a specified period for payment of rent, conferred by the owner, whether state or private.

Glossary

LEGAL PLURALISM
The multiple, often overlapping, and even contradictory bases for claims on a resource (e.g., state law, customary law, religious laws, project regulations, and local norms).

LEGITIMACY
Rightfulness; the property of decision makers that improves voluntary compliance, usually based on conformity of these expectations about rule. This confers on a command or law an authoritative or binding character, implying a duty to obey (Heywood, 1997).

LESSEE (or TENANT)
Person who leases in land.

LESSOR (or LANDLORD)
Owner who leases out land.

LOCAL LAW
Dominant local interpretations of customary law, religious law, and other relevant normative and legal frameworks (Benda-Beckmann et al., 1996).

LOCAL LEVEL
Usually the village or its equivalent.

MANAGEMENT TRANSFER
Formal transfer of management responsibility over natural resources from the state to other organizations, with the state withdrawing from its former role.

MORAL HAZARD
Moral hazard is the fact that a party insulated from risk may behave differently from the way it would behave if it were fully exposed to the risk.

MORTGAGE
A contract by which a borrower commits land as a security for a loan.

MORTGAGEE
The lender who accepts the land as security.

MORTGAGOR
The borrower who mortgages land.

MOVABLE PROPERTY
Property other than real property (European usage).

NGOs
Non-governmental organizations, usually referring to voluntary and non-profit organizations which pursue public interests. Sometimes, NGOs are distinguished from community-based organizations (CBOs).

NON-RIVAL
Non-rivalry of consumption (= indivisibility of benefits). A good in non-rival when a unit of the good can be consumed by one individual without detracting, in the slightest, from the consumption opportunities still available to others from the same unit (Cornes and Sandler, 1986).

NORMS
Rules of conduct which specify appropriate behavior in a given range of social contexts. A norm either prescribes a given type of behavior or forbids it. All human groups follow definite types of norm, which are always backed by sanctions of one kind or another — varying from informal disapproval to physical punishment or execution (Giddens, 1997).

OPEN ACCESS
Use of a commons without controls.

Glossary

OPEN-ACCESS RESOURCE
A resource to which access is open and uncontrolled.

ORGANIZATION
A team of individuals who seek some agreed upon collective goals within the framework of collective choice rules.

PARCEL
A continuous area of land acquired as a unit under one title.

PARTICIPATION
"One or more processes in which an individual (or group) takes part in specific decision-making and action, and over which s/he may exercise specific controls. It is often used to refer specifically to processes in which primary stakeholders take an active part in planning and decision-making, implementation, learning and evaluation. This often has the intention of sharing control over the resources generated and responsibility for their future use" (Source: www.ifad.org, accessed 01/06/05).

PARTITION
Breaking up a parcel into smaller parcels, by division in inheritance or by sale of part of the parcel.

PERSONAL PROPERTY
Property other than real property (Anglo-American usage).

PLOT
A synonym for parcel; also used to indicate a piece of land within a parcel managed by someone other than the parcel owner.

PLURALISM
System in which numerous groups or actors exhibit autonomy of action within the state, which influences the character of governance (Dahl, 1982). The term is also used more generally to describe a belief in, or a commitment to, diversity and multiplicity (Heywood, 1997).

POLICIES
Instruments, rules, and regulations on various levels, especially by government. Policies typically define a course of action to reach certain objectives.

POLITICS
The activity through which people make, preserve, and amend the general rules under which they live (Heywood, 1997).

POLITY
The political system; the set of power relationships of a society — e.g., a democratic polity, a monarchical politics, etc. Those aspects of society by which occurs the exercise of political authority (Heywood, 1997).

POSSESSION
Having control of land or another resource.

POSSESORY MORTGAGE (or ANTICHRESIS)
A mortgage under which the land is held by the lender until the loan is repaid, usually in lieu of interest.

POWER
The ability of individuals, or the members of a group, to achieve aims or further the interests they hold. Power is a pervasive aspect of all human relationships. Many conflicts in society are struggles over

power, because how much power an individual or group is able to achieve governs how far they are able to put their wishes into practice at the expense of those of others (Giddens, 1997).

PRESCRIPTION (or PRESCRIPTIVE ACQUISITION)
Acquiring ownership of land by possession over a long period of time, which is open and without permission of the owner during which the possessor acts as if she or he were the owner.

PRESCRIPTION PERIOD
The minimum time that land must be held to acquire it by prescription, usually in the range of 15-30 years.

PRIVATE PROPERTY
Property held by private persons, natural or legal.

PRIVATIZATION
Transfer of rights and responsibilities from the public sector to private groups or individuals. This can include non-profit service organizations (grassroots or external NGOs) and for-profit firms (Uphoff, 1998).

"Denotes transfers of responsibility for public functions to voluntary organizations or private enterprises" (Rondinelli and Nellis, 1986).

Transfer of responsibility for certain governmental functions to non-governmental organizations, voluntary organizations, community associations, and private enterprises.

Selling to the public or to workers of government-owned assets or enterprises meant for the production of goods or services, also referred to as denationalization (Dahal, 1996).

PROPERTY
A set of rights and responsibilities concerning a thing, often stated as rights against everyone.

PROPERTY RIGHTS
"The capacity to call upon the collective to stand behind one's claim to a benefit stream" (Bromley, 1991).

"An enforceable authority to undertake particular actions in a specific domain" (Commons, 1968).

"Actions that one individual can take in relation to other individuals regarding some 'things'" (Agrawal and Ostrom, 2001).

"The claims, entitlements and related obligations among people regarding the use and disposition of a scarce resource" (Furubotn and Pejovich, 1972).

System of property rights. "A method of assigning to particular individuals 'authority' to select, for specific goods, any use from an unprohibited class of uses" (Alchian, 1965).

PUBLIC GOODS
Goods that are non-rival — consumption by one person does not reduce the supply available for others-and non-excludable — people cannot be prevented from consuming them. These characteristics make it impossible to charge consumers for public goods, so the private sector is not interested in supplying them. Instead, they are often supplied by government. Public goods are usually national or local. Defense is a national public good, benefiting the entire population of a country. Rural roads are local public goods, benefiting a smaller group of people. There can also be global public goods, benefiting most of the world's

population, for example global peace and security, or information needed to prevent global climate change. Providing such goods (and services) is a function of international organizations (Soubbotina and Sheram, 2000).

Collective goods. Non-excludable goods (both tangible and abstract) from which a person may benefit without having to contribute to the production or maintenance of the good (McCay et al., 1999).

Non-rivalry. Non-rivalry of consumption (indivisibility of benefits): A good in non-rival when a unit of the good can be consumed by one individual without detracting, in the slightest, from the consumption opportunities still available to others from the same unit (Cornes and Sandler, 1986).

PUBLIC PROPERTY
Property held by any level of government.

REAL PROPERTY
Property in land and attachments (Anglo-American usage).

RENT
(verb) The act of leasing; (noun) payment by a tenant to a landlord for temporary use of land under a lease.

RESOURCE TENURE
Right(s) in land and other resources including water and forests.

RIGHTS
Legal or moral entitlements to act or be treated in a particular way; civil rights differ from human rights. (Heywood, 1997).

RULE OF LAW
The principle that law should "rule" in the sense that it establishes a framework within which all conduct or behavior takes place (Heywood, 1997).

SCHEME OF INTESTACY
The heirs, their priority, and their shares, as specified by law for cases in which there is no will or wills are not permitted.

SECURITY
Property of the borrower promised to the lender if the loan is not repaid on time.

SECURITY OF TENURE (or TENURE OF SECURITY)
Tenure held without risk of loss; alternatively, tenure held without risk, and for a long time (preferred use of the term); alternatively, tenure resembling full private ownership.

SEPARATION OF POWERS
The principle that legislative, executive and judicial power should be separated through the construction of three independent branches of government (Heywood, 1997).

SHARE OF TENANCY
A tenancy with a share rent.

SHARE RENT
A rent consisting of a percentage of the production of the land.

SHARECROPPING
Farming land as a tenant under a share rent.

Glossary

SOCIAL CAPITAL
See Capital.

SOCIAL EXCLUSION
"A multidimensional concept, involving economic, social, political, cultural, and special aspects of disadvantage and deprivation, often described as the process by which individuals and groups are wholly or partly excluded from participation in their society, as a consequence of low income and constricted access to employment, social benefits and services, and to various aspects of cultural and community life. A key component is the framing of the issue as social and community exclusion, rather than individual and personal responsibility" (www.childpolicyintl.org).

SOCIAL GROUPS
Collections of individuals who interact in systematic ways with one another. Groups may range from very small associations to large-scale organizations or societies. Whatever their size, it is a defining feature of a group that its members have an awareness of a common identity. Most of our lives are spent in group contact; in modern societies, most people belong to groups of many different types (Giddens, 1997).

SOCIAL STRUCTURE
Patterns of interaction between individuals or groups. Social life does not happen in a random fashion. Most of our activities are structured: they are organized in a regular and repetitive way. Although the comparison can be misleading, it is handy to think of the social structure of a society as rather like the girders which underpin a building and hold it upright (Giddens, 1997).

> Structure. Refers generally to constructed frameworks and patterns of organisation which, in some way, constrain or direct human behaviour (Bilton et al., 1996).

SPILLOVER EFFECTS
Spillover effects are externalities of economic activity or processes upon those who are not directly involved in it. Odors from a rendering plant are negative spillover effects upon its neighbors; the beauty of a homeowner's flower garden is a positive spillover effect upon neighbors.

SPORADIC REGISTRATION
Registration of a parcel separately from the others in the area, voluntarily and generally at the initiative and expense of the owner.

SQUATTER
Someone who occupies land without any legal authority.

STATE
The organization that has jurisdiction over all property and persons in the modern world. "States" are the institutional underpinning of modern governments, and have legal and practical acceptance as the political association that holds "sovereign" jurisdiction within defined territorial borders, characterized by its monopoly of legitimate violence (Heywood, 1997).

STATE-BUILDING
Creation of new government institutions and the strengthening of existing ones.

STATUTORY LAW
Law of the state; official government law.

SUBDIVISION
Breaking up a parcel into smaller parcels, by division in inheritance or by sale of part of the parcel.

Glossary

SUBSIDIARITY

"Principle requiring that the distribution of power and responsibility should be in favor of lower-level governmental institutions and smaller jurisdictions (Vanberg, 1997) and political authority to be always allocated at the lowest possible institutional level, that is, close to the citizens, who are the ultimate sovereign. Moreover, it must be compatible with efficiency and accountability" (Swift, 1995).

SUCCESSION

The legal process by which land or other property passes from a deceased owner to his or her heirs.

SUSTAINABILITY / SUSTAINABLE DEVELOPMENT

Originally a concept developed in forestry and then more widely applied in environmental management, referring to the ability of an ecosystem to maintain a defined/desired state of ecological integrity over time. Drawing on this idea, the Brundtland report defined sustainable development as a form of development "that meets the needs of present generations without compromising the ability of future generations to meet theirs" (WCED, 1987). Sustainable Development was made an international commitment at the Earth Summit in Rio 1992, and reaffirmed at the Johannesburg Summit in 2002.

SYSTEMATIC REGISTRATION

Registration of all parcels in an area at the same time, usually compulsory and therefore without charge to the owner.

TENANCY AT SUFFERANCE

A tenancy that can be terminated by the landlord at any time.

TENANCY YEAR-TO-YEAR

A tenancy that the parties must agree to renew each year.

TENURE

Right(s) in a landholder's resource.

TENURE NICHE

An area with a distinctive tenure arrangement, usually related to the particular use to which the land is put.

TENURE REFORM

The attempt to alter and so improve the rules of tenure.

TESTATE SUCCESSION

An inheritance under a will.

TITLE DEED

The contract transferring ownership (title) to land.

TITLE REGISTRATION

A land registration that confers a guarantee of the title by the government.

TRANSACTION COSTS

Costs incurred for using the price mechanism for coordinating economic activity (Coase, 1960). In most definitions, transaction costs include the costs of searching for information, the costs of bargaining and making contracts, and the costs of monitoring and enforcing contracts. They also include the costs of defining and enforcing property rights.

TRUST

Emphasising the fact that modern life requires people to rely on large-scale, abstract systems of knowledge, expertise and social organisation beyond their full understanding or control (see risk and reflexivity) (Bilton et al., 1996).

UNIMODAL AGRARIAN STRUCTURE

A distribution pattern for land in which most land is owned by holders with average-sized holdings.

USER GROUPS

Membership organizations composed primarily of natural resource users.

USURFRUCTUARY RIGHTS (or USURFRUCT)

Individual or household rights of use which exist under communal tenure systems.

VALUES

Ideas held by human individuals or groups about what is desirable, proper, good, or bad. Differing values represent key aspects of variations in human culture. What individuals value is strongly influenced by the specific culture in which they happen to live (Giddens, 1997).

WILL (or WILL AND TESTAMENT)

A document executed by the owner before his or her death, specifying heirs and what portion of the estate each is to receive, after debts are paid.

References

Agrawal, A. and E. Ostrom. 2001. Collective Action, Property Rights, and Devolution of Forest and Protected Area Management. In Meinzen-Dick, R., A. Knox, M. Di Gregorio ed. *Collective action, property rights and devolution of natural resource management: Exchange of knowledge and implications for policy.* Feldafing, Germany: Zentralstelle fur Ernaehrung und Landwirtschaft (ZEL), Food and Agriculture Development Centre (DSE).

Alchian, Armen A. 1965. Some Economics of Property Rights. *Il Politico* 30(4):816-829.

von Benda-Beckmann, F., K. von Benda-Beckmann, and H.L.J. Spiertz. 1996. Water rights and policy. In *The role of law in natural resource management*, ed. H.L.J. Spiertz and M.G. Wiber, 77-99. Gravenhage, the Netherlands: VUGA.

Berger, Peter L. and Thomas Luckmann. 1967. *The social construction of reality.* Harmondsworth: Penguin.

Bilton, Tony, Kevin Bonnett, Pip Jones, Tony Lawson, David Skinner, Michelle Stanworth and Andrew Webster. 1996. *Introductory Sociology*, 3rd edition. London, Macmillan:670.

Bromley, D. 1991. *Environment and economy: Property rights and public policy.* Cambridge, MA: Basil Blackwell, Inc.

Bruce, J.W. 1998. Review of tenure terminology. *Tenure Brief* 1. Available at http://ageconsearch.umn.edu/bitstream/12814/1/ltctb01.pdf accessed 10/30/09.

Carney, D. (ed) 1998. Sustainable Livelihoods: what contribution can we make? Papers presented at DFID's Natural Resources Advisers' Conference, July 1998. London: DFID

Coase, Ronald H. 1960. The problem of social cost. *The Journal of Law and Economics*, 3: 1-44.

Coleman, J.S., E.Q. Campbell, C.J. Hobson, J. McPartland, A.M. Mead, F.D. Weinfeld, and R.L. York 1966. *Equality of Educational Opportunity.* Washington, DC: U.S. Department of Health, Education, and Welfare, p. S98.

Commons, J.R. 1968. *Legal foundations of capitalism.* Madison: University of Wisconsin Press.

Cornes, R. and T. Sandler. 1986. *The theory of externalities, public goods, and club goods.* Cambridge: Cambridge University Press.

Dahal, D.R. 1996. *The challenge of good governance: Decentralization and development in Nepal.* Kathmandu, Nepal: Center for Governance and Development Studies.

Dahl, R.A. (1982): Dilemmas of Pluralist Democracy, New Haven: Yale University Press.

Eggertsson T. 1990. *Economic behaviour and institutions.* Cambridge University Press: 40-41.

Ensminger, Jean. 1992. *Making a Market.* Cambridge University Press NY.

Evans, A.1993. 'Contracted out': Some reflections on gender, power and agrarian institutions. *IDS Bulletin*, 24(3).

References

Furubotn, E.G. and S. Pejovich. 1972. Property rights and economic theory: A survey of recent literature. *Journal of Economic Literature* 10(4):1137-1162.

Giddens, Anthony. 1997. *Sociology.* London: Polity Press.

Heywood, A. (1997): Politics, London: MacMillan Press.

Hesseling, G. 1996. Legal and institutional incentives for local environmental management. In *Improved natural resource management: The role of formal organizations and informal netwoks and institutions.* Henrik Secher Marcussen, ed. International Development Studies, Rosklide University. Occasional Paper No. 17, pp. 98-134.

Kirk, M. 1999. *Land tenure, technological change and resource use: Transformation process in African agrarian systems.* Frankfurt: Peter Lang.

Lachmann, Ludwig M. 1978. *Capital and its structure.* Kansaa City, MO: Sheed Andrews & McNeel.

Maniates, M. 1990. Organizational designs for achieving sustainability: The opportunities, limitations, and dangers of state-local collaboration for common property management. Paper presented at the First Annual Meeting of the International Association for the Study of Common Property, Durham, NC, Sept. 27-30, 1990.

Marshall, G. 1998. *A dictionary of sociology.* New York: Oxford University Press.

McCay, Bonnie, Louise Fortmann, Fikret Berkes, Meg McKean Antonio Diegues, Charlotte Hess. 1999. Useful Definitions for the Study of Common Property Theory. Prepared for the Conference on Common Property Theory, Zonguene, Mozambique, July 20-24.

Meade, J. E. 1973. *The theory of Economic Externalities. The Control of Environmental Pollution and Similar Social Costs.* Leiden, Sweden: Sijhoff.

Meinzen-Dick, Ruth, Anna Knox. 2001. Collective Action, Property Rights, and Devolution of Natural Resource Management: A Conceptual Framework. In Meinzen-Dick, R., A. Knox, M. Di Gregorio ed. *Collective action, property rights and devolution of natural resource management: Exchange of knowledge and implications for policy.* Feldafing, Germany: Zentralstelle fur Ernaehrung und Landwirtschaft (ZEL), Food and Agriculture Development Centre (DSE).

Mearns, R. 1996. Community, collective action and common grazing: The case of post-socialist Mongolia. *Journal of Development Studies* 32(3): 297-339.

North, D. C. 1990. *Institutions, institutional change and economic performance.* Cambridge: Cambridge Univ. Press.

Ostrom, Elinor. 1999. Social capital: A fad or a fundamental concept? In *Social capital: A multifaceted perspective*, ed. Partha Dasgupta and Ismail Seraeldin, 172-214. Washington, DC: The World Bank.

References

_____. 1994. Constituting social capital and collective action. Journal of Theoretical Politics 6(4) 527-562.

Ostrom, E., L. Schroeder, and S. Wynne. 1993. *Institutional incentives and sustainable development: Infrastructure policies in perspective.* Boulder, CO: Westview Press.

Page, N. and Czuba, C.E. (1999): Empowerment – What is it? Journal of Extension, Vol. 37 (5), http://www.joe.org/joe/1999october/comm1.html

Pomeroy, R. S. 2001. Devolution and Fisheries Co-Management, in Meinzen-Dick, R., A. Knox, M. Di Gregorio (eds.), *Collective action, property rights and devolution of natural resource management: Exchange of knowledge and implications for policy.* Feldafing, Germany: Zentralstelle fur Ernaehrung und Landwirtschaft (ZEL), Food and Agriculture Development Centre.

Putnam, Robert, with Roberto Leonardi and Raffella Nanetti. 1993. *Making democracy work: Civic traditions in modern Italy.* Princeton, NJ: Princeton University Press.

Rondinelli, D. and J. Nellis. 1986. Assessing decentralization policies in developing countries: The case for cautious optimism. *Development Policy Review* 4(1): 3-23.

Rondinelli, D., J.S. Mcculloch, and R.W. Johnson. 1989. Analyzing decentralization policies in developing countries: The case for cautious optimism. *Development and Change*,20(1): 57-87.

Sandler, Todd. 1992. *Collective Action: Theory and application.* Ann Arbor: The University of Michigan Press.

Schmoller von, G. 1920. *Grundriss der Allgemeinen Volksw*Duncker und Humblot.

Soubbotina, T.P., and K. Sheram (2000): Beyond Economic Growth: Meeting the Challenges of Global Development. Washington DC, World Bank.

Swift, J. 1995. Dynamic ecological systems and the administration of pastoral development. In *Living with uncertainty: New directions in pastoral development in Africa*, pp. 153-173, I. Scoones, ed. London: Intermediate Technology Publ.

Uphoff, N.T. 1998. Community-based natural resource management: Connecting micro and macro processes, and people with their environments. Paper presented at International Workshop on Community-Based Natural Resource Management, The World Bank, Washington, DC, 10-14 May.

UNDP (United Nations Development Programme). 1997. Governance for sustainable human development: A UNDP policy document. New York: UNDP.

University of Richmond. A Social Psychology Glossary. http://www.richmond.edu/%7Eallison/glossary.html.Accessed 5-6-02

References

Vanberg, V. 1997. Subsidiarity, responsive government and individual liberty. In *Subsidiaritaet: Idee und Wirklichkeit*, pp. 253-270. Knut Wolfgang Noerr and Thomas Oppermann, eds. Tuebingen, Germany: J.C.B. Mohr.

Vedeld, T. 1996. Enabling local institution-building: Reinventing or enclosing the commons in the Sahel. In *Improved natural resource management: The role of formal organizations and informal networks and institutions*, pp 135-189. H.S. Marcussen, ed. Occasional Paper No. 17 Roskilde, Denmark: International Development Studies, Rosklide University.

Vermillion, D. 2001. Property rights and collective action in the devolution of irrigation system management. In Meinzen-Dick, R., A. Knox, M. Di Gregorio (eds.), *Collective action, property rights and devolution of natural resource management: Exchange of knowledge and implications for policy*. Feldafing, Germany: Zentralstelle fur Ernaehrung und Landwirtschaft (ZEL), Food and Agriculture Development Centre.

WCED (World Commission on Environment and Development) 1987. Our Common Future. Oxford University Press, Oxford.

Woolcock, M. and A. T. Sweetser. 2002. Bright Ideas: Social Capital—The Bonds That Connect. *ADB Review* 34 (2).

Contributors

A.M. Roldan
amroldan@wwf.org.co

Abdul B. Kamara
a.b.kamara@afdb.org

Agnes Quisumbing
A.Quisumbing@cgiar.org

Amrik Heyer
amrik_h@yahoo.com

Andre Devaux
a.devaux@cgiar.org

Andrea Rizvi
arizvi@worldbank.org

Anna Knox McCulloch
annak@rdiland.org

Anne Weingart
anneweingart@googlemail.com

Annet Abenakyo
a.abenakyo@cgiar.org

Anthony Bebbington
anthony.bebbington@man.ac.uk

Beatriz Armendariz de Aghion
barmend@fas.harvard.edu

Bekele Hundie
bekelehu@yahoo.com

Benedikt Korf
benedikt.korf@geo.uzh.ch

Bert Visser
bert.visser@wur.nl

Boureima Drabo
psb.gtz@fasonet.bf

Brenda Katon
bmkaton@skyinet.net

Brent Swallow
b.swallow@cgiar.org

Bruce Campbell
B.CAMPBELL@CGIAR.ORG

Bryan Bruns
BryanBruns@BryanBruns.com

Carol J. Pierce Colfer
c.colfer@cgiar.org

Celine Dutilly-Diane
celine.dutilly-diane@cirad.fr

Christopher A. Scott
cascott@email.arizona.edu

Christopher Gibson
Christopher_Gibson@brown.edu

Clarence Chitemi
chitemic@yahoo.com

Clarissa Augustinus
clarissa.augustinus@unhabitat.org

Claudio Velasco
c.velasco@cgiar.org

Cosmas M.O. Ochieng
ochiengodhiambo@gmail.com

David Edmunds
edmundsdavid@lycos.com

David J. Spielman
d.spielman@cgiar.org

Douglas Horton
d.horton@mac.com

Douglas L. Vermillion
douglas_vermillion@yahoo.com

Elias Zerfu
e.zerfu@cgiar.org

Elinor Ostrom
ostrom@indiana.edu

Elly Kaganzi
ekaganzi@champ.org.rw

Esther Mwangi
e.mwangi@cgiar.org

Eva Wollenberg
l.wollenberg@cgiar.org

Evan Dennis
emdennis@indiana.edu

Eve Crowley
eve.crowley@fao.org

Frances Stewart
frances.stewart@qeh.ox.ac.uk

Francis Alinyo
kapchorwa@actionaiduganda.bushnet.net

Contributors

Frank Place
f.place@cgiar.org

Gaston Lopez
g.lopez@cgiar.org

Graham Thiele
g.thiele@cgiar.org

Hailemichael Taye
hailat2003@yahoo.com

Helen Markelova
h.markelova@cgiar.org

Helle Munk Ravnborg
hmr@diis.dk

Juanita Gonzalez
juanita.gonzalez@gmail.com

James Barham
james.barham@usda.gov

Javier Ekboir
jekboir@prodigy.net.mx

Jean-Paul Vanderlinden
jeanpaul.vanderlinden@c3ed.uvsq.fr

Jemimah Njuki
J.Njuki@cgiar.org

John Hoddinott
J.Hoddinott@cgiar.org

Jon D. Unruh
jon.unruh@mcgill.ca

Jon Hellin
j.hellin@CGIAR.ORG

Jonathan Murdoch
jonathan.morduch@nyu.edu

Joseph Tanui
JTanui@cgiar.org

Julie Van Domelen
Julie.Van.Domelen@gmail.com

Julio A. Berdegue
jberdegue@rimisp.cl

Kassahun Aberra
waga966@yahoo.com

Kelsey Moore
kelseyameliamoore@gmail.com

Kiflu Bedane
kiflu-b@yahoo.com

Klaus Deininger
kdeininger@worldbank.org

Konrad Hagedorn
k.hagedorn@agrar.hu-berlin.de

Krishna P. Acharya
kpacharya1@hotmail.com

Kristin Davis
k.davis@cgiar.org

Lorena Cantillo
lorenacantillo@gmail.com

Laura German
L.German@cgiar.org

Lauren Pandolfelli
lpandolfelli@gmail.com

Leulseged Begashaw
lbegashaw2005@yahoo.com

Liz Alden Wily
lizaldenwily@gmail.com

Margaret Polski
mpolski@indiana.edu

Marie Godquin
mgodquin@googlemail.com

Martha Negash
Martha.negash@yahoo.com

Martina Padmanabhan
Martina.padmanabhan@agrar.hu-berlin.de

Mesfin Tsegaye
mesfin_tsgy@yahoo.com

Michael Kirk
kirk@wiwi.uni-marburg.de

Michael Woolcock
mwoolcock@worldbank.org

Miguel Ordinola
cipincopa@cgiar.org

Monica Di Gregorio
m.di-gregorio@lse.ac.uk

Nancy Johnson
N.Johnson@cgiar.org

Nancy McCarthy
nancy.mccarthy1@gmail.com

Contributors

Niels P. Louwaars
niels.louwaars@wur.nl

Nina Lilja
n.lilja@ksu.edu

Pablo Eyzaguirre
P.Eyzaguirre@cgiar.org

Pakping Chalad Bruns
bruns@cm.ksc.co.th

Parvin Sultana
parvin@dhaka.agni.com

Pascal Sangiga
psanginga@idrc.or.ke

Patricia Kameri-Mbote
pkameri-mbote@ielrc.org

Patricia Shanley
p.shanley@cgiar.org

Paul Thompson
paul@agni.com

Paula Silva-Ochoa
polsil@hotmail.com

Peter Hazell
P.Hazell@cgiar.org

Philippe Dongier
pdongier@worldbank.org

Pramila Krishnan
Pramila.Krishnan@econ.cam.ac.uk

Rajendra Pradhan
rpradhan@soscbaha.org

Roberta Centonze
robertacentonze@hotmail.com

Rosemary Thorp
rosemary.thorp@qeh.ox.ac.uk

Ruth Meinzen-Dick
r.meinzen-dick@cgiar.org

Sabina Alkire
sabina.alkire@qeh.ox.ac.uk

Scott McNiven
mcniven@primal.ucdavis.edu

Shaun Ferris
s.ferris@cgiar.org

Shenkut Ayele
shenkutayele@yahoo.com

Sheona Shackleton
s.shackleton@ru.ac.za

Simon Anderson
simon.anderson@iied.org

Simon Nyangas
nyangassimon@yahoo.co.uk

Stefan Dercon
Stefan.Dercon@economics.oxford.ac.uk

Stephan Dohrn
stephandohrn@gmail.com

Talib Esmail
tesmail@worldbank.org

Tassew Woldehanna
wtassew@econ.aau.edu.et

Thomas Bernet
t.bernet@cgiar.org

Tiadiane Ngaido
t.ngaido@cgiar.org

Waga Mazengia
waga966@yahoo.com

Wendmsyamregne Mekasha
w.mekasha@yahoo.com

Wendy Wakeman
wwakeman@worldbank.org

Wilberforce Tirwomwe
wtirwomwe@yahoo.com

Zenebe Admassu
zenebeteferi@yahoo.com

Zewude Jote
zewdieqpo@yahoo.co.uk

Printed in Dunstable, United Kingdom

91340609R00185